THE FORGOTTEN KIN

Although much is written about contemporary families, the focus is typically limited to marriage and parenting. In this path-breaking assessment of families, sociologist Robert M. Milardo demonstrates how aunts and uncles contribute to the daily lives of parents and their children. Aunts and uncles complement the work of parents, sometimes act as second parents, and sometimes form entirely unique brands of intimacy grounded in a lifetime of shared experiences. *The Forgotten Kin* explores how aunts and uncles support parents, buffer the relationships of parents and children, act as family historians, and develop lifelong friendships with parents and their children. This is the first comprehensive study of its kind, detailing the routine activities of aunts and uncles, the features of families that encourage closeness, how aunts and uncles go about mentoring nieces and nephews, and how adults are mentored by the very children for whom they are responsible. This book aims to change the public discourse on families and the involvement of the forgotten kin across generations and households.

Robert M. Milardo is Professor of Family Relations at the University of Maine. He has published extensively in the field of family studies in leading journals and books and is currently editor of the *Journal of Family Theory & Review* owned by the National Council on Family Relations, of which he was elected a Fellow in 2005. He is the former associate editor of the *Journal of Social and Personal Relationships* and the former editor of the *Journal of Marriage and Family*. Professor Milardo is active in the developing science of personal relationships and served as the first president of the International Association for Relationship Research. His interviews and commentaries on family issues have appeared in a wide array of venues, including *Psychology Today*, the *Guardian*, the *Wall Street Journal*, the *Washington Post*, *USA Today*, and a variety of local and regional media.

The Forgotten Kin

AUNTS AND UNCLES

Robert M. Milardo

University of Maine

CAMBRIDGE
UNIVERSITY PRESS

CAMBRIDGE UNIVERSITY PRESS
Cambridge, New York, Melbourne, Madrid, Cape Town, Singapore,
São Paulo, Delhi, Dubai, Tokyo

Cambridge University Press
32 Avenue of the Americas, New York, NY 10013-2473, USA

www.cambridge.org
Information on this title: www.cambridge.org/9780521516761

First published 2010

Printed in the United States of America

A catalog record for this publication is available from the British Library.

Library of Congress Cataloging in Publication data

Milardo, Robert M.
The forgotten kin : aunts and uncles / Robert M. Milardo.
    p.   cm.
Includes bibliographical references and index.
ISBN 978-0-521-51676-1 (hardback)
1. Aunts – Family relationships.   2. Uncles – Family relationships.   3. Nieces – Family
relationships.   4. Nephews – Family relationships.   I. Title.
HQ759.94.M55   2010
306.87–dc22   2009037298

ISBN   978-0-521-51676-1 Hardback

CONTENTS

LIST OF TABLES

PREFACE

[My aunt and I] spent hours together at her country house, weeding, watering, planting. No question of mine was too repetitious or unworthy. "No," she smilingly answered once, "peat moss is not a person."
Paula DiPerna, 1998

A STORY FOUND

I was raised in a typical Italian-American family. It was large and sociable. Family gatherings were frequent, offered occasions to visit and for children to play, and always centered on food and talk. Our home was near town, and within a short drive were the homes of my mother's six sisters and two brothers and my father's sister and three brothers. The sisters talked daily; the brothers played cards every week. Nearly all of my aunts and uncles, as well as my father, worked in what Eisenhower called the nation's "military industrial complex," although I'm not sure my family thought of it in this way, and they looked at me kind of oddly when I brought it up one Christmas. I don't think I was an especially difficult child, certainly not any more difficult than my brothers or cousins, but I did at the time think my parents were occasionally, and without justification or provocation, entirely unreasonable. At these times, I visited Aunt Bea with my list of complaints. Bea is my mother's youngest sister. She had five daughters, one son, and a husband who played the clarinet. Bea listened, acknowledged, and encouraged, and then she would convince me that my parents were wonderful people, kind and generous, and I returned home comforted. I imagine my parents were a bit relieved to have their youngest son out of the house for a day.

My earliest recollection of an uncle occurred one summer evening. I had only recently gotten a new Schwinn bicycle. It was red with blue and white trim. I was speeding around our home, failed to make a sharp turn, went airborne, and landed in a heap in the midst of a hedgerow that separated the front lawn from the sidewalk. At the time, Uncle Tom happened to be walking over for a visit, reached into the hedge, lifted me up, and carried me around the house and into the kitchen, where first aid was administered, consisting of multiple bandages and Bactine. Recently I saw my Uncle Tom, who is now elderly but still has the same wiry smile. (Uncle Tom knows about the military industrial complex. I'm sure of it.) Tom has always asked how I was and how work was going. "Do you like teaching?" he queried, and I replied in the affirmative. "Good," he replied, "as long as you like it. That's what's important." I would be remiss in suggesting our conversations were short-lived, as often they were not. My uncles and aunts were each in their own way remarkable, intelligent, articulate people. But I would be equally remiss not to acknowledge that our conversations always began with an expression of interest and usually followed with a measure of support. This is not to say that they were not sometimes critical – they were – but the wellspring was always clear. I had a passel of second mothers and fathers who were encouraging, supportive, interested, playful, and always there. There were exceptions. There always are. Uncle so-and-so was nice enough when he was sober, but at times he had difficulty managing his intake of alcohol, and at such times became abusive. From my parents' perspectives, although I never had the opportunity to ask them directly, I suspect they would view their siblings as part occasional irritation, part fun, and in larger part supportive of themselves, their parenting, and their children. But most important for my parents, their siblings were central to the mix of ingredients that defined what it meant to be a family.

I did not intend to write a book about aunts and uncles or their nieces and nephews, at least not initially. I began with a simple interest in uncovering instances of men other than fathers in caregiving roles. My own uncles were positive influences in my life, and I simply wondered whether uncles were important in the lives of others. This was in the late fall of 2001. The University of Maine, my academic home for more than two decades, offered a one-year leave from teaching, advising, and other routine duties to initiate a new program of research. Jan Pryor, my friend and colleague, to whom I will be forever grateful, encouraged me to accept a visiting research appointment at Victoria University in Wellington, New Zealand. The appointment in a psychology department brimming with talent included a stipend, an apartment with cleaning service, and an office situated in a city with more cafés per capita than any other city in the world, including San Francisco. I packed immediately.

Sometimes interest and opportunity collide, and in this case, it was a remarkably smooth entry into a new research venture. I began with a handful of questions and arranged interviews with a small group of uncles and nephews in New Zealand. What do the relationships of uncles and nephews look like? Are uncles important to nephews, especially supportive, but possibly, occasionally critical? How do uncles understand their responsibilities to their nephews, or their siblings, the parents of nephews? Do they routinely complement the work of parents or occasionally act as surrogate parents, especially in cases in which one parent is absent? In my own experience, uncles were important adult role models. Most I emulated, and others suggested lifestyle choices to avoid, like alcoholism. In my conversations with nephews, I asked how they regarded their uncles and what qualities they especially admired, as well as those they did not admire. The stories these uncles and nephews told were rich descriptions of their relationships and their families, richer than I had ever imagined.

I continued the project on returning to Maine and interviewed yet another group of uncles and nephews. As the project grew, it became clear that I couldn't stop with uncles and nephews. I thought of my own aunts, and their wonderfully warm, quirky, inquisitive selves. Some were full-time homemakers, like my own mother; some combined childrearing and careers; some were single and childless. They all voted, which is to say they shared a common feminist sensibility. On Easter Sundays during the formative years of my childhood, we gathered together as was the family's tradition. My uncles wore suits, gaudy silk ties, and shiny wingtips. The aunts wore skirted suits, stylish hats, and matching gloves. From this I learned the importance of the ensemble, and the ensemble of this family included aunts as well as uncles.

In the subsequent year, I began interviewing aunts and nieces about their relationships. In all I interviewed 104 aunts, uncles, nieces, and nephews and accumulated more than 80 hours of recorded interviews, and many hundreds of pages of text wherein those interviews were transcribed. This book is the story of the participants, their relationships, and their families.

As social science projects go, 104 participants is a relatively small number of people and certainly unrepresentative of any known group. Qualitative research, which is often based on in-depth interviews, excels at representing a few people well, in their own words and rooted in their own experience, and suggests the range of possibilities that may further characterize larger groups. Nonetheless, I selected participants with an eye toward maximizing the diversity of the families and relationships they represented. I wanted to discover varieties of family relationships – and especially the forms of relationships among aunts and nieces, and uncles and nephews – that are potentially widespread.

The sample comprises largely nominate white families and includes a number of Franco-Americans, the largest minority group in Maine, and smaller numbers of Native Americans, Asians, Pacific Islanders, and Hispanics, as well as gays and lesbians. It does not include Black Americans, nor does it represent an array of other groups central to the mix of North American families – or New Zealanders for that matter. Overall the aunts, uncles, nieces, and nephews described a range of relationships, some close and some relatively distant, and they did so with remarkable consistency and nuance.

Although aunts, uncles, nieces, and nephews occasionally reported disagreements and conflict, none described a relationship that was highly conflictual or abusive. Nonetheless, uncles, relative to other family members, are a common perpetrator of the sexual abuse of nieces and, more rarely, nephews.[1] In the effort to understand the contributions of uncles, as well as other family members, I do not wish to overlook the very destructive ways in which men sometimes prey on children. Nevertheless, in the mix of relationships described here, there is little question of a decidedly generative culture of aunting and uncling.

The book is written for a broad audience, including researchers, specialists in family policy, family counselors, college teachers and their undergraduates, and graduate students who are in some way interested in moving beyond the nuclear family unit and expanding the realm of family to include the study of multiple households and issues of kinship and friendship, where the culture of aunting and uncling practically resides.

Curiously, family scholarship is surprisingly lacking in this regard. The study of families is largely restricted to relationships among parents, parents and children, and siblings, typically in childhood and adolescence with relatively little directed at relationships among adult siblings.[2] Studies of kinfolk are limited to the contributions of grandparents.[3] But aunts and uncles are of a different generation, uniquely influential, and largely forgotten. In a review of 10 leading introductory family textbooks, I found no reference to aunts, uncles, nieces, or nephews. This is the first book to address the relationships of aunts and uncles in depth.

---

[1] Chiroro, Viki, Frodi, Muromo, & Tsigah, 2006; Margolin, 1994; Russell, 1986.
[2] Robertson, 1995; Walker, Allen, & Connidis, 2005.
[3] C. L. Johnson, 2000.

By omitting aunts and uncles from our inquiries of families, we inadvertently simplify how families actually operate across households, and we omit an important area of some people's individual lives – one that influences their personal development and their understanding of themselves, as well as the remarkable ways they can influence their siblings and their siblings' children. To fully understand families – when they are distressed and when they are resilient – we need to know about how they are actually lived and experienced. The view of two parents raising young children independently is largely mythic.[4] For many, families are not self-contained private enterprises, tidy households largely closed off from community; given the realities of merging childrearing with dual-worker families, or single-parent families, private enterprise is hardly an option.[5] Rather, families are organized across multiple households. A sister learns of her niece's academic accomplishments not directly from her niece but from her older sister, who happened to call their brother, father to the niece. A simple detail about a niece travels across several households, each maintained by a sibling, before finally arriving at the doorstep of an aunt, and in many instances such chains of communication often include grandmothers. And as many parents know, nieces and nephews can be important conduits of information about adolescent children. A mother, and aunt, learns from a niece that her son has a new romantic partner, for instance. Nieces and nephews are influenced by their aunts and uncles, and, just as important, they influence their aunts and uncles. Like parenting, the effects of aunting and uncling are bidirectional. The organization of families across households describes a configuration of highly interdependent family units inclusive of adults and children. Articulating the relationships of aunts and uncles changes the way we understand families.

I hope this book will be of interest to aunts and uncles, nieces and nephews, who may find experiences and voices similar to their own. The participants often commented on how being a part of the study altered their views of themselves and family members, or otherwise sharpened their understandings of the importance of a particular aunt, niece, uncle, or nephew. Many participants were quick to point out the unusualness of my queries. Aunt Sylvia explained, "There aren't too many people like you who come around asking 50 questions [about aunting]." As participants told their stories, perhaps they came to understand their families, their siblings and parents, and their uncles and aunts more deeply. Perhaps readers will as well. Unquestionably, and if nothing else, this book demonstrates how

[4] Smith, 1993.   [5] Hansen, 2005.

aunts and uncles are important in the lives of children – how aunts and uncles are important to parents and how aunts and uncles are, just as importantly, influenced by the children for whom they are responsible. Whether a researcher or family professional, teacher or student, aunt or uncle, niece or nephew, or simply an interested party, I hope you will find the stories participants shared with me as intriguing and enlightening as I did.

A READER'S GUIDE TO THE FORGOTTEN KIN

The book is organized into nine chapters that can be read sequentially or not, depending on the reader's interests. Chapter 1 frames this inquiry within the field of family studies. At the outset, families are viewed broadly as configurations of multiple interdependent households and relationships. The chapter details what we know from the limited available literature on aunts and uncles, as well as summarizing literatures that indirectly inform our explorations, including research on adult siblings, grandparents, and, more generally, kinship, and on the typical patterns of gendered differences that consistently appear in the realm of relationships with kin. This material is paired with a dynamic view of families as socially constructed enterprises, an understanding of intergenerational solidarity, and a focus on the concept of generativity, which proves to be central to an understanding of the relationships of aunts and uncles with nieces and nephews, as well as their parents. The chapter questions the common belief that contemporary families are isolated nuclear units and suggests that, for some families, ties to kin are generative, active, and influential.

Chapter 2 describes how the study was conducted, the questions that were asked, and the methods used to distill essential findings. It provides detailed descriptions of the participants in terms of their ages and family backgrounds. This material is useful for placing the current study within a context and suggesting where and for whom the findings may be generalized. The chapter also includes a lexicon or quick guide to the participants by name (actually pseudonym) and key characteristics such as age and marital status. Throughout the book, readers may find the quick guides to the *dramatis personae* useful in understanding their essential life circumstances.

Chapter 3 explores basic features of the relationships of aunts and nieces, uncles and nephews, describing how often they visit, what they do together, and how access to new mediums such as cell phones and e-mail influence their relationships. The chapter details how families negotiate geographic distances that separate them and continue their relationships, how they stay informed of one another's circumstances, and how sometimes they establish distinctly close ties. We detail the array of social and personal factors that influence the closeness of aunts and uncles with nieces and nephews, including the all-important relationships between adult siblings, or the parents of nieces and nephews, as well as personal features of aunts and uncles, such as childlessness, or highly regarded qualities such as "being fun" or holding strong family values. Each of these realms of family experience illuminate when aunts and uncles are apt to develop influential relationships with their nieces and nephews.

Aunts and uncles described their roles in a variety of ways, often seeing themselves as adjuncts to parents, as third parties with unique perspectives, or, in some cases, as surrogate parents. Chapter 4 explores each of these roles. The chapter first considers how aunts and uncles view the importance of their relationships in general terms, how such relationships change over time, and how aunts and uncles supplement parents, act as objective third parties, or act as surrogate parents, often when biological parents are unavailable or entirely absent. Parental separation and divorce is an important factor that can influence relations among extended family members; aunts and uncles can function effectively in helping children come to understand their parents' marital struggles.

Chapters 5 through 7 explore the relationships of aunts and uncles in greater detail by addressing the question of how such relationships are generative. Generativity, or a concern for future generations as it is typically defined, can be thought of in terms of four essential components of generative families, communities, and cultures. These essential components include mentors, meaning keepers or family historians, intergenerational buffers, and fellow travelers or friends. *Mentors* are the practical guides, individuals who model action, teach skills, provide guidance or support, and generally facilitate the advancement of others. Direct mentoring of nieces and nephews, a cornerstone of generative action, occurred in nearly all areas of personal and relational life. Chapter 5 describes how aunts and uncles actively mentor their younger charges, how they express support, and how they are occasionally critical. In some areas, aunts and uncles differed in the focus of their mentoring. For instance, aunts and nieces were more likely to discuss relationships with romantic partners and issues regarding sexual activity, and they did so in greater depth than uncles and nephews. The chapter also discusses how aunts and uncles mentor parents by simply providing a listening ear or, at other times, providing direct support for parents who are dealing with sensitive issues regarding their children; chief among these issues was the sexual activity of adolescents. Finally the chapter explores the issue of *reverse mentoring* – occasions when nieces and nephews mentored their aunts and uncles, for instance, by offering advice in dealing with other family members. Although generativity is usually viewed as "a concern for future generations," in fact generative actions are frequently lived and expressed among all generations.

Chapter 6 explores *intergenerational buffering* as a form of family work. Aunts and uncles act as buffers by mediating the occasional disputes between family members, acting as partisan supporters or critics, sharing knowledge about family members without qualification, and otherwise enacting their third-party perspectives as nieces and nephews seek to better understand their parents or other family members. Aunts and uncles participate in family work by fostering a sense of family togetherness. Building a sense of family togetherness occurs directly as aunts and uncles encourage nieces and nephews to be appreciative of their family members or through the organization of family visits or reunions; it occurs more indirectly as aunts and uncles share stories about family members, particularly the parents of nieces and nephews, and in doing so realize the family's unique history.

In Chapter 7, we explore how family relationships occasionally take on the character of a close friendship. Some aunts and nieces, uncles and nephews, report exceptionally close relationships in which they share similar interests and simply enjoy one another's company. Like a good friendship, their relationships are often marked by reciprocity, mutual support, advice giving, and occasional criticism. They are people who have known each other for long periods of time (sometimes since the birth of a niece or nephew), shared nearly all major life transitions, and readily expressed the expectation that their relationships would continue well into the future. Their friendships are unique and irreplaceable because of their shared biographies founded in family ties. For some aunts and uncles, the friendships that develop with nieces and nephews are redemptive in that they alter the course of a life. For instance, a recovering alcoholic uncle finds new meaning in his life as a result of a developing relationship with his nephew. In helping her niece, an aunt finds that she comes to understand her own life in new ways.

Chapter 8 centers on the social reproduction of aunting and uncling as we examine how aunts and uncles understand their roles, whether they talk about aunting and uncling and with whom and to what effect, and how their personal experience of their own aunts and uncles informs their current relationships with nieces and nephews. Overall we find considerable continuity across generations in the expression of aunting and uncling.

The concluding chapter summarizes what this book has to offer in how we go about thinking about families, especially the contributions of aunts and uncles. Given the limited research on families as social configurations of multiple households, it is not so surprising that many of the key findings were previously unanticipated and unreported. We do not know how often the relationships of aunts and uncles with nieces and nephews are realized, but we do now know that when they are active, they are fundamental in building strong, resilient, healthy families.

ACKNOWLEDGMENTS

There are multitudes of people I should thank because they, knowingly or not, influenced the production of this book. Katherine, a well-regarded qualitative researcher and feminist scholar, is among the unknowingly influential. I mentioned to her in November 2001 that I was thinking about interviewing uncles. The sum total of her response was an enthusiastic "Great!" and I thought that an interesting comment both in its brevity, clarity, and fit. I hope it was also a prophetic comment.

My aunts and uncles had no idea I would eventually write about them, however obliquely, although they have been present throughout this production. In some regards, they provided the initial impetus for the project, and some of my initial ideas about the focus of interview questions were based on my experiences with them. You will see mention of them along the way; they provide the pseudonyms for many of the aunts and uncles I interviewed, as did my cousins for the nieces and nephews.

John Coltrane inspired much of the writing over a period of three years and plays again today, mostly *A Love Supreme*, first released when I was ambling the halls of high school in search of a beat in 1965. And as much as I am inspired by *Bringing It All Back Home*, Dylan's fifth studio album released in the same year, I am not able to write to it as it is more of a sing-along kind of mix, with the likes of "Subterranean Homesick Blues." I can't sing along to Coltrane, which explains in part why jazz is a perfect accompaniment to silent thought and active keyboards. While we are on the subject of Subterranean, I should mention my parents, who never objected to either hard pop, free jazz, or shock folk, and for this, as well as many things, including introducing me to their siblings, I thank them. My nieces Nicole and Angela and my nephew Seb are spectacular people and provided my first experiences in the sheer fun of uncling, with the occasions brought

xxi

about by my brothers Nicholas and Sebastian and their partners, Virginia and Peg.

Rosemary Blieszner, Heather Helms, Michael Johnson, and Stephen Marks have been supportive of this project throughout. They are the very best of colleagues, brilliant scholars, thoughtful in all regards, and appreciative of the importance of understanding and advocating for people and their relationships.

This project began in earnest in Wellington, New Zealand, at Victoria University, where I was a resident visiting scholar in the School of Psychology. Jan Pryor, my wonderful colleague and friend, hosted the visit. Jan now serves both as the director of the Roy McKenzie Centre for the Study of Families housed at Victoria University and as Commissioner of Families for the government of New Zealand.

Janice Bacon is the administrative assistant in the Department of Human Development and Family Studies at my home institution, the University of Maine, and was instrumental in solving the dilemma of the week, usually accompanied by a smile, if not an outright chortle. Ruth-Ellen Cohen is a journalist who managed to pen several articles on the project over the years, one of which appeared on the front page of the *Bangor Daily News*, which I thought spectacular. These articles helped gain volunteers for the project. My thanks to the many talented undergraduate and graduate students who helped with the project in a variety of ways, including Sarah Beaudette, Sarah Bourget, Jennifer Downs, Laurie Farkas, Meghan Hannington, Nika Landry, Meredith McIntire, Rebecca Riccio, Amy Skelton, Katie Vigue, and Terry Watson.

My partner, Renate Klein, inspires, quips, and generally comments on this American life, and for this I irregularly thank her. Perhaps I should do so more often.

To the aunts, uncles, nieces, and nephews who allowed me to pry, I thank you for the inspiration and all that you do.

1

Relational Landscapes

Oddly enough, aunting and uncling have little clear representation in the public discourse about families. The relationships of aunts and uncles with nieces and nephews are rarely discussed or examined in any comprehensive way. Yet relationships among siblings are among the more resilient, long lasting, and intimate of family ties, and with the introduction of children, the roles of aunt and uncle are added to the mix of bonds linking siblings and their partners or spouses.

Even the terms *aunting* and *uncling* are relatively new; they appeared only recently in the popular and academic literatures on families, and then amid some controversy. Among the early appearances of the terms was an article I wrote and submitted for review to a leading academic journal. The article was published in due time, but not without some spirited exchanges.[1] One of the reviewers questioned the terms aunting and uncling and lamented over their inclusion in the family lexicon, perhaps thinking they were unnecessary, unusual, or simply dreadful. The story illustrates the invisibility of the family work of aunts and uncles because specific terms to describe what they do are not in common usage. We have heretofore no common terms by which to describe our expectations of aunts and uncles or their typical activities and to differentiate them from the expectations and activities of other family members such as parents or grandparents. Terms such as aunting and uncling have a clear linguistic parallel with the term *parenting*, a word in common usage, but the former still sound foreign to some ears, as they did to the journal reviewer. The gap in our common language is suggestive of how the family positions of aunts and uncles are rarely discussed or acknowledged in any formal way. The family work of aunts and uncles, nieces and nephews is neatly hidden from public view and

[1] Milardo, 2005.

1

acknowledgment, although as we shall see, aunts and uncles routinely dis-cuss, among themselves and their intimates, their relationships with nieces, nephews, and other family members, and their contributions to family work are varied, consequential, and apparently commonplace.

The invisibility of aunts, uncles, nieces, and nephews, as well as relation-ships among adult siblings more generally,[2] in the field of family studies contrasts sharply with the lived experience of actors who know quite clearly the importance of each to the other. Family members rather commonly talk among themselves, visit, phone, e-mail, circulate family photos in person or via Web sites, and celebrate holidays, birthdays, and anniversaries. In their contacts, they share news and gossip, and all of this occurs across households of grandparents, parents, adult siblings (some of whom are sin-gle), and close friends, including coworkers. To be sure, not all families are in frequent communication, but then not all exist as isolated households. One need only recall travel patterns on major North American holidays to confirm this.

In one curious instance, the everyday and academic discourse on families fuses implicit acknowledgment of what aunts and uncles typically do and how these positions are commonly understood. The Aunties and Uncles Co-operative Family Project Ltd. is a program developed to service disadvan-taged children in Sydney, Australia.[3] The program matches adult volunteers with children typically from single-parent families headed by women. The adult volunteers agree to spend one weekend per month with their assigned child and are expected to help build the child's self-esteem and confidence. Volunteers become mentors to parents as well. The program staff refers to volunteers as aunties and uncles and the children who are served by the program as nieces and nephews. At least some of the volunteers come to think of the families they are assigned to as extensions of their own families. That is, they regard themselves as aunts or uncles and the children as nieces or nephews. As one adult volunteer remarked, "We have become family and would continue to be, even if [the program] ceased to exist." At least some of the families served agree: "With all we receive from the auntie, we feel she and her family is like a family to us."[4]

The Aunties and Uncles Program is unusual in several respects. First, by labeling the volunteers as aunties and uncles, the organizers are implicitly identifying a meaning or definition of these family positions – aunts and uncles mentor children and children's parents. In doing so, the organizers

---

[2] For reviews of the adult sibling literature see Mauthner, 2002; Mikkelson, 2006.
[3] Wilkes, Beale, & Cole, 2006.   [4] Wilkes et al., 2006, p. 299.

recognize what family scholars have often overlooked – the integral role aunts and uncles can play in family life. Second, the organizers assume a common meaning to aunting and uncling that parents and children will recognize and in this way implicitly define a common culture of aunting and uncling. Third, the program facilitates the social construction of kinship, what we might call *chosen* or *fictive kin*.[5] Volunteers may come to view themselves as chosen kin, or as uncles and aunts connected by virtue of their responsibilities to parents and children rather than ties of blood or marriage; serviced families may come to regard their assigned providers as being like kin. In this way, chosen kin are created through a deliberate intervention program that implicitly recognizes a definition of what it means to be an aunt or uncle and applies such labels to participants. In ordinary family life, the positions of aunt and uncle may be rooted in relational ties of blood or marriage, or they may be rooted in ties of friendship, shared expectations, and values. Just as we sometimes regard a close friend as *like a brother or sister*, we may come to regard such a friend as a chosen uncle or aunt. Fourth, in the same way that not all aunts and uncles are actively involved with their nieces and nephews, not all volunteers and serviced families come to view themselves as being like kin. Simply applying the label of auntie or uncle to a volunteer does not ensure a mentoring relationship will develop or that participants will come to actually think of each other as kin. This circumstance suggests that we refrain from *essentializing* aunting or uncling, or viewing the enactment of these social positions as entirely consistent and invariable. As we shall see throughout this book, there is great variety in the depth of relationships that develop among aunts, uncles, parents, and their children. Aunts and uncles can develop lifelong friendships with their nieces and nephews, just as they can fail to develop even the most superficial of relationships.

In the pages that follow, I review a select few literatures that help inform our interest in aunts and uncles. Research on kinship is sparse but most certainly helps provide essential background, and we can usefully draw on understandings developed by sociologists – and, to a lesser extent, evolutionary psychologists and anthropologists. I follow this initial literature review by introducing two core theoretical perspectives: the concept of intergenerational solidarity and ideas about generativity taken from developmental psychology. Each of these perspectives is cast within feminist concerns about the social construction of families, and each helps frame the study of aunts and uncles, suggesting initial research questions while

[5] Carrington, 1999; Muraco, 2006; Spencer & Pahl, 2006.

enriching our developing understanding of the importance of aunts and uncles and the organization of family systems.

Family scholars and practitioners are rather late in coming to understand aunts and uncles and the varied ways they influence their siblings, the children of their siblings, and themselves. There are, of course, exceptions and some fine initial studies of aunts and uncles, nieces and nephews, as well as developing literatures on relationships among adult siblings, grandparents, and grandchildren. I consider these literatures as they informed the development of this project and the questions asked in *The Forgotten Kin*. First I consider the more general area of kinship.

UNDERSTANDING KINSHIP

The field of family studies has advanced substantially in the past several decades in terms of the major areas of inquiry, ways of thinking about those areas, and ways of gathering and analyzing data.[6] Yet in some regards, the field is underdeveloped, and one instance of this underdevelopment is the literature on families and their involvement within networks of kin or other close associates.[7] In a comprehensive review of the kinship literature, social anthropologist Coleen Johnson[8] noted the near absence of a literature on relationships between family and kinship members, with the exception of the literatures on grandparenting and caregiving for the elderly. Johnson's evaluation is supported by a recent study of the mainstream scholarship on families.

Family scholars Karen Fingerman and Elizabeth Hay, in an analysis of research published on relationships, found that the vast majority of literature focuses on spouses, heterosexual romantic partners, parents, and children.[9] The remaining forms of family relationships compose less than 10% of the published research, including relationships with grandparents, grandchildren, in-laws, stepparents and stepchildren, siblings, cousins, and other forms of personal associates such as family friends, neighbors, coworkers, and service providers. To be sure, relationships among primary partners (e.g., spouses) and parents and children are among the most important of personal relationships; family professionals and laypersons alike continually rate these two domains highly,[10] and they are clearly consequential. It makes sense that intimate relationships among adult partners (e.g., spouses

[6] Milardo, 2000.
[8] Johnson, 2000.
[10] Fingerman & Hay, 2002.
[7] Milardo & Helms-Erikson, 2000.
[9] Fingerman & Hay, 2002.

or unmarried couples living together) and relationships among parents and children should command our attention. However, relationships with grandparents are important for children, parents, and the grandparents.

Similarly, when volunteers are asked to rate the importance of relationships with collateral kin – aunts, uncles, nieces, and nephews – they rate these relationships as relatively important. For instance, Fingerman and Hay asked respondents in their study to rate the importance of a wide variety of kin and nonkin on a 10-point scale. Spouses, children, and parents are rated typically very high in importance with average ratings of 8 or higher, siblings about 7.5, and collateral kin somewhat less in importance, with average scores in the range of 5 to 7.[11] Yet these scholars find that research on siblings represented less than 5% of available research, with most of that focused on children, approximately 1.5% focused on grandparents, and less than 0.1% on collateral kin.[12] The imbalance of what people consider important in their lives and what social scientists tend to study is clear. This study is designed to correct that imbalance, however modestly.

The significance of a wider tracing of kin is apparent when we question beliefs about a sense of obligation due individual family members. What, for example, are the rules governing relationships with kin, and collateral kin in particular? In times of family crisis, do adults generally feel compelled to provide relatives with comfort or financial support; for that matter, on occasions of family celebrations such as anniversaries or birthdays, do adults feel compelled to provide relatives with gifts or to visit? Felt obligations to kin can be strong or weak, consistent across a variety of relationships, or relationship-specific and stronger for some relationships than others. Felt obligations can be consistent across people (e.g., nearly all people agree about a sense of obligation to particular types of kin) or relatively inconsistent, in which case individuals are free to act in ways they feel appropriate. Family sociologists Alice and Peter Rossi explored these questions in a now-classic study of families across three generations.[13] They asked a large and representative sample of people living in the greater Boston area to estimate the degree of obligation they felt to provide comfort, money, gifts, or visitation to a variety of kin. The obligation to provide support was rated for

[11] Fingerman & Hay, 2002.

[12] These figures are best interpreted as estimates because although the number of articles Fingerman and Hay (2002) surveyed was large (n = 1,000), the number of journals was limited to 6, all of which were published in North America, and without the inclusion of gerontological journals where studies of extended kin may appear more regularly, although certainly not frequently.

[13] Rossi & Rossi, 1990.

a variety of kinfolk on the usual multipoint scale, ranging from 0 (*no sense of obligation*) to 10 (*a very strong sense of obligation*). From this manner of questioning, we can judge variations in felt obligation to various kin relations, and from this infer a normative structure and perhaps glean some idea of the importance of kin. Parents' sense of obligation to children can be compared with that of grandparents, aunts, and uncles; conversely we can compare a sense of obligation by adult children to care for their siblings, parents, grandparents, aunts, and uncles. Of course, understanding normative beliefs about obligations to kin does not guarantee a relationship will ensue. Much like close friendship, for instance, relationships among siblings are in part the result of personal discretion, values, and opportunity and, in this way, the consequence of social or relational constructions.[14]

In general, respondents feel obligated to provide support for kin. Mean obligation ratings fall in the range of 6 to 7, indicating fairly high levels of felt obligation.[15] Average ratings to provide a kin relation with financial aid, comfort, a gift, or visit were all in this range; the forms of aid are highly interrelated. Kin that evoke a strong obligation to visit are also the kin who evoke an obligation to exchange a present or provide financial aid in a crisis. This does not mean all kin are rated in similar ways. Parents evoke a greater sense of obligation than cousins. We can use this information to examine how aunts and uncles compare with other kin.

As we might expect, people generally feel a strong sense of obligation to parents and to children. Parents and children are rated 8 or higher for most items.[16] In times of crisis, we regard providing comfort or financial aid to parents and children a distinct obligation; in times of celebration, most regard providing gifts or visiting an obligation. Following parents and children are a core of kin members including siblings, grandparents, and grandchildren, who are relatively high in levels of felt obligation.

Several intriguing patterns arise from these descriptive comparisons of felt obligation toward nieces, nephews, aunts, and uncles. Siblings evoke a stronger level of obligation to act in supportive ways than the children of siblings (i.e., nieces and nephews). Participants are more inclined to provide support to their siblings than they are to the children of their siblings. This suggests that close ties among siblings may not entirely translate to close ties between siblings and their nieces and nephews.

Close friends can evoke significant obligations to provide support that in several instances exceed those to nieces, nephews, aunts, uncles, and

---

[14] Hansen, 2005.   [15] Rossi & Rossi, 1990, table 4.7, p. 173.
[16] Rossi & Rossi, 1990, table 4.7, p. 173.

cousins. This finding is yet another indicator that close friends and close kin evoke similar expectations. There is one exception in that nieces and nephews, as well as aunts and uncles, evoke a stronger gift-giving norm than friends. Individuals are apparently more inclined to acknowledge an aunt or nephew's birthday, or other cause for celebration, by exchanging gifts. Perhaps exchanging gifts serves to solidify a family connection, however symbolically, without requiring a level of intimacy consistent with providing comfort or of geographic proximity consistent with permitting visiting.[17]

Along with a general expectation to provide aid to nieces and nephews, there is also a parallel expectation to provide uncles and aunts with aid when needed, including financial aid. This suggests that over time, the relationships of aunts and uncles with nieces and nephews are balanced, or at least not entirely one-sided. In contrast, others have suggested that exchanges of support, including affection, are stronger downward (e.g., from parent to child or uncle to nephew) than upward (e.g., from nephew to uncle).[18] We feel more obligation toward our children, grandchildren, nieces, and nephews than they perhaps feel toward us. The varied findings regarding the reciprocal nature of relationships among collateral kin, or grandparents and grandchildren, may well depend on the ages of the participants. Whereas younger nieces and nephews may be less inclined and less able to provide support for aunts and uncles, older nieces and nephews may be more inclined and able to do so.[19] At any one point in the life span, relationships among kin may appear asymmetrical, whereas over the long term, they are more apt to be balanced.

In addition, kin relationships vary in terms of the flexibility of the norms ascribed to them. For instance, we expect parents to support their children with few exceptions. Within the Rossi and Rossi's multigenerational study, this is reflected in a relatively high mean score on each of the measures of felt obligation (a rating of 8 or higher), as well as a relatively low range of scores within the parent group (less than half a point). Obligations to parents and children are high and uniform.

Some of the highest ranges of scores appear among the two groups of most interest: (a) aunts and uncles and (b) nieces and nephews. Apparently, on average people feel a considerable sense of obligation to provide for their collateral kin, but there is significant variation, with some reporting a much greater sense of obligation and others a much lower sense of obligation. This finding suggests that there is substantial individual discretion in providing

[17] Rossi & Rossi, 1990.
[19] Schnieder & Cottrell, 1975.

[18] Bengtson, 2001; Bianchi, 2006.

support for nieces and nephews or aunts and uncles, and more so than we find among other kin relations, with the possible exception of relations among stepkin.[20]

Relationships with kin vary systematically in other ways, and especially in regard to gender differences. As we might expect, gender plays an important part in understanding relationships among kin, and women generally report more knowledge of kin, a greater sense of obligation to kin, and more direct involvement. At all ages, women report larger networks of kin, and they are able to name larger numbers of kin than men.[21] Men and women seem to know similar numbers of close kin (i.e., grandparents, parents, grandchildren, and children), but on average women know a broader array of more distant kin, including aunts, uncles, nieces, and nephews, as well as more of the potentially vast array of cousins (e.g., grandparents' cousins, parents' first cousins, personal first cousins, first cousins' children, grandchildren, and so on), and in-laws. In one inquiry, the average number of kinfolk known by women was 183, whereas for men the average was 135.[22] These figures are interesting because they illustrate the typical gender difference, but also temper any conclusions we make. Men on average are not completely isolated from kin. They may know fewer kin than women on average, but they still know many, and there are some men who are apt to be actively involved with kin. The issue is important because when men are more involved with kin, they tend to report higher levels of marital satisfaction, as do their wives. Involvement with kin is in some way connected to the particulars of marital quality.[23]

Comparatively, in most cases, women report a greater sense of felt obligation toward kin than men and a greater sense of obligation to provide for their nieces and nephews, as well as their elderly aunts and uncles.[24] This sense of obligation is paired with a greater knowledge of kin and more activity. Sisters, for instance, can name more kin than brothers.[25] Women visit with kin more often, especially with other female kin,[26] and they are more likely to include aunts and uncles in their networks of intimates and near intimates.[27] These simple facts illustrate the greater salience of kin in the daily lives of women.

[20] Sarkisian, 2006.   [21] Schnieder & Cottrell, 1975.
[22] Schnieder & Cottrell, 1975.
[23] Burger & Milardo, 1995; Helms, Crouter, & McHale, 2003; Perry-Jenkins & Salamon, 2002.
[24] Rossi & Rossi, 1990, table 4.14, p. 193.   [25] Salmon, 1999; Salmon & Daly, 1996.
[26] Gerstel & Gallagher, 1996; Rainie, Fox, Harrigan, Lenhart, & Spooner, 2000; Schnieder & Cottrell, 1975.
[27] Wellman & Wortley, 1989.

Women in their roles as mothers, daughters, wives, and sisters serve to connect family members. They are central in encouraging men to develop closer relationships with their own kin, encouraging relationships among children and grandparents, and encouraging relationships between their siblings (aunts and uncles) and their children. Women are in many regards *kin keepers*,[28] key figures in the development and routine maintenance of family relationships within and across households. The significance of women as kin keepers is suggested in the reflections of men and women regarding who is considered important when growing up. Grandmothers and aunts are likely to be cited as more important to respondents than grandfathers and uncles, and maternal grandmothers and aunts are the closest of all.[29] This attention to kin keeping suggests mothers and sisters, relative to fathers and brothers, are more central in encouraging relationships among aunts and uncles with nieces and nephews.

Of course, kinship is not the sole domain of family sociologists; anthropologists have long recognized the variable importance of kinship in framing the social, economic, political, and religious organization of family groups and the communities in which they live.[30] They have extended considerable effort in understanding complex issues of lineage and descent (i.e., who is considered kin and with what significance), postmarital residence patterns (e.g., where couples are expected to reside in relation to one partner's or the other's kin), and the organization of family households (e.g., who lives with whom).

Largely absent from this impressive accounting of the world's array of conventions regarding kinship and their significance for the organization of societies is an accounting of aunting and uncling in the daily life of families as well as a recognition that kinship bonds are inherently both personal and relational in nature in three important regards. Aunts are aunts only because of the presence of their nieces and nephews, and conversely. Second, people almost universally fudge who is considered kin and who is not.[31] At times, and perhaps routinely, close friends who are unrelated by blood or marriage come to be viewed as aunts, uncles, nieces, or nephews.[32] Conventions may provide some guidelines, but essentially relationships are socially constructed and based on a degree of personal discretion. We develop close relationships with people we like and who like us, and aunts, uncles,

[28] Leach & Braithwaite, 1996; Rosenthal, 1985.
[29] Dubas, 2001; Monserud, 2008; Schnieder & Cottrell, 1975, p. 197; Silverstein & Marenco, 2001.
[30] Parkin & Stone, 2004.   [31] Faubion, 2001.
[32] Carrington, 1999; Muraco, 2006; Oswald, 2002; Spencer & Pahl, 2006.

nieces, and nephews are no exception. This also means that some kin, including aunts and uncles, may not be acknowledged or readily identified as such. Third, relationships among aunts, uncles, nieces, and nephews develop (or fail to develop) in a family context involving multiple relationships and households. Parents, grandparent, other siblings, and their partners can all influence the relationships that develop. To be sure, family members are notoriously opinionated, their relationships both potentially supportive and potentially problematic.[33]

More recently, evolutionary psychologists have begun examining kinship issues in attempts to better understand the biological basis for kinship selection. In essence, by helping those to whom one is sure of being related, we advance the replication of our own genetic identity.[34] From an evolutionary perspective, this means that individuals should invest more in the offspring of daughters and sisters because they can be more assured of being related. Among primates and humans, for instance, there is a strong preference for associating with maternally related kin.[35] In a series of studies, all of which are based on college students, living distance is unrelated to the frequency of visiting grandparents, aunts, and uncles. Although students and their parents generally live closer to paternal relatives, including grandparents and the siblings of fathers, they have more contact with maternal relatives, including both visiting and phoning, a finding that is generally consistent across a variety of research. Maternal grandmothers, for instance, experience more contact with their grandchildren relative to their paternal counterparts,[36] and grandchildren report being closer to maternal than paternal grandparents.[37]

Although the evolutionary perspective is one of the more controversial theories of human behavior,[38] this research is suggestive of the importance of collateral kin and the greater importance women place on relationships with kin. We can hypothesize that aunts and uncles are more likely to develop relationships with the offspring of sisters regardless of how near or far they live, that aunts should develop closer relationships with nieces and nephews than uncles, and that female kinfolk (mothers, grandmothers, and sisters) are more likely to encourage relationships among aunts, uncles, and children. Perhaps evolutionary factors such as natural selection and a preference for investing in the offspring of daughters and sisters have some influence, although I wonder if social constructions such as gender and

[33] Fingerman, Hay, & Birditt, 2004.
[34] Harvey & Wenzel, 2006; Kenrick & Trost, 1997.
[35] Stone, 2000.   [36] Cox, 2003.
[37] Dubas, 2001; Monserud, 2008.   [38] Harvey & Wenzel, 2006.

negotiated family roles cast a broader, more dynamic, and more immediate influence on the conduct of personal relationships.

Taken together, our brief foray into the varied literatures on kinship suggests that although there is little public discourse – and surprisingly little research – on the relationships of aunts, uncles, nieces, and nephews, generally they are not entirely remote, diffuse, or categorically undifferentiated relationships. Americans report rather high levels of felt obligation to collateral kin, as well as obligations to provide support in times of personal need and in recognition of significant events such as birthdays and holidays. Then, too, there is considerable variation from person to person, with some individuals endorsing a substantial obligation to provide for their collateral kin and some endorsing little sense of obligation. We can anticipate that not all aunts and uncles develop relationships with nieces and nephews, and considerable personal discretion is likely involved in doing so or not. Research, however limited, is mixed regarding whether relationships among collateral kin are balanced or asymmetric, although quite possibly aunts and uncles provide more support to nieces and nephews during the formative years of childhood and adolescence; perhaps nieces and nephews reciprocate that support as they become older.

Gender differences repeatedly occur, and women display more knowledge of kin, more direct involvement, and a greater sense of obligation relative to men. Nonetheless, there is notable variation. For instance, although sisters can name more kin on average than their brothers, some brothers name as many kin as their sisters, and a few name more. For instance, in a study of 24 sibling pairs, sisters named more kin than brothers in most cases – 20 of 24. In two cases, sisters and brothers named identical numbers of kin, and in another two cases, brothers named more kin than sisters.[39] There is little doubt women are more involved with kin, but it is equally clear that there are exceptions. Although women are generally closer to kin, some men will likely report more interest in kin, as well as greater knowledge of and involvement with them. One purpose of this study is to identify men who are perhaps uniquely involved with kin, especially their nephews.

THE RESEARCH QUESTIONS

At the heart of this book is an interest in understanding the relationships of aunts and nieces, as well as uncles and nephews, and to do so within the context of an ensemble of family relationships. In developing a set of research

---

[39] Salmon & Daly, 1996.

questions, I draw on several theoretical perspectives: a model of intergenerational solidarity, a feminist perspective on the social construction of family relationships, and generativity theory. Each perspective informs the development of specific research questions.

Intergenerational Solidarity

The model of *intergenerational solidarity* was first developed by social gerontologist Vern Bengtson and his colleagues,[40] and directed at characterizing "the behavioral and emotional dimensions of interaction, cohesion, sentiment, and support between parents and children, grandparents and grandchildren, over the course of long-term relationships."[41] The framework, although originally directed at vertical relationships between parents and children of multiple generations, can usefully be applied to collateral kin, including the relationships of parents with their siblings and the children of siblings, and thereby framing the perspective as a matter of solidarity within and across generations.

Intergenerational solidarity comprises six related dimensions that I have modified to be more inclusive of a broader range of relationship phenomena while preserving the essential meaning of each dimension. *Affectual solidarity* refers to expressed sentiments including demonstrations of affection and intimacy. *Associational solidarity* refers to the frequency of interaction between family members and the forms those interactions take (e.g., in-person contacts as well as computer-mediated contacts). *Consensual solidarity* refers to similarity or dissimilarity in the attitudes and values of members. *Functional solidarity* directs our attention to the exchange of social support, criticism, and the refusal to provide support, in acknowledgment that family members can be highly supportive as well as critical of one another's activities. *Normative solidarity* refers to the sense of obligation members feel toward one another. Finally, *structural solidarity* refers to that component of intergenerational ties derivative of proximity, which can be viewed in terms of both physical space and social space.

The intergenerational solidarity perspective is useful because it helps organize many of the issues previously identified as important and perhaps characteristic of the relationships of aunts and uncles with their nieces and nephews, as well as relationships with parents and grandparents, and because the model is inherently relational. The relationship of any two

---

[40] Bengtson, 2001; Silverstein, Giarrusso, & Bengtson, 1998.
[41] Bengtson, 2001, p. 8.

family members is in part dependent on and influenced by relationships with other family members.

The intergenerational solidarity model has been criticized to the extent that it implies a normative directive regarding how families should be organized rather than how they are actually lived.[42] Family members should be uniformly nice, consistently supportive, active listeners, and unquestionably honest; they are not. Paradoxically the people with whom we experience our closest relationships are often those with whom we experience the most conflict.[43]

Feminist scholars have usefully criticized conceptualizations of families that ignore the variety of forms in which people construct their relationships.[44] The enactment of family roles, as partners, parents, siblings, aunts, or uncles, is at once normatively prescribed and individually negotiated within a unique constellation of personal relationships that span multiple households. An uncle may express some degree of belief in the importance of maintaining relationships with his sister's children, but the enactment of his relationships with nieces and nephews is dependent on his relationships with his sister, his parents, other siblings, and perhaps interactions with additional family members including partners or spouses and children of siblings. In short, the roles of aunt and uncle are socially constructed within a relational context.

Traditional views of families, their membership, the course of family life cycles, and gender often misrepresent how relationships actually develop.[45] Drawing attention to the variety of ways in which intergenerational solidarity is constructed should not limit our attention to failures to achieve closeness, dissimilarities in personal beliefs, refusals to provide support, or exchanges of direct criticism. Families are likely composed of measures of affection and disaffection, association and distance, consensus and discontent, functional support and interference. Traditional views of families distort the relationship structures and processes as they are actually lived and negotiated. There are several consequences we might well avoid, and chief among these are unrealistic portraits of the interior character of families that dismiss the full range of expressions of solidarity that enhance relationships or distance members. We might well avoid unrealistic portraits of the exterior character and composition of families that assume a view of families as households composed of parents and children, separate from their

[42] Katz, Lowenstein, Phillips, & Daatland, 2005.
[43] Fingerman et al., 2004.
[44] Allen, Fine, & Demo, 2000; Roberto, Allen & Blieszner, 2001.
[45] Hansen, 2005; Smith, 1993; Thorne & Yalom, 1992.

connections to kin and other close associates. We might also well avoid an invariant portrait of the players and gendered roles they enact. Undoubtedly women are often, as we shall discover, central figures in the maintenance of relationships among kinfolk, but this should not preclude examination of the exceptions in which men are deliberately involved with kin. The dominant discourse on families rightly views women as more actively engaged in family relationships, but then it often misrepresents or simply ignores the contributions of men as caregivers. Simultaneously considering issues of intergenerational solidarity and the social construction of family relationships permits us to view families in the full array of ways in which they are enacted, and that is precisely our goal – to uncover the understudied roles of aunts and uncles in the relational sphere of mutual interdependencies. Our questions are informed by normative prescriptions of family responsibilities and obligations, but we shall see how our players conform and expect that they will disrupt tidy views of the standard all-American family.

With a broad view of intergenerational solidarity and its components, we begin with several initial questions. Do aunts and uncles routinely develop close relationships with their nieces and nephews, and are they regarded as such by nieces and nephews? How are aunts and uncles influential in the lives of their nieces and nephews, and perhaps in the lives of parents? These essentially descriptive questions frame much of the purpose of this book. To understand and predict the movements of heavenly bodies, we need to first describe the core celestial players and their movements.

A second set of questions concerns how aunts and uncles view their roles with regard to nieces and nephews, as well as other family members, and especially parents. Do they, for instance, view themselves as supplementing parents or acting in ways that are unique and complement the work of parents? Do they regard themselves at times as advocates for the interests of parents, and at other times for their children? Having examined the question of how aunting and uncling is expressed, we can also examine why some develop more active relationships than others. What personal and relational features influence the development of active relationships among aunts, uncles, nieces, and nephews? These concerns are paired with questions about how aunts and uncles learn their roles – if and when they talk about aunting and uncling and with whom.

Generativity

In our attempt to understand the contributions of aunts and uncles, we can usefully turn to the vast literature on parenting for guidance. Although the contributions of aunts and uncles are apt to be unique in some ways, in many regards, they may complement those of parents. Generally the literature on parenting focuses on how mothers and fathers contribute to their children's development, how the contributions of mothers and fathers are distinct, and how parenting contributes to the personal development of parents.[46]

One emerging perspective examines the roles of mothers and fathers in the context of life-span development and as an instance of generativity defined as an "adults' concern for and commitment to the next generation, as expressed through teaching, mentoring, leadership, and a host of other activities that aim to leave a positive legacy of the self for the future."[47] Generativity has been viewed as a stage of midlife development, as originally proposed by psychologist Eric Erikson, or, more typically, as a salient concern, elements of which appear throughout the adult life course.[48]

We can speak of generative individuals, and thus place generativity in the mix of personality attributes,[49] as well as generative parents, on whom most research efforts have centered.[50] In addition, we may speak of generative roles and in so doing open the inquiry to a variety of relationships with family members, coworkers, and friends where generativity is expressed,[51] as well as generative societies and cultures.[52] Oddly enough, applications of generativity to families are limited, and research has largely been silent regarding the potential contributions of relatives, including grandparents, uncles, and aunts, as well as nonkin, including fictive kin and friends.[53] Parents are certainly important purveyors of generativity, but they may not be entirely unique in this regard. By conceptualizing generativity as an element of individual development, we risk overlooking the relational context in which generativity appears, and kin are apt to be central in that context.

In applying the concept of generativity to the culture of aunting and uncling – the caring for nieces and nephews – I borrow from John Kotre's conceptualization of generative cultures in which four forms of cultural mediators are viewed as essential.[54] *Mentors* are the practical guides,

[46] Arendell, 2000; Marsiglio, Amato, Day, & Lamb, 2000.
[47] de St. Aubin, McAdams, & Kim, 2004, p. 4.
[48] Cohler, Hostetler, & Boxer, 1998; McAdams & Logan, 2004.
[49] Keyes & Ryff, 1998; McAdams, Hart, & Maruna, 1998.
[50] Hawkins & Dollahite, 1997; McAdams & Logan, 2004; Snarey, 1993.
[51] McDermid, Franz, & De Reus, 1998.   [52] Kotre, 2004.
[53] Applications of generativity to grandparenting appear in the work of Pratt, Norris, Hebblethwaite, & Arnold (2008) and Thiele & Whelan (2008).
[54] Kotre, 2004.

individuals who model action, teach skills, and provide guidance or support and who generally facilitate the advancement of others. The *keeper of meaning* refers to individuals concerned with preserving a family's traditions. *Intergenerational buffers* are family members who have firsthand knowledge of parents and their children and can intercede on behalf of a parent with a child, or conversely. This view of buffering is somewhat broader than the concept's original reference to family members who, for example, directly protect children by interrupting decidedly abusive cycles.[55] For our purposes it is more useful to think of intergenerational buffers as individuals who are motivated to protect or enhance the well-being of others. For instance, an aunt may intervene in a conflict between a niece and her parent and in this way act as an intergenerational buffer. Finally we can call on the idea of *fellow travelers* or, more commonly, friends or intimates, in reference to peers who share common interests and help us cope with significant life events such as illness, divorce, or the death of an intimate.

This model of generativity is useful for gaining an understanding of the relationships of aunts and uncles with nieces and nephews because each of the four forms of cultural mediators serve as a *sensitizing concept*,[56] potentially alerting us to the significance of kin and their relationships. In addition, applying a model of generativity to family relationships can serve as a means to identify new dimensions of generativity that may not readily fit existing conceptualizations. Although generativity is largely regarded as a psychological construct – an element of individual development that makes its debut in adulthood – viewing generativity in a relational context may suggest an entirely new understanding of generative actions and their significance.

Like parents, aunts and uncles may act as teachers and mentors of their nieces and nephews. For example, an uncle may offer advice or criticism regarding a nephew's relationships with family members or friends or with regard to performance in school or career plans. Aunts and uncles may be similar in how they enact mentoring, or they may differ. Relative to mothers, fathers are more apt to engage in problem solving with their adolescent sons and to provide advice regarding educational or career plans; they are less likely to discuss emotions or relationship issues.[57] Similar differences are found in the activities of grandmothers and grandfathers with grandchildren.[58] Grandfathers do provide occasional social–emotional

[55] Kotre & Kotre, 1998.
[56] Ambert, Adler, Adler, & Detzner, 1995; Marsiglio, 2004.
[57] Hosley & Montemayor, 1997.   [58] Silverstein & Marenco, 2001.

support, including advice regarding relationships, but perhaps more commonly, they provide counsel regarding intellectual and academic development and support regarding physical and athletic development,[59] as well as acting as spiritual or religious advisors.[60] The mentoring of aunts and uncles may differ in similar ways, with uncles being more attune to problem solving and aunts to relationship work. Each of these activities is an example of mentoring, and they are all suggestive of how aunts and uncles may serve as important models for nieces and nephews and supplement the work of parents, a position consistent with earlier inquiries of aunts and uncles as well as the views of nieces and nephews.[61]

Aunts and uncles may serve unique functions relative to parents. Examples include occasions in which uncles act as family historians and relate stories to nephews concerning their parents' early biographies. These narratives may help nephews understand their parents as individuals who were once young adults in addition to offering insights into their parents' motivations for acting the way they do. Among younger and older generations, grandparents are viewed as important sources of family history and tradition,[62] although by virtue of their relationships as siblings or peers of nieces' and nephews' parents, aunts and uncles can share a unique version of family history. Aunts and uncles are free to relate their own versions of family histories, including the personal biographies of siblings (e.g., the parents of nieces and nephews) and parents (i.e., nieces' and nephews' grandparents). Their knowledge is unique and, to a certain extent, unburdened by the conventional expectations held of parents. This may be especially true of childless aunts who are free to deviate from traditional views of mothering, domesticity, and femininity.[63]

In their role as intergenerational buffers, uncles, and perhaps more typically aunts, may engage in *emotion work* with nieces and nephews by providing them with opportunities to process conflicts or other concerns regarding parents or other family members. Emotion work refers to deliberate attempts to alter emotions or feelings about persons or relationships.[64] Inquiries directed at wives and their friendships find that women routinely share their concerns about their marriages with close friends and in this way engage in a form of emotion work.[65] Spouses, and especially women, talk

[59] Roberto et al., 2001; Snarey, 1993.
[60] Hanks, 2001; Hawkins & Dollahite, 1997; Snarey, 1993.
[61] Chebra, 1991; Ellingson & Sotirin, 2006.
[62] Copen & Silverstein, 2007; Pratt & Fiese, 2004; Robertson, 1977.
[63] Sotirin & Ellingson, 2006.   [64] Hochschild, 1979.
[65] Oliker, 1989.

to their close friends about their marriages and in doing so improve their understanding of their relationships with effects on their marriages.[66] Similarly nieces and nephews may engage in a form of *family work* in which they disclose their concerns about their parents or other family members with aunts and uncles and in doing so enrich their understanding of themselves or their families.

Aunts and uncles may also act as buffers by directly advocating for the interests of nieces and nephews, or they may mediate in conflicts between nieces and nephews with their parents or siblings. Network members, including parents and friends, are found to act as partisan supporters, and occasionally as critics, of the positions intimate partners adopt in their conflicts, and they influence the tactical positions partners take in their conflicts.[67]

Companionship is a common theme in the relationships of mothers and fathers and their adult children.[68] Similarly, the relationships of aunts with nieces and uncles with nephews may include elements of shared common interest and mutual support, both characteristic of friendship. Although whether friendship themes routinely appear among uncles and nephews is unknown, in a longitudinal study of the elderly, social gerontologists Clare Wenger and Vanessa Burholt report that shared common interests highlight the relationships of elderly uncles and their adult nephews and nieces.[69]

In the chapters that follow, we explore how generativity – a concern for future generations – is expressed in the relationships of aunts and uncles with their nieces and nephews. Four relational features, taken from John Kotre's definition of the requirements of generative cultures, frame the primary research questions regarding how aunts and uncles serve as mentors, family historians, intergenerational buffers, and friends of their nieces and nephews.

DESCRIBING THE RELATIONSHIPS

Undoubtedly aunts and nieces, uncles and nephews will vary in the frequency of their interaction and the meaning that interaction takes in defining their relationships. In one of the first direct investigations of uncles and aunts, then–graduate student Janice Chebra reported contact with nieces and nephews averaged "monthly or several times per year or less," although the 64 aunts and 30 uncles in this study typically rated the relationships as

---

[66] Helms et al., 2003.
[68] Miller-Day, 2004; Snarey, 1993.

[67] Klein & Milardo, 2000.
[69] Wenger & Burholt, 2001.

"important" and "moderately" close.[70] Chebra reported elements of responsibility for disciplining young nieces and nephews (over half of whom were under age 11), caretaking, and mentoring, as well as a certain degree of indulgence. This pattern of responsibilities is similar to ties between grandparents and grandchildren,[71] although aunts and uncles are likely to evidence some distinct qualities relative to grandparents because they are often of the same generation as the parents of nieces and nephews and know and understand parents as siblings or peers.

Popular treatments characterize the relationships of aunts and uncles with nieces and nephews as a unique blend of roles that sometimes parallel those of parents, complementing and supplementing what parents ordinarily do, and at other times share characteristics of peer-based friendships.[72] These basic themes reappear in the few direct inquiries with aunts, uncles, nieces, and nephews.

In an exploratory study of elderly Welsh uncles, Clare Wenger and her colleagues reported several factors that affect the closeness of elderly uncles with their adult nieces and nephews.[73] Their relationships appeared strongest when uncles acted as substitute parents for their nieces and nephews as children, when nieces or nephews lived in close proximity to their uncles, when there was frequent quality contact between uncles and their nieces or nephews, when the uncles felt a need for a substitute child, when no child or children served as a direct heir, and when uncles were in need of a caregiver and the niece or nephew was the only living or available relative. This work suggests that proximity, personal need, and a history of interaction promote cross-generational relationships with important consequences for all parties.

Complementing earlier work, more recent studies examine aunting from the perspective of nieces and nephews who clearly value aunts as mentors and elder confidants, while at the same time valuing them as recreational partners and nonjudgmental intimates. Family communication scholars Laura Ellingson and Patricia Sotirin asked nieces and nephews to respond to an open-ended question about communication with their aunts and in this way described how they understood the roles of their aunts and their importance.[74] The participants in this study, who were undergraduate students, were asked to write an essay in response to the directive:

[70] Chebra, 1991, p. 43.
[71] Nahemow, 1985; Robertson, 1995; Silverstein & Marenco, 2001; Thomas, 1986.
[72] Cogan, 2002; Sturgis, 2004; Traeder & Bennett, 1998.
[73] Wenger, 2001; Wenger & Burholt, 2001.
[74] Ellingson & Sotirin, 2006; Sotirin & Ellingson, 2006.

"Please describe communicating with one or more of your aunts."[75] This straightforward query yielded a surprising array of responses and insights into how young women and men (averaging 21 years of age) view their aunts. They described their aunts as mentors and role models, confidantes and trusted advisors, older peers, and occasionally second mothers. Nieces and nephews described how their aunts provided welcome gifts or treats, helped in maintaining family connections, and communicated an overall climate of encouragement. For many participants, aunts represent a valued confidant. For others, and especially those nieces and nephews who were close to their aunts in age, aunts were often viewed as experienced and "savvy peers." Then, too, nieces and nephews describe some aunts whom they did not admire or wish to emulate; although the authors are unclear how often nieces and nephews identify undesirable qualities in their aunts, they wisely recognize this possibility.

In general, this array of findings is consistent with a depiction of aunts as positive role models complementing parents and encouraging nieces and nephews. As a journalist remarked anecdotally about her own family experience, "She was my aunt, and perhaps more than mothers, aunts exist to give the message that all things are equally possible and permissible."[76]

Ellingson and Sotirin found that when aunts were not acting as surrogate parents, aunts were viewed as more neutral relative to parents with little responsibility for enforcing family rules.[77] Aunts were regarded as less judgmental, and as a result nieces and nephews were more comfortable confiding in aunts in ways they might not with parents.

Nieces and nephews were not specifically questioned about the interventions of aunts on their behalf. For instance, when inevitable conflicts occur between parents and their children, especially in adolescence, we might anticipate that aunts, as well as uncles, act as advocates for the interests of parents or children. Nonetheless, the student volunteers spontaneously reported that aunts occasionally acted as a refuge when conflicts with parents emerged. Additionally, we can anticipate that parents may seek the counsel of aunts, and uncles, in dealing with their children, or parents may directly encourage aunts and uncles to intervene with their children and in this way supplement the work that parents do. In certain circumstances, aunts, and uncles, may serve to help nieces and nephews cope with abusive childhoods, a stark reminder that family members can occasionally

[75] Sotirin & Ellingson, 2006, p. 88.   [76] DiPerna, 1998, p. 152.
[77] Ellingson & Sotirin, 2006.

engage in decidedly harmful activities with children; aunts, uncles, and grandparents can and do effectively intervene on behalf of their nieces, nephews, and grandchildren.[78]

Although basic inquiries of aunting and uncling are limited, the few existing studies are suggestive of how aunts and uncles on some occasions and in some families actively mentor their nieces and nephews and advise parents on matters of child care. Many additional questions remain, and key among them is the issue of identifying the features of families and their members that directly affect the development of relationships between aunts and nieces, and uncles and nephews. The question is intriguing and one for which we can draw on several indirect or informal sources.

PREDICTING CLOSENESS

Elizabeth Bott, in her now classic study of working-class London families, identified several features that seem to influence closeness with kin, including the physical accessibility of kin, type of genealogical relationship, connectedness of the kinship network, presence and preferences of connecting relatives who are typically grandmothers and elder sisters, perceived similarities and differences in social status, and idiosyncratic combinations of needs and attitudes.[79] All of these features may influence whether relationships among aunts, uncles, nieces, and nephews develop.

Geographic and Virtual Accessibility

Accessibility facilitates strong ties among kin, but it is not sufficient or entirely necessary. Kin who live in close proximity report more active relationships, and their easy accessibility facilitates ongoing relationships. Then, too, it may well be that the closeness or intimacy of a relationship prompts relatives to establish neighboring residences. On the other hand, many accessible ties – kin who live near one another – are not strong ties, and many near intimates are relatively distant geographically. In short, geographic distance seems to have less impact on the depth of relationships with kin than we might expect, and often distance and closeness are only weakly related, if at all, a finding with a long pedigree in family studies that has been reported in recent work by evolutionary psychologists,[80] the work of social

---

[78] Doyle, 2001; Johnson-Garner & Meyers, 2003.
[79] Bott, 1971.   [80] Salmon, 1999.

gerontologists on grandparenting,[81] as well as in much earlier studies by sociologists on kinship.[82]

With the advent of personal and batch e-mail (i.e., *family spam*), instant messaging, cell phones and text messaging, chat rooms, blog sites, family Web sites, web cams, and other features of digital technology, we can expect geographic dispersion to be even less consequential as a primary factor in accounting for the closeness of ties with kin. In fact, the use of cell phones and e-mail in particular seem to have a very positive effect on family communications. Recent studies of daily Internet use are establishing that rather than replace in-person contact, new mediums such as Internet access and cell phones enhance communication with intimates by increasing the frequency and variety of contacts.[83] Computer-mediated communications, including e-mail sent to individuals or groups, facilitate the maintaining of existing relationships as well as the expanding of the range of kin and other personal associates contacted.[84] Because of the convenience, low cost, and asynchrony of e-mail, individuals are able to carry on conversations at their leisure and at different times. In a recent study, participants believed their Internet use increased the number of core intimates, near intimates, and casual acquaintances with whom they communicated, increasing the range of contacts by approximately 30%. Geographically distant kin and friends were among the most active e-mail users.[85] Among those who maintain long-distance relationships and are unable to interact routinely in person, computer-mediated communications facilitate intimacy.[86]

In summary, although accessibility can facilitate relationships among adult siblings and their children, the effects of geographic dispersion are limited. Contemporary mediums such as cell phones, personal or family Web pages, and e-mail ameliorate the challenges of maintaining long-distance relationships by offering a convenient means through which family members can observe frequent contact and keep informed of one another's daily lives. In many cases, as we shall see, social distance – or how close or distant family members feel to one another – trumps geographic distance as an influential factor in the initiation, development, and maintenance of relationships among aunts and uncles with their siblings and the children of their siblings.

---

[81] Roberto et al., 2001; Silverstein & Marenco, 2001.
[82] Bott, 1971; Fischer, 1982; Litwak & Kulin, 1987; Waite & Harrison, 1992.
[83] Igarashi, Takai, & Yoshida, 2005.
[84] Boase, Horrigan, Wellman, & Rainie, 2006; Boase & Wellman, 2006.
[85] Boase et al., 2006.   [86] Stafford, 2005.

Relationships among Adult Siblings

Yet another factor likely to be influential in the development of relationships among aunts and uncles with their nieces and nephews is the tenor of relationships among adult siblings and their spouses or partners. Adult sibling ties are unique if for no other reason than their longevity, paired with elements of normative obligation to provide support and a certain degree of personal discretion to maintain close ties or not on the basis of similarities of lifestyles and personal likes and dislikes.[87] With the longevity of sibling relationships comes the potential for instability as life circumstance brings partners closer together or drives them further apart over time.[88] Significant life transitions, including changes in occupation, marriage and partnership statuses, divorce, and the death of a parent, create opportunities for increasing closeness or distance. In comparison, the arrival of children on the part of one sibling or another more consistently increases closeness.[89] A single 41-year-old sister explained: "When we were the two of us together [as sisters] . . . we were quite close and then . . . things got more distant by the time she married. . . . And then, with the baby, things have come closer because I have been so deeply involved."[90] In this case, and perhaps for many other aunts and uncles, the arrival of a child had the effect of renewing a relationship between siblings that had lapsed in closeness. When both siblings become parents, their children can serve as a raison d'être, offering opportunities for contact premised on providing mutual help in child care based on similar needs.[91] Siblings can provide both practical help in child care and opportunities for their children to establish playmates with their cousins. New parents may encourage the involvement of their siblings and welcome the additional help in child care they can provide. We find similar processes among young adult parents in their relationships with their own parents. Closer relationships among young parents and their own parents are associated with closer ties among grandchildren and their grandparents.[92]

For childless siblings the arrival of a niece or nephew can represent a welcome opportunity to engage with young children that might not otherwise be available and occasion a closer bond between siblings. In a popular treatment of aunts, a childless aunt reckoned that with her niece she was able "to receive and express the kind of unquestioning affection parents

---

[87] Eriksen & Gerstel, 2002; Igarashi et al., 2005; Matthews, 2005; Mikkelson, 2006.
[88] White, 2001.   [89] Connidis, 1992.
[90] Connidis, 1992, p. 976.   [91] Segura & Pierce, 1998.
[92] Fingerman, 2004; Monserud, 2008; Ruiz & Silverstein, 2007; Silverstein & Marenco, 2001.

get to enjoy every day" and later added that "aunts can go home when the child gets testy."[93] Then, too, single and childless individuals engage in more contact with their siblings, relative to their married counterparts, and they report more routine exchanges of emotional support and practical support with household labor.[94] In her insightful study, sociologist Karen Hansen describes how parents construct family networks and on some occasions draw heavily on their siblings for support in child care.[95] It is perhaps no accident that the most active aunts and uncles are often those who are relatively established, single, and childless. Quite possibly single and childless individuals are more inclined to develop ties with their nieces and nephews, and especially if they, and parents, value a strong sense of family, are child oriented, and adopt an ethos of provisioning mutual support.

Ties between siblings are influenced by a variety of additional life transitions with the potential to spill over onto relationships between aunts, uncles, nieces, and nephews. Divorce can intensify the relationships of siblings and potentially influence the relationships of aunts and uncles with the children of the divorced sibling. When reflecting on her divorce, a middle-aged women said: "[My siblings] were pretty crucial to getting through that time period. . . . They were truly superb with my kids and they probably helped me out a lot more than I knew at the time."[96] This example suggests that aunts and uncles serve to help their nieces and nephews with adjusting to the divorce of their parents, perhaps becoming important confidants for their nieces and nephews, as well as parents. Parallel functions are found among grandmothers who mentor families experiencing divorce by actively supporting parents and children.[97] On the other hand, for noncustodial parents, divorce can lead to a deterioration of grandchildren's relationships with grandparents, typically paternal grandparents.[98] Young adults who are less influenced by issues of custody (e.g., because they are living largely independently of either parent) may be freer to continue relationships with maternal and paternal grandparents because custody issues are not quite as salient,[99] and they may be freer to maintain relationships with aunts and uncles regardless of the tenor of relationships among adult siblings. To date, the role of aunts and uncles in ameliorating the adjustment of parents or their children to divorce has yet to be examined, although it is apt to be significant.

---

[93] DiPerna, 1998, p. 154.

[94] Gerstel & Sarkisian, 2006; Sarkisian & Gerstel, 2008.

[95] Hansen, 2005.　　　　　　　　　　[96] Connidis, 1992, p. 978.

[97] Copen & Silverstein, 2007; Hanks, 2001; Johnson, 1988.

[98] Cherlin & Furstenberg, 1986; Kruk & Hall, 1995.

[99] Cooney & Smith, 1996.

In short, there is good reason to expect that the relationships among adult siblings are influential in promoting or impeding the development of ties among aunts and uncles with their nieces and nephews. Strong relationships among siblings are apt to encourage the development of relationships with children. In comparison, distant relationships among siblings may deter the development of relationships of aunts and uncles with children. For some, childlessness may prove to be an important factor and provide welcome opportunities for nurturing children that might not otherwise be available. The exchange of support among sisters and brothers prompted by a deteriorating marriage illustrates how events occurring among parents and children reverberate across households, potentially influencing relationships among siblings and between siblings and their nieces and nephews. Significant transitions such as marriage and divorce are experienced across households, and they may intensify relationships with siblings and their children or distance them.

Gender and Kin Keeping

Comparing adult sisters and brothers, we see that, as is often the case, women are more active in the care and maintenance of family relationships. Sisters provide more and a wider array of help to their siblings, and they are more apt to provide help with practical tasks such as laundry, household labor, caring for a sick child, or more generally providing child care.[100] This wider involvement of sisters with kin suggests that aunts may be more involved with their nieces and nephews relative to uncles and that the relationships among sisters as well as sisters and brothers may be more important in facilitating relationships among all family members. There is considerable evidence that women are more involved with kin on average, relative to men. Averages, however, can be misleading.

The greater involvement of women with kin is easily demonstrated. Women have more contact with kin, and especially other womenfolk. They provide more practical help in matters of household labor and child care and, not surprisingly, more emotional support.[101] Women send more greeting cards – nearly 85% of the billion cards sent annually, in recognition of anniversaries, birthdays, holidays, and special events; this practice illustrates their participation in the ongoing maintenance of family relationships.[102] Women are more apt to communicate with kin by e-mail, including aunts

---

[100] Eriksen & Gerstel, 2002; Voorpostel & Van Der Lippe, 2007.
[101] Gerstel & Gallagher, 1996; Leach & Braithwaite, 1996.
[102] di Leonardo, 1987; Gibbs, 2008.

and uncles, and believe such communication mediums have served to improve their connections to siblings, distant kin, and friends.[103]

Women clearly engage in more kin keeping than men, on average, as we
have documented throughout this chapter. This suggests that aunts will be
more involved with nieces and nephews than uncles and, on average, that
they will communicate more often and exchange more resources with their
siblings and the children of their siblings. Because women are more likely to
engage in kin-keeping activities with other women, we can expect that ties
between aunts and nieces will be among the strongest and most resilient.
That is what the averages tell us to expect. However, a more detailed look
at the available evidence suggests a far more interesting and nuanced story.
In nearly all cases, there are exceptions, occasions when men seem to be
involved in kin keeping and occasions when the differences between men
and women are relatively modest. For instance, while women are most often
identified as kin keepers, much smaller but still significant proportions of
men also actively engage in kin keeping. On the order of 15% to 28% of
kin keepers are men based on the available research.[104] Although women
provide routine help to a greater number of kin and invest more hours in
doing so, some men are more involved than others.[105] The most active men
may eclipse the least active women. Traditional rules of engagement apply,
but on occasion gender is undone.[106]

Inquiries of grandparents typically find grandmothers are more involved
with their grandchildren, relative to grandfathers, and they do so by providing short- and long-term child care, acting as family historians, and
providing instrumental and emotional support to parents.[107] Nonetheless,
this does not mean grandfathers are uniformly uninvolved; they at times are
highly involved, influential, and find their activities with grandchildren personally rewarding.[108] By concentrating on grandmothers, we inadvertently
apply a "feminized lens" that underreports and undervalues the contributions of grandfathers. A singular attention to gendered family roles discounts
the deliberate relationships men and women create of their own agency, and
given their own predispositions and circumstance.

Recent investigations of Internet use clearly demonstrate the greater
involvement of women with kin, but again some gender differences are
modest. Although women report that e-mail has brought them closer to

[103] Rainie et al., 2000.
[104] Leach & Braithwaite, 1996; Rosenthal, 1985.
[105] Gerstel & Gallagher, 1996.   [106] Blume & Blume, 2003; Deutsch, 2007.
[107] Fingerman, 2004; Monserud, 2008; Silverstein & Marenco, 2001.
[108] Roberto et al., 2001.

their families (43% of female e-mail users), improved their family relationships (41%), and improved their knowledge about family members (27%), the differences between women and men are slight, less than 7%.[109] Significant proportions of men believe e-mail use has brought them closer to their families (37%), improved their relationships (34%), and increased their knowledge of family members (23%). Centering on comparative averages obfuscates the landscape of families and their lived diversity.

One important purpose of this study is to identify men who are actively engaged in kin keeping by virtue of their relationships with their siblings and their nephews. They may well represent a minority of men, those with a feminist sensibility who recognize the importance of caregiving, and they may well be outnumbered by active aunts, but by design and purpose, this study seeks to describe the full range of aunting and uncling and to uncover instances of active aunting and uncling where they exist.

Personal Experience and Preference

Taken together, the issues of proximity and accessibility, the closeness of siblings, presence of kin keepers as connecting relatives, and engagement in the work of developing and maintaining family relationships are all potentially important factors influencing the relationships among siblings and their children. Undoubtedly, additional features of families and their members are influential. We may expect families who value their common ancestry and celebrate their unique family identity will encourage relationships among members, including collateral kin. Cross-generational ties experienced in the formative years of childhood can influence the future engagements of adults. For instance, uncles may model their own experience of being uncled in developing their relationships with nephews, perhaps compensating for any shortcomings they may have experienced in their own relationships, much as fathers do,[110] or they may develop models from a number of male role models including fathers, grandfathers, other kin, and peers, again as fathers do.[111] Similarly aunts may model women who were important in their lives.

Personal preferences will additionally play a role. Relationship scholars are quick to point out that we like people with whom we share similar interests and values.[112] This essential underpinning to personal relationships is

---

[109] Rainie et al., 2000.
[111] Daly, 1993.

[110] Marsiglio, 2004; Pleck, 1997.
[112] Blieszner & Adams, 1992.

apt to influence the connections between adult siblings in which relationships are built on a mix of obligation and personal volition. We can expect
that close relationships among siblings spill over to children, encouraging
relationships among aunts, uncles, nieces, and nephews. Among older nieces
and nephews, common interests and recreational pursuits held in common
with aunts and uncles may become an additional feature that encourages
their relationships to continue into adulthood, taking on the character of a
mutual friendship.

The mix of normative customs and relational and personal features
that characterize relationships among kin are interdependent, and no one
feature is apt to explain why relationships flourish and why they fail. Uncles
may develop relationships with young nephews because the uncles generally
have strong relationships with their siblings, because their sisters encourage
such relationships, because they live near their nephews, and because their
families have a tradition of strong relationships with nephews and nieces.
They may continue the relationship into adolescence and adulthood because
both uncle and nephew find commonality in their personal interests, enjoy
one another's company, and come to view themselves as friends. The relative
weight or importance of any one feature likely depends on the configuration
of combined features as well as the age of participants.

CONCLUSION

The contemporary discourse on families has largely ignored the contributions of aunts and uncles, and yet there is good reason to believe they
are active and consequential. In a large and representative sample of the
U.S. population, sociologists Lynn White and Agnes Riedman find approximately half of all adults report seeing and talking with their siblings at least
once per month, and about two thirds consider at least one sibling among
their closest friends.[113] When sisters are present, contact is even greater. The
most common exchanges among siblings is advice giving and providing
child care to nieces and nephews. It seems entirely likely that aunts and
uncles are rather commonly active and important in one another's lives and
in the lives of children.

In framing this study we explored several relevant literatures including
the limited research available on personal beliefs about the importance of
ties with kin and obligations to immediate and extended kin. Literatures on

---

[113] White & Riedman, 1992.

adults siblings, grandparents and grandchildren, and the few direct studies of aunts and uncles illustrate how we might come to understand uncling and aunting, or how aunts and uncles influence the lives of children and their parents. We drew on the concept of intergenerational solidarity, feminist ideas about the social construction of families, and generativity, modifying these perspectives to better accommodate the breadth of research questions concerning individuals and relationship processes. Consistent with this conceptual grounding, we assume families are best represented as configurations of interdependent relationships organized across multiple households. In short, family members talk, and in doing so, they build relationships. They share news, gossip, evaluate, seek confirmation; they offer advice, sometimes criticism, and sometimes interference. Wherever we look, women are more active and oriented toward building connections. We can expect aunts to be no different and to build stronger ties to their siblings and their nieces and nephews compared with uncles. Wherever we look there are exceptions – men who express an interest in kin and establish ties with their siblings and perhaps their nephews. While appreciating how gender guides the construction of family relationships, we can simultaneously acknowledge personal agency and how individuals construct their family relationships on the basis of personal preferences and opportunity. Our design is to recover what aunts and uncles do, how they think about their positions, and how they are consequential.

2

The Study

The 104 volunteers for this study included aunts, uncles, nieces, and nephews who were interviewed in their homes, offices, or occasionally in a public café. The interviews ranged widely from under a half hour to nearly two hours. Often the volunteers had much to say in response to my questions about their experience being an uncle or aunt, niece or nephew. In all, I recorded more than 83 hours of material, which was later transcribed verbatim into text files. Here I describe the volunteers in some detail, the kinds of questions I asked, and the method I used to come to some understanding of what they shared. Some readers may be more interested in the actual findings and less in the details of the inquiry's design. Feel free to move right along to the findings presented in the chapters that follow.

THE DESIGN OF THE STUDY

Because we know so little about what aunts and uncles do, or how nieces and nephews experience uncling or aunting, the most direct approach seemed the most appropriate. I simply asked them to describe their relationships in their own words. In this way, the *data* of the study are the voiced experiences of participants. Experiences include descriptions of how often they visited, chatted by phone, or e-mailed. Some were in frequent contact, some were not. Some were exceptionally close and described relationships like that between a parent and son or daughter, or between intimate friends. They described ordinary experiences of daily life, experiences of shared amusements, and details of their relationships with each other as well as relationships with other family members.

All of the interviews were directed around a favored niece, nephew, aunt, or uncle. I asked each aunt to identify a favored niece and each uncle to identify a favored nephew. When interviewing nieces or nephews,

I did the same and asked each to identify a favored aunt or uncle and to answer all questions with reference to that individual. Participants typically responded to this request quite easily, with some exceptions. Two uncles identified favored nephews who were twins (one pair of 7 year olds and one pair of 13 year olds), and one aunt identified twin 7-year old nieces. Uncles and aunts often mentioned additional nephews and nieces, other than their nominated *favorite*, and they were encouraged to do so particularly when there was no clearly favored person or to illuminate differences in their respective relationships. Where a favored person could not be identified, participants were asked to identify the person they saw most often.

The aunts and uncles were unrelated to one another and represented very different families. The nieces and nephews were in nearly all cases unrelated to the aunts and uncles. In two cases I interviewed an aunt and then later her niece; these were exceptions to the typical practice I used. The decision to interview one party to a relationship rather than pairs suits the study's purpose by maximizing the number of relationships being described and therefore the potential range of relationship types, their closeness, conduct, and overall diversity.

For perhaps no other reason than simplicity, each uncle described a relationship with a particular nephew and each aunt described a relationship with a particular niece. I did not specifically ask uncles about their nieces or aunts about their nephews, although they did occasionally mention them. In the same way, when interviewed, nieces described a particular aunt, and nephews described a particular uncle. Throughout the interviews, participants often spoke about other family members, including other uncles or aunts, nieces or nephews, grandparents, parents, and siblings.

One consistent finding of the study is the variety of relationships that link family members. As I demonstrate in the chapters that follow, families are often organized across multiple households. Aunts learn about their nieces by talking with their sisters, and conversely parents sometime rely on their siblings to communicate with their children or otherwise represent the interests of parents. Uncles learn how to deal with a particularly thorny issue having to do with a sibling by talking with their nephews. In some cases family intimacies transcended household boundaries, and this was especially true of sisters who interacted frequently, even daily, and included adult nieces in their multiplex relationships.

Although the purpose of the study is to explore one particular class of family relationships, our conversations often ranged more widely and were governed by the experiences of participants. A distinct advantage of qualitative research design is the ability to inquire about a particular class of personal relationships while permitting the respondents to govern just how those stories are told, and often this means adding details regarding other family members. In many regards, families are in fact not well represented by singular pair relationships such as that between husband and wife, parent and child, or aunt and niece; rather they are pairs set in a community of interdependent relationships from which they draw personal meaning and a shared collective biography.

The interviews were designed to elicit information on basic descriptive features of the respondents and their families, as well as each of the specific research interests defined earlier. I asked each respondent about his or her personal background such as age, ethnicity or race, education, occupation, partnership or marital status, and sexual orientation. This provided the essential background material. The aunts and uncles were asked how often they had interacted with a niece or nephew over the previous year, as well as how their relationship changed over the course of their niece's or nephew's lives. They were asked to describe the kinds of activities in which they engaged; whether they provided advice, criticism, or partisan support; any instances of family work; family storytelling; and mentoring. They were asked to describe significant events that were especially important to them or events they believed were important to their niece or nephew. Nephews were asked a similar set of questions about a favored uncle, and nieces about a favored aunt.[1]

Additional questions were fashioned to address whether uncles or aunts ever talk about their roles, or if they model their own experiences in how they enact their respective roles of aunt or uncle. To address each of these questions I asked aunts and uncles to describe any instances of talk about what it means to be an aunt or uncle or whether they shared their experiences with friends or kin. I asked them to describe their relationships with their own aunts and uncles during their childhood or adult lives. With the exception of these two sets of issues, similar questions were asked of both generations.

THE VOLUNTEERS

Uncles and nephews were drawn from two locations. The New Zealand sample consists of 10 uncles and 19 nephews; the Maine sample consists of 11 uncles and 12 nephews. The two samples of uncles did not differ

---

[1] The range of questions is depicted in the Interview Coding Protocol presented in the Appendix.

significantly in demographic characteristics such as their average age (M = 46), race (95% White), sexual orientation (86% heterosexual), or partnership status (66% married or cohabiting) (see Table 2.1). Annual incomes averaged $55,000 USD ($SD$ = $22,600) for the Maine uncles, of whom 73% were professionals and 64% were college educated. Income estimates were unavailable for the New Zealanders, of whom 60% were professionals and 78% were college educated. Forty-eight percent of the uncles were childless.

In addition, the samples of uncles did not differ in terms of their nephews' characteristics such as the nephew's average age of 20 (range = 7–43), sexual orientation (heterosexual 95%), or frequency of interaction, with 24% visiting biannually or less often, 33% bimonthly to monthly, and 43% greater than monthly. Five of the uncles (24%) described relationships with nephews whose fathers were absent, typically through death or divorce. One uncle reported his nephew's mother had recently died, and one reported a nephew's alcoholic mother was absent from the family.

The Maine interviews with uncles (M = 52 minutes) were somewhat longer than the interviews with New Zealand uncles [M = 36 minutes, $t(19) = 2.64$, $p < .02$]. Additional comparative details are presented in the Appendix (Table A1).

Independent of the uncles, separate samples of nephews were interviewed, all of whom ranged in age from 18 to 28. The Maine nephews were somewhat older (M = 23) than their New Zealand counterparts [M = 19, $t(29) = 4.4$, $p < .001$] but otherwise were similar in terms of demographic characteristics: race (90% White), partnership status (93% single), occupation (90% students), and sexual orientation (97% heterosexual). All of the nephews were childless. Their uncles were aged on average 46 years and heterosexual (100%). They ranged widely in terms of frequency of interaction, with 23% visiting biannually or less, 52% visiting bimonthly or monthly, and 26% visiting several times per month.

The majority of uncles and nephews were related through an uncle's sibling and typically a sister (approximately 50%) or brother (approximately 30%). Uncles who were related by marriage are not well represented (i.e., a parent's brother-in-law or a nephew's father's sister's husband), perhaps indicating that such uncles are less likely to develop relationships with their nephews.

In many ways the aunts were similar to uncles (see Table 2.2). The 31 aunts who were interviewed were on average 48 years of age, largely White (93.5%), and heterosexual (87%). Five of the aunts were of Franco-American heritage, and two were Native American. Most were employed in professional (76%) or managerial positions (10%) with annual household incomes of approximately $54,500. Most were married or living with their

Table 2.1. *Descriptive statistics for uncles (n = 21) and nephews (n = 31)*

Variables	Uncles	Nephews
Age, Mean (SD)	46 (10.7)	20.7 (2.8)
White, non-Hispanic	95	90
Education		
High school	5	3
Some college	25	90
College degree(s)	70	7
Occupation		
Professional	67	3
Blue collar	10	7
Student	14	90
Retired/disabled	10	0
Annual income (in thousand USD), Mean (SD)[a]	55.00 (22.60)	11.80 (4.0)
Heterosexual	86	97
Marital status		
Single	24	93
Married/cohabiting	66	7
Divorced	10	0
Childless	48	100
Uncle's nephew's age, Mean (SD)	20 (8.35)	N/A
Nephew's uncle's age, Mean (SD)	N/A	46.1 (9.5)
Uncle's nephew's sexual orientation		
Heterosexual	95	N/A
Nephew's uncle's sexual orientation		
Heterosexual	N/A	100
Frequency of interaction		
Annually or less	14.3	9.7
Biannual	9.5	12.9
Bimonthly	23.8	35.5
Monthly	9.5	16.1
Biweekly	14.3	9.7
Weekly or greater	28.6	16.2
Nephew's father absent	23.8	9.7
Uncle's relationship to nephew's parents		
Mother's brother	52.4	51.6
Father's brother	28.6	32.3
Brother-in-law	19.1	16.1
Length of interview (in minutes), Mean (SD)	44.6 (16.2)	22.7 (14.1)

Note: All figures are in percentages unless otherwise noted.
[a] Incomes are not available for the New Zealand sample.

Table 2.2. *Descriptive statistics for aunts (n = 31) and nieces (n = 21)*

Variables	Aunts	Nieces
Age, Mean (SD)	48.0 (7.6)	27.7 (10.6)
White, non-Hispanic	93.5	90.0
Education		
High school	3.2	0
Some college	12.9	42.9
College degree(s)	83.8	57.2
Occupation		
Professional	75.9	23.8
Managerial	10.3	0
Student	6.9	66.7
Retired	6.9	4.8
Unemployed	0	4.8
Annual income (in thousands USD), Mean (SD)	54.50 (18.3)	25.0 (13.2)
Heterosexual	87.1	100
Marital status		
Single	12.9	47.6
Married	54.8	23.8
Cohabiting	16.1	19.0
Divorced	16.1	9.5
Childless	54.8	81.0
Aunt's niece's age, Mean (SD)	21.83 (9.63)	N/A
Niece's aunt's age, Mean (SD)	N/A	52.62 (15.39)
Aunt's niece's sexual orientation		
Heterosexual	100	N/A
Niece's aunt's sexual orientation		
Heterosexual	N/A	95.2
Frequency of interaction		
Annually or less	12.9	33.3
Biannual	19.4	9.5
Bimonthly	29.0	14.3
Monthly	3.2	19.0
Biweekly	6.5	4.8
Weekly or greater	29.0	19.1
Niece's father absent	6.4	23.8
Aunt's relationship to niece's parents		
Mother's sister	51.6	57.1
Father's sister	38.7	33.3
Sister-in-law	6.4	4.8
Other	3.2	4.8
Length of interview (in minutes), Mean (SD)	75.86 (15.4)	48.97 (20.99)

Note: All figures are in percentages unless otherwise noted.

partner (71%), and slightly more than half of the aunts were childless (55%). They described nieces who were on average 22 years of age, and, with one exception, they ranged in age from 7 to 41. One aunt with a 7-month-old niece was interviewed to explore her views about this newly achieved status and newly developing relationship. Approximately one third visited biannually or less (32%), nearly one third visited bimonthly or monthly (32%), and the remainder visited several times per month (35.5%). Most of the aunts and nieces were related through an aunt's sister (52%) or brother (39%). Aunts related to nieces through marriage (i.e., a parent's sister-in-law) were uncommon and occurred in only two cases.[2] Like the uncles, this suggests that such relationships rarely develop. Two of the aunts (6%) described relationships with nieces whose fathers were absent; none described relationships with nieces whose mothers were absent.

Twenty-one nieces were interviewed. They were on average 28 years of age with a range of 19 to 54. They were largely White (71%) or of Franco-American background (19%). The sample included one Hispanic niece and one Native American. Most were students (67%) or working in professional positions (24%). Nieces were typically single (48%), married, or living with partners (43%). Most were childless (81%). They were heterosexual and described aunts who were on average 53 years of age. One of the aunts was a lesbian and in this instance was also interviewed. Visits with aunts were occasional for some, averaging biannually or less (43%), and a third reported visiting bimonthly or monthly (33%); others reported visiting several times per month (24%). Five of the nieces (24%) and three of the nephews (10%) reported their fathers were absent for most of their lives, typically as a result of a divorce; none reported absent mothers.

The Interviews

All interviews were digitally recorded and later transcribed verbatim by myself or a very talented team of student research interns to whom I shall be eternally grateful. Interviews were semistructured and open-ended; conducted in homes, offices, or public areas; and took an average of 45 minutes for uncles ($SD = 16$) and 23 minutes for nephews ($SD = 14$). One uncle was interviewed by phone. Interviews were substantially longer for the women and averaged 76 minutes ($SD = 15$) for aunts and 49 minutes ($SD = 21$) for

---

[2] One aunt, Dorthea, is actually a cousin to her niece, although she views herself as an aunt and is referred to as such by her niece, for whom she is a legal guardian. The niece is Dorthea's father's sister's child.

nieces. This feature is one of the more consistent findings in the study. The women talk more and in greater detail about their relationships, with a niece or aunt as the case may be, but also about other family members. In some regards, this is not a surprising finding because women are consistently found to be more relationship oriented relative to men, more articulate about their relationships, and more concerned about kin.[3] Nonetheless, as we will see in the following chapters, it would be an error to assume that men do not establish close, intimate ties with their nephews. In many regards, they are certainly intimate, and on occasion more so than some aunts with their nieces.

Aunts and uncles were recruited through advertisements and word-of-mouth, with a preference for those who had nieces or nephews of at least school age to allow for opportunities to discuss issues concerning school, families, and friendships. In fact, 81% of the nephews referenced by uncles were teens or young adults, and 65% of the nieces referenced by aunts were teens or young adults (i.e., in the age range of 13–29). The samples of nieces and nephews were solicited through newspaper ads and campus announcements. Their only requirement for participation was being 18 or older and having a living aunt or uncle regardless of how often they visited or how close they felt to that person.

The tactic of identifying a favored nephew or niece, or uncle or aunt, could have introduced some bias by eliciting descriptions of relationships that are unusually close. There is no attempt in this study to represent a population or to characterize an *average* relationship. Rather, the purpose here is to uncover how relationships among collateral kin are organized, expressed, and potentially influential for nieces, nephews, parents, and other family members. We are interested in both the potential diversity of relationship forms, and whether generative relationships exist, as well as identifying properties of the relationships of aunts and uncles with nieces and nephews when they are generative.

There is considerable variability in the data, and not all aunts or uncles, nieces or nephews described close relationships. Twenty-four percent of uncles ($n = 5$) described relationships with nephews whom they saw very infrequently (biannually or less), and some described relationships that were relatively modest, involving little intimacy or common interest, although they still characterized the nephew in question as a favorite. Similarly 23% of the nephews ($n = 7$) described relationships that involved minimal contact and little intimacy.

---

[3] di Leonardo, 1987; Gerstel & Gallagher, 1996; Milardo & Helms-Erikson, 2000.

Like the uncles, aunts described relationships that varied in closeness. Thirty-two percent ($n = 10$) described relationships in which they visited with their nieces irregularly (biannually or less) and as a consequence had limited knowledge of their nieces' daily lives. Forty-three percent of the nieces ($n = 9$) described visiting with aunts relatively infrequently and less than biannually.

The current design efficiently addresses the primary research questions concerning the potential contributions of aunts and uncles and the nature of their relationships. It yields relationships that vary from decidedly intimate to decidedly superficial and includes instances of occasional conflict and disagreement, but it does not represent relationships with high levels of conflict or abusive relationships.

PLAN OF ANALYSIS

In conducting the analysis and the interviews on which they are based, the goal was to search for theoretical saturation[4] – that is, an outcome in which no new constructs are being revealed and no new properties of the existing constructs are being developed. In analyzing the transcripts, I used a combination of content analysis, which assumes the theoretical dimensions of interest have been identified a priori, and an inductive procedure often referred to as a *grounded theoretical* approach that makes no such a priori assumptions.[5] The analysis proceeded in several stages. In the first stage, each unit – or *meaning unit* – of text was subjected to a constant comparative analysis.[6] Typically, a meaning unit is equivalent to a sentence or several paragraphs. In this way, the transcripts were divided into units of meaning or thought as conveyed by the interviewee, and each meaning unit was assigned to one of several codes or relationship dimensions (e.g., mentoring, buffering). Through an iterative process of constant comparison, the coding scheme and the domains each code represented were further refined as illustrated in the transcripts. Some of the themes represented in the interviews were not entirely anticipated (e.g., instances of reciprocal friendships in which nephews provided advice to uncles, or instances where aunts sought out the advice of nieces), and in this way new codes were developed to best represent respondents' comments. As a means to develop and refine the coding scheme, all transcripts were entered into *N6* (NUD* IST6 or Non-numerical Unstructured Data Indexing, Searching, and

[4] Strauss & Corbin, 1990.
[5] Ambert et al., 1995; Glaser & Strauss, 1997; LaRossa, 2005; Strauss & Corbin, 1990.
[6] Strauss & Corbin, 1990.

Theorizing), a program designed for the analysis and management of text-based interview data. The scheme for coding interviews is summarized in Table 2.3 and detailed in the Appendix. All direct quotes of participants represent themes found in a majority of cases unless otherwise noted.

Three theoretical perspectives including intergenerational solidarity, a feminist perspective on the social construction of family relationships, and generativity informed the kind of questions asked of participants and the initial coding of their responses. As themes unfolded that were not entirely anticipated or predicted, new codes were developed. The outcome of this constant comparative method of coding interview transcripts is *theoretical extension* and *theoretical refinement*.[7] Theoretical extension occurs when preexisting models are applied in new ways, to new groups, or to new social phenomena – applications that were not entirely anticipated in the original model. Theoretical refinement occurs when themes emerge from the interviews that call for change or modification of the existing theory. As we shall see in the chapters that follow, the interviews with aunts, uncles, nieces, and nephews call for both extensions and modifications, especially in regard to how we are to understand the essentials of intergenerational solidarity, generativity, and the social construction of families.

SAMPLE LIMITATIONS

A variety of obvious questions arise from the interviews, some of which can be successfully addressed and some of which cannot. Two limitations of the study are derivative of the relatively small, nonrepresentative samples. Given that the uncles and nephews were drawn from two cultures, there is the obvious question of how New Zealand uncles and nephews compare with their American counterparts. This is an intriguing question, but it is not one that can be addressed with the current design. No doubt both cultures are complex, and we cannot hope to represent their diversity with small convenience samples. In reading the transcripts, however, it would be difficult to distinguish one from the other, with the exception of colloquialisms, and this similarity in the two cultures will be apparent in the voices quoted herein and in the themes they represent.

In addition, there is the obvious question of how aunts and uncles compare. This is an important question. It is a difficult one to address accurately with this study and its reliance on fairly small and nonrepresentative samples. Any difference in the relationships that appears in the chapters that follow may represent an actual difference, one to be found in any

---

[7] Snow, 2004.

Table 2.3. *A summary of individual and relational dimensions*

Dimension	Definition	Sample components
Individual and Relational Descriptors	Describing individuals, relationships, and activity patterns	• Age, marital status • Frequency of interaction • Closeness • Common activities
Aunt/Uncle Roles	Family members' beliefs and expectations regarding aunts and uncles and their relationships with nieces and nephews	• Supplemental parents • Third-party perspectives • Substitute parents • Influence of ethnicity, sexual orientation, or parental status
Mentoring	Direct exchanges of support and advice	• General support • Criticism • Supportive listening • Spiritual advice • Mentoring gender • Nefarious activity • Reverse mentoring • Mentoring parents
Meaning Keeping and Family Work	Communications that influence a family's solidarity or knowledge about family history, as well as communications about particular individuals or in regard to particular relationships with family members	• Storytelling • Managing family traditions • Family work or talk about family members • Child minding talk
Intergenerational Buffers	Acting as an intermediary in relationships between family members	• Mediating disputes between family members • Expressing empathy
Friendship	Basic friendship themes in the relationships of uncles and aunts with nieces and nephews	• Companionship themes • Shared interests • Mutual support
Personal Development	The influence of nieces and nephews on aunts and uncles, or changes in the way aunts and uncles view themselves as a result of aunting or uncling.	• Experiences of aunting or uncling that are life changing
Role Socialization	An aunt's or uncle's formal and informal preparation for the role.	• Aunts' or uncles' memories of their own aunts and uncles • Talk about being an aunt or uncle

Table 2.4. *A Summary of the minority status and sexual orientation of participants* (n = 104)

Status	Aunts	Nieces	Uncles	Nephews	Total
White, non-Hispanic/non-Franco	24	15	20	26	81.7% (85)
Hispanic	0	1	0	0	1.0% (1)
Franco	5	4	0	2	10.6% (11)
Asian	0	0	0	1	1.0% (1)
Pacific Islander	0	0	1	1	1.9% (2)
Native American	2	1	0	1	3.8% (4)
Gay/Lesbian	4	0	3	1	7.7% (8)

Table 2.5. *Descriptive features of aunts*

Id No.	Aunt	Aunt's age	Marital status	No. of kids	Visits per year	Niece	Niece's age	Comment
501	Francesca	45	Single	0	>12	Maria	11	
502	Connie	50	Married	0	>12	Brice	22	Franco
503	Theriza	52	Married	0	<3	Liz	23	
504	Sandy	40	Married	0	>12	Mimi	16	
505	Denise	41	Single	0	>12	Lauren	7	Twin nieces
506	Kathryn	56	Married	2	<3	Nicole	16	
507	Barbara	50	Married	0	>12	Sarah	21	Franco
508	Sylvia	68	Divorced	0	3–6	Anna	30	
509	Debbie	36	Single	0	>12	Emma	58	Franco
510	Alexandra	38	Cohabiting	0	3–6	Julia	24	Lesbian Aunt
511	Beatrice	53	Divorced	2	3–6	Cindy	16	
512	Rebecca	46	Cohabiting	0	>12	Lauren	23	Lesbian Aunt
513	Harriett	53	Married	2	3–6	Tonya	41	
514	Stella	52	Married	2	>12	Elise	18	Franco
515	Susan	38	Married	1	3–6	Nika	26	
516	Ilse	50	Cohabiting	0	3–6	Lana	16	Lesbian Aunt
517	Carla Lyn	54	Married	2	<3	Margo	14	
518	Olympia	52	Married	1	<3	Ruth	35	Father Absent
519	Dora	52	Single	0	<3	Lois	19	
520	Dorthea	28	Married	0	>12	Florence	14	
521	Gladys	50	Married	2	3–6	Bess	41	
522	Raye	44	Divorced	4	>12	Sunshine	17	Native Amer.
523	Roxy	44	Married	0	<3	Chloe	12	
524	Elena	44	Cohabiting	2	<3	Marge	26	Franco
525	Maya	53	Married	1	>12	Vicky	41	
526	Lena	50	Married	1	3–6	Beth	17	
527	Addie	46	Divorced	1	>12	Heather	20	Native Amer.
528	Roslyn	55	Cohabiting	0	3–6	Nina	30	Lesbian Aunt
529	Erma	27	Divorced	0	<3	Iris	23	
530	Isabella	58	Married	1	<3	Lila	32	
531	Rosemary	43	Married	0	7–12	Katie	25	Father Absent

Table 2.6. *Descriptive features of nieces*

Id no.	Niece	Age	Marital status	No. of kids	Visits per year	Aunt's age	Comments
401	Janice	27	Single	0	>12	48	Father Absent
402	Diana	54	Married	2	<3	98	Father Absent
403	Angela	21	Single	0	>12	50	Franco
404	Patricia	53	Divorced	0	>12	86	
405	Michele	31	Married	2	<3	48	
406	Leigh	22	Single	0	7–12	40	
407	Natalie	32	Married	0	<3	60	Franco
408	Elspeth	19	Single	0	<3	40	
409	Marty	23	Single	0	7–12	59	
410	Nicole	24	Married	0	<3	61	Father Absent
411	Estella	28	Cohabiting	0	<3	48	Hispanic
412	Una	23	Cohabiting	0	>12	46	
413	Shenna	23	Single	1	>12	41	
414	Sabina	23	Single	0	7–12	49	
415	Hattie	22	Single	0	3–6	60	
416	Cora	24	Single	0	3–6	45	
417	Nan	23	Married	0	<3	52	
418	Tess	48	Cohabiting	1	<3	58	Native Amer.
419	Zoey	22	Single	0	3–6	43	
420	Yvette	21	Cohabiting	0	<3	42	Franco
421	Fiona	19	Single	0	7–12	31	Franco, Father Absent

representative study of such relationships, or it may reflect the particulars of the people constituting each of the samples. Nonetheless, where differences between aunts and uncles are apparent, and consistent with gender differences reported in other forms of personal relationships, I cautiously suggest how the relationships of aunts and uncles may substantively differ.

Attempts were made to introduce some diversity in the various samples by encouraging the participation of minorities when available, including those with a Franco-American heritage (a group that comprises about 25% of the population of Maine),[8] those with Native American backgrounds (1% of the Maine population),[9] and those who identified themselves as gay and lesbian. In addition, the New Zealand samples include small numbers of Pacific Islanders and Asians (see Table 2.4).

[8] U.S. Census, 1990 Census of Population and Housing, Maine, Summary Tape File 3A, June 1993. For additional discussion of Franco-Americans in Maine, see Langellier & Peterson, 2004.
[9] U.S. Census. Table DP-1: Profile of General Demographic Characteristics 2000. Retrieved October 18, 2005, from http://censtats.census.gov/data/ME/04023.pdf.

Table 2.7. *Descriptive features of uncles*

Id no.	Uncle	Uncle's age	Marital status	No. of kids	Visits per year	Nephew	Nephew's age	Comments
001	Benny	48	Married	3	<3	Thad	21	
002	Robert	48	Single	0	<3	Zak	17	Father Absent
003	Lou	40	Married	0	7–12	Jag	19	
004	Chris	60	Cohabiting	0	>12	Sumner	43	Gay Uncle & Nephew
005	John	35	Single	0	3–6	Josh	16	Gay Uncle
006	Nick	28	Cohabiting	0	>12	Beckett	11	Father Absent
007	Tom	44	Divorced	1	>12	Will	7	
008	Billy	39	Cohabiting	0	3–6	Oliver	13	Father Absent
009	Stephen	22	Single	0	>12	Paul	17	Samoan, Mother Deceased
010	Danny	54	Married	2	>12	Finn	14	
101	Ricky	39	Single	0	>12	Coop	19	Gay Uncle
102	Evan	59	Married	2	>12	Ansel	16	Mother Absent
103	Jimmy	40	Married	2	7–12	Loni	18	
104	Al	49	Married	1	<3	Carlo	15	
105	Mark	60	Married	2	<3	Kurt	36	
106	Pat	60	Married	1	<3	John-Paul	28	
107	Sammy	50	Married	0	3–6	Sean	28	Father Absent
108	Greco	53	Divorced	2	>12	Serge	17	
109	Michael	53	Single	0	3–6	Joey	19	
110	Freddie	44	Married	5	>12	Toby	27	Father Absent
111	Jessie	34	Married	3	>12	Ace	18	

By introducing some diversity in the samples of uncles and aunts, nephews and nieces, I hope to increase the likelihood of discovering variations in the ways such relationships are constructed and the dimensions of intergenerational solidarity and generativity that emerge, which is a primary goal of this study. It is not a goal to generalize to any known population or minority group, or to represent the distinct proportions of aunts, uncles, nieces, and nephews who maintain intimate relationships. The purpose is to explore how these kin establish personal relationships with one another, the nature and impact of those relationships for family members, if those relationships include elements of generativity, and how *uncling* and *aunting* – the process of caring for nephews and nieces – parallels parenting and grandparenting and how it is unique.

Table 2.8. *Descriptive features of nephews*

No. Id	Nephew's name	Nephew's age	Marital status	No. of kids	Visits per year	Uncle's age	Comments
202	Andy	18	Single	0	3–6	60	
203	Lee	21	Single	0	>12	45	Asian
204	Ted	19	Single	0	<3	37	
205	Art	19	Cohabiting	0	<3	47	
206	Dirk	18	Single	0	3–6	45	
207	Rusty	19	Single	0	<3	63	
208	Brig	20	Single	0	3–6	41	Father Absent
209	Taika	19	Single	0	>12	23	Maori
210	Archie	20	Single	0	<3	59	
211	Silas	18	Single	0	<3	47	
212	Van	20	Single	0	>12	55	
213	Buddy	19	Single	0	7–12	39	
214	Jerry	18	Single	0	>12	46	
215	Hy	19	Single	0	3–6	50	
216	Ian	18	Single	0	3–6	24	
217	Rog	19	Single	0	3–6	50	
218	Bruce	18	Single	0	7–12	45	
219	Heath	24	Single	0	>12	41	Father Absent
220	Davie	18	Single	0	<3	40	
301	Jonnie	27	Single	0	3–6	40	Gay
302	Nat	21	Single	0	7–12	45	Franco
303	Mario	23	Cohabiting	0	3–6	45	Father Absent
304	Barry	24	Single	0	7–12	59	
305	Jamie	21	Single	0	>12	45	Franco
306	Mark	25	Single	0	3–6	39	
307	Sherman	28	Single	0	>12		Native Amer
308	Peter	20	Single	0	3–6	49	
309	Art	21	Single	0	<3	55	
310	Tony	20	Single	0	3–6	43	
311	Gaston	21	Single	0	7–12	59	
312	Raymond	26	Single	0	>12	46	

NAMING THE RESPONDENTS

All of the respondents were given pseudonyms, and certain identifying features (e.g., the names of persons or places) were changed to ensure the privacy of participants. Tables 2.5 through 2.8 present basic descriptive features of each participant such as ages and relationship status. Readers may find it helpful to refer to these tables throughout the presentation of the findings.

3

Describing the Relationships

In this chapter, I detail the relationships of aunts and nieces, uncles and nephews, describing their essential qualities, including how often they visit and, just as important, how new mediums such as cell phones and e-mail influence their relationships. We explore how families negotiate geographic distances that separate them and continue to engage one another, stay informed of one another's circumstances, and sometimes maintain distinctly close ties. In attempting to cast light on the factors that influence closeness, we explore in greater depth the all-important relationships between adult family members and especially siblings, or the parents of nieces and nephews. We examine the impact of divorce on extended family members and the importance of aunts and uncles in helping children come to understand their parents' marital struggles. Other key features of families can encourage contact and the development of close relationships, including careers and family obligations, personal features such as childlessness, highly valued qualities like being fun, and family values that encourage contact, or fail to do so. Each of these broad features of families and their members illuminate when aunts and uncles are apt to develop extended relationships with their nieces and nephews.

TOGETHER NEAR AND FAR

Aunts, uncles, nieces, and nephews varied widely in their frequency of interaction, from the occasional family gatherings to weekly or even daily contact, and they vary in the purpose of their visits (see Table 3.1).

Nearly a third (30%) of respondents described relationships with minimal contact in which visits were biannual or less often. In nearly all cases low levels of contact were associated with significant distances separating family members. All of the aunts, uncles, and nieces, and most of the nephews,

Table 3.1. *Frequency of face-to-face interaction*

	Aunts	Uncles	Nieces	Nephews
Low contact Biannual or less	32.3% (10)	23.8% (5)	42.9% (9)	22.6% (7)
Moderate contact Bimonthly to monthly	32.3 (10)	33.3 (7)	38.1 (8)	54.8 (17)
High contact Biweekly to daily	35.5 (11)	42.8 (9)	19.0 (4)	22.6 (7)

who reported low levels of face-to-face contact, described relationships with favored others who lived out of state or overseas. Where contact was relatively low or infrequent, it often took the form of family visits over significant holidays. For some nephews and nieces, even infrequent contact was meaningful.

> I always remember Christmases growing up because I was five when [my uncle's] daughter died and after that he always spent every Christmas with us. He would bring his family all the way over and it would be awesome. Our Christmases were great. We have a huge gathering on Christmas Eve and on Christmas we'd spend the whole day as a family. I always remember liking what my uncle gave me most, and I hate saying this, but better than what my parents gave me. (Jamie)

In contrast, nearly all cases of those with high levels of face-to-face contact (30%) lived in the same or neighboring communities. Exceptions to this rule were an uncle and nephew who lived a considerable distance from one another, about a 5-hour drive, but still managed monthly visits and nearly daily e-mail and phone contact. The nephew (age 43) and uncle (age 60 and retired) are gay, and the uncle is a major support figure and benefactor for his nephew, who was recently diagnosed HIV positive.

Face-to-face interaction tells only part of the story, explains only part of how uncles and nephews, aunts and nieces, keep informed of each others' lives and those of other family members. An aunt speaks to her niece, who is away in graduate school, "every week or two" because the niece has a cell phone with unlimited night and weekend calling time. When I asked what they talked about, Aunt Theriza described how her niece had only recently moved to her own apartment and is now learning how to cook. "So we talk about that a lot," she said. In fact, Aunt Theriza, with her husband, had driven her niece from Maine to a school in the midwestern United States and helped her move into a new apartment. Aunt Theriza acts as a muse and mentor, teaching her niece life skills laced with abundant support via the airwaves.

For others e-mail becomes a means to supplement communication when personal contact is relatively infrequent. Beatrice is married and has two sons. She visits with her 16-year-old niece, Cindy, "about once every six weeks," but they e-mail one another every week. In her words, "e-mail has changed our relationship . . . it's opened things up." Their relationship became closer over the past several years and especially while Cindy was living in China for a year with her family. During this period, aunt and niece e-mailed one another daily. Cindy's family could not afford the tuition of private schools, and the children were home-schooled. In Beatrice's words, "it was a very, very lonely year" for the children. She says, "up to that point we were kind of an extended family but it wasn't that personal. It became very close in the year that she was away." In this case, a niece had a need; an aunt had the time, inclination, and skill to respond; and the accessibility of e-mail made the development of their relationship possible. Aunt Beatrice was able to act on the needs of her niece. In a recent exchange, Cindy described to her aunt how her boyfriend was struggling with depression and the difficulties this was presenting to her. Aunt Beatrice responded by suggesting to her niece that she can be "a very loving person and have some boundaries around what she takes on" and then followed this by sending some literature to read on depression. In this instance, the act of writing via e-mail provided the niece with a way to reflect on her challenges in school and with her boyfriend and a safe way to explore issues; fortunately, her aunt is both responsive and wise.

Although nearly all aunts and uncles talk on the phone and visit however frequently, not all value communicating by e-mail. For many it is clearly a valued medium of expression, a convenient way to stay in touch; for Beatrice it is a unique and positive influence in her relationship with her niece. For others, e-mail is not available or not especially valued because "it's always nice to hear somebody's voice" (Aunt Alexandra). E-mail can be considered insecure or lacking in privacy, as in the case of a niece and her boyfriend who share the same e-mail address and about whom Aunt Erma remarked: "I would not be one hundred percent comfortable that he's not reading the stuff." Or it can be considered potentially intrusive. "I think I'm very respectful that [my niece's] got two little kids and the last thing I need to do is burden her with an e-mail message" (Aunt Harriett). In contrasting her relationship with her niece and son, Aunt Beatrice remarked, "E-mail is great, but it's definitely not a substitute for just sitting at the table doing homework. I've really noticed that with my oldest son because so much of the intimacy with him is silent. I never have that with [my niece]; there is no silent intimacy with her."

Exchanges by phone or e-mail supplement direct contact, and often these lines of communication filter through third parties, usually sisters of aunts or uncles, or grandmothers (of nephews and nieces).

[My nephew lives overseas] and is setting up a business. He has lived there 3 years. I keep in touch with him through my sister and she tells me what he is doing or we e-mail back and forth once in awhile. Not a lot but once in a while. I always know what he is doing. Either my sister tells me or her husband tells me or I check out [my nephew's] latest Web site. (Uncle Pat)

One uncle described how he exchanges e-mail with his sister several times per week and speaks on the phone monthly, although they are able to visit only a few times per year, usually over Christmas and summer vacations. "They are not long [e-mail] notes," he says. "That's how I know what [my nephew] is doing. [My nephew] is in the dog house right now about his math grades" (Uncle Al).

Another uncle visits with his nephew three or four times annually, but he is kept informed through his weekly contact with his sister (the nephew's mother), and daily e-mail contact with his mother (the nephew's grandmother).

My mother is the hub. Everybody communicates with her and she disperses [news] out mostly by e-mail these days. She emails at least once a day to each of us . . . often two or three times a day. I always reply, even if it is very succinct. . . .

In the last year my nephew came to neither Thanksgiving nor Christmas. People were very upset about that.

RM: Who communicates with [your nephew] about this?

Probably both my mother and my sister to let him know they are not happy about that.

RM: Would your sister let you know that she was not happy?

Oh, yes. (Uncle Sammy)

These exchanges demonstrate how families routinely share information and communicate their expectations of one another across multiple households, a stream of communication that occurs with or without the benefit of face-to-face interaction. E-mail, home phones, and cellular phones provide ways for family members to easily maintain contact with one another. The newer mediums of Internet and cellular-based communications can and do enrich personal relationships. They are readily used to supplement relationships with relatively frequent direct interaction and those in which geographic distance or personal circumstance, as in commitments to families, children, and careers, limit personal contact. Under these circumstances, they are welcome alternatives.

It is tempting to use measures of direct personal interaction and distance as predictors of closeness or intimacy; most certainly many of the respondents who lived near one another maintained intimate relationships with frequent contact, and many who were more distant did not. Although living near one another can facilitate a relationship between aunts, uncles, nieces, and nephews, social distance often trumps geographic distance. In some cases, pairs of uncles and nephews and aunts and nieces failed to develop close relationships even though they lived relatively close to one another, and yet others maintained close relationships over great distances. Uncle Sammy is a highly successful professional well established in his career. His nephew is 28 and works as a mechanic; although they live within a 2-hour drive, their relationship is modest. Sammy describes a lack of common interests and experiences that limit their relationship.

> I don't know. To be honest there is such a difference. For him it wasn't even easy to get through vo-tech school and my wife and I are both university professors. There is a fair difference there that makes me wonder to what extent we are effective [role] models.

In this instance, the uncle is informed about his nephew's activities largely through his sister and mother but believes he has little in common with his nephew. Here social distance is perhaps more important as an influential factor than geographic distance.

For others, a limited relationship, in the sense of limited communication, does not necessarily imply an unimportant one, or a relationship without consequence. For instance, a 28-year-old nephew who lived in the same household as his uncle described surprisingly little contact but an important relationship nonetheless. In his words: "We talk some, not really too much. [My uncle] mainly talks with my grandfather. I'm off doing my own thing" (Nephew Sherman). Sherman goes on to describe his uncle as "an excellent man. He has a heart of gold and he would do anything for you. I really admire him for that." This interview suggests that closeness and importance are distinct dimensions of relationships; a nephew may not report a close relationship with his uncle, but this does not necessarily mean the relationship is unimportant or inconsequential to the nephew.

In contrast, many described close relationships with favored others who lived at a distance. Aunt Sylvia is a retired college teacher who recently moved from the midwestern United States to Maine to be near her sister. Sylvia is childless; she divorced at a young age and never remarried. Her niece is single and recently completed a doctorate at a New Zealand university and currently works in a leading laboratory in Great Britain. Sylvia takes great pride in describing her niece's talents and successes. She recently spent a summer vacation visiting with her niece in the United Kingdom. Although Sylvia never lived in the same state as her sister during her niece's childhood, she has managed to maintain a relationship and continues to do so through her occasional visits with her niece, her niece's annual visits home, her monthly e-mail communications, and, importantly, her frequent visits with her sister, who communicates regularly with her daughter. Perhaps the relationship of Sylvia with her niece would be even closer were they to live in neighboring communities; nonetheless, a variety of additional factors contribute to their closeness. Sylvia has the time and inclination. She has a close relationship with her sister and, following her professional retirement, recently relocated to the same rural community. Sylvia, her sister, and her niece share a variety of common interests much like good friends. In this case, as in many others, the closeness of siblings encouraged the relationship of aunt and niece to develop in ways that eventually led to a configuration of reciprocal interdependencies. This is a configuration that spans three households and the relationships of mother and daughter, sisters, and aunt and niece. It would be difficult to appreciate fully any one relationship without considering the others.

BECOMING CLOSE

Throughout the interviews four broad sets of factors seem to influence the closeness of kin relationships, or the lack of it: relationships between family members, careers and family obligations, personal conditions, and family norms regarding the responsibilities of members to one another. I consider each in turn.

Family Gatekeepers and Relationship Spillover

The tenor of relationships between aunts or uncles and their siblings can have an important influence on the frequency of interaction with nieces and nephews, their closeness, or even if they have a relationship at all. Some described contested relationships with siblings and, as a consequence, minimal relationships with nieces or nephews. Uncle Al is a professional and maintains a relationship with his sister's 15-year-old son. The families are distant but visit several times per year. Al exchanges e-mail with his sister a "couple of times per week," and they talk on the phone monthly. Al manages to stay informed of his nephew's activities, including his progress in school and participation in sports. Al contrasts his relationship with his sister's son with that of another nephew, the son of his brother:

> When you first called, I was thinking about it and contrasting how much I know about my nephew and how little I know about Rob, who is my older brother's son. My relationship with Rob is not as close and I think that's a function of my relationship with my brother. We had a contested relationship as kids. We fought often. He doesn't keep in touch. I send him notes and cards and hear from him maybe once a year. So I know little about Rob and have maybe seen him three or four times.

Aunt Lena maintains a close relationship with her sister, whom she speaks with several times per month. "When my sister and I talk," she says, "it's usually a two-hour phone call." During these occasions Lena also speaks with her niece. They share news about school, sports, and their common interest – interior design. They "compare decorating notes" and chat about recent episodes of the home and garden show they both watch regularly. The attachment Lena feels toward her sister, and their frequent communications, facilitates the relationship of aunt and niece. Although her calls are to her sister, she also speaks with her niece, and Lena's sister clearly encourages these contemporaneous occasions. Later in the interview, she mentions a second niece, the daughter of her brother-in-law, about whom she says: "We don't really get along with [my husband's] family all that well. I've never had a relationships with [my husband's] niece. . . . We went to visit [them] one Thanksgiving. We'll never do that again."

Uncle Mark describes a contested relationship with his brother, which in his mind has influenced his relationship with his nephew.

> I don't consider [my relationship with my nephew] close at all. The reason is that probably for the first 15 years that my brother was married our relationship was not that great. We would be in contact, but not a lot of contact. In terms of writing or talking by phone, it would be monthly, but mostly conversations about caring for my mother. . . . For the first 12 years, my brother visited Maine once.

In this case, the relationship with the uncle's brother and nephew was complicated by the brother's divorce, the estranged relationship that existed between the brothers, and the estranged relationship between the brother and sister-in-law with whom the nephew lived.

> I think when [my nephew] was in high school he was having some real complicated relationships with his father and stepfather. He was not living with my brother; he was living with his mother [and stepfather]. In a sense we sort of stayed out of that complexity, partly because I didn't have a real strong relationship with [my nephew]. Calling and writing didn't seem like much of an option.

The relationship between Mark and his nephew improved in time when Mark decided to establish more contact. During the interview, I asked him what led to this change in his relationship with his nephew.

> Well I think there were several factors. My relationship with my brother had definitely improved. I felt that I had not done a real good job as an uncle. I felt that I needed to be more involved with him than I had been. It was just something I wanted to do.

Mark goes on to describe his involvement in therapy and interest in improving his own life and relationships with family members.

> I was just trying to look at the family constellation, my involvement with my brother, with his family, and how to improve in a sense my own life. I saw [my relationship with my nephew] was one of the things that was sort of an undone piece that I wanted to begin to work on.

More recently, Mark has taken a greater interest in his nephew, who is now married and a young parent.

Mark's experience of his sibling's divorce and the negative consequences it had on his relationship with his nephew was not typical of the people I interviewed, but neither was his experience entirely unique. Divorces were common and reported in at least 30% (32 of the 104 cases) of the families I interviewed. In most cases, aunts or uncles provided support for nieces and nephews as they struggled to understand their parent's divorces, their own divorces in the case of adult nieces and nephews, or those of other family members. In at least four cases, the divorces of parents (siblings of aunts and uncles), or the threat of divorce, had a chilling effect on the relationships of aunts and uncles with their nieces and nephews.

Francesca is a 45-year-old single and childless professional working in the public school system. Her niece, Maria, is 11, and the daughter of her brother. They live across the street from one another and visit frequently. Their relationship is remarkable because of the amount of time they spend together, its diversity and intensity, and the way Francesca integrates Maria into her life and even her friendships. "We have a relationship beyond the family [connection]," she says. "We do a lot of stuff together, and I have always invited her along [when I go] hiking with friends or to a restaurant." Francesca and her niece have frequent dinners together at home; "soak in the hot tub" and talk about family, friends, and school; occasionally shop together; and engage in outdoor activities or attend sporting events. Francesca says: "She is really part of my life [and] every aspect of it," and she goes on to comment, "I have been more significant in her life on a day-to-day basis than her own mother."

Maria's father and mother frequently work evenings and Saturdays, and Francesca fills in on these occasions. Their marriage is troubled, the parents recently separated, and Maria has asked her aunt whether they are going to divorce. Francesca provides support and, perhaps most important, a listening ear, but she is concerned. The possibility of being separated from her niece would be "devastating to everyones" and, she adds, "a real anxiety for me." The situation is complicated by the estranged relationship between Francesca and her sister-in-law, and they have not talked in months. Toward the end of our interview Francesca returns to the issue and shares her concerns and wishes.

> I really worry about [divorce] because I've seen how, from an educator's point of view, divorces can go. I've seen people do really foul things. I've said to my brother we can do some things to make it not be ugly, we can talk frankly, talk to the family. If there's something I can do, I don't want [my sister-in-law] to feel that I still wouldn't take Maria if she doesn't have a sitter or is stuck at work. I would never want her to feel that even though she's divorced from my brother that there's still not this connective tissue that we have. Maybe it will be okay. . . . I don't want Maria to be put in the middle and not feel comfortable with both her parents. That's pretty good if you can do that.

For Uncle Mark and Aunt Francesca, marital distress spills over to affect the children as well as their relationships with other family members – relationships that supplement what parents do for their children and that are important to both the children and their extended kin. Such relationships are irreplaceable. Francesca is concerned and well aware of the potentially negative consequences of a deteriorating marriage. Nonetheless, her relationship with her niece is at risk should the parents actually divorce, bringing to bear a change in residence of either parent, or otherwise exacerbating the already strained relationship between mother and aunt.

In some ways, it is not surprising that most aunts and uncles described siblings (typically sisters and sisters-in-law) and occasionally grandmothers who directly encouraged or facilitated relationships with nieces and nephews. Strong, healthy relationships between adult siblings spill over and affect the relationships between adults and children. Kathryn describes close relationships with her sister and brother who live in the midwestern United States. She remarks: "My sister she was just amazing. She was halfway around the world and she was very involved with my boys and encouraging them, and I think she really fosters the relationship between me and her kids. She has encouraged them to write to me and things like that." Kathryn takes great pride in describing how her brothers had taken an active interest in her oldest son and recently orchestrated a special weeklong visit in which they "took him to every sporting event known to mankind."

Aunts and uncles occasionally mentioned their appreciation of their siblings' generosity in sharing their children, and this was especially true of those who were childless. Aunt Barbara describes her and her husband's continuous involvement since birth with their 21-year-old niece. The niece lived with her aunt and uncle for a couple of years and additionally often visited during extended summer vacations. Barbara says of her brother and his wife: "They were most generous with their child." Other childless aunts spoke of the excitement they felt with the birth of a niece and their appreciation that the niece's parents encouraged a close relationship. One uncle, who was gay and childless, described his lifelong relationship with his 16-year-old nephew as the closest he would ever come to being a father. He clearly valued the relationship with his nephew, a relationship that his sister encourages.

A brother encouraged the relationship between his sister and his daughter by suggesting they take a two-week holiday in Europe. Aunt Carla Lyn, a mother of two grown children, was thrilled and dutifully planned the tour of great European cities, which her brother financed. The young teenage niece was apparently less thrilled, by the aunt's account, particularly with an early morning walking tour of the *égouts* of Paris, otherwise known as sewers. (Perhaps she was wearing sandals; although fetching in most Parisian venues, they would have been insecure on this particular walk. I neglected to ask.)

Individual Circumstance: Career and Family Obligations

The personal commitments of aunts and uncles, including their family obligations, parental statuses, and careers, influenced their relationships with nieces and nephews, as did the personal commitments of adult nieces and nephews to their own relationships and careers. Marriages, newborn children, and careers requiring relocations all affect the relationships of kin – sometimes in positive ways and sometimes not.

Aunt Barbara maintains a close relationship with her 21-year-old niece Sarah, the daughter of her brother. They have maintained a lifelong relationship and lived in the same community throughout Sarah's childhood. Sarah recently moved out of state to attend college. Aunt and niece visit on holidays and college breaks but otherwise largely communicate by e-mail and, less frequently, by phone.

> Now we keep in touch mostly by e-mail. Well, she is kind of buried, as you know college students can be. So I hear from her about once a month now, sometimes more. We call each other periodically, especially when there's some upheaval in the family.... I probably write her once a month, you know, long-winded things. Whereas from her I get "I'm so busy." You know, "I'm doing this project or this test," that type of thing. She does a lot of photography and she has what they call a photo-log [a Web site]. I go there often and leave little notes.

Barbara does not visit as often with her niece as she once did, but they still manage to keep in contact. Barbara has firsthand knowledge of Sarah's activities, her academic interests, her friends, and her art. Her niece has access to the activities of family members and an important person with whom to share her concerns.

Later in the interview, I asked Barbara if her niece was important to her. She replied immediately: "Extremely. She and [her sister] own my heart." In this case a lifelong history of interaction, a strong commitment to family, shared personal interests, and accesses to the Internet permit a relationship to develop and adapt to changes in personal circumstance. It is perhaps not inconsequential that Barbara is childless, which in her words "gave me the time to give to her," although she adds "I think we were just simpatico from the get go." I return to the issue of childlessness later.

In the course of a family's development, a mix of career and relational changes affects relationships between kin. Aunt Olympia is now 52, married with an 11-year-old daughter, and a successful and active university faculty member. Her niece, Ruth, is a law school faculty member, married, and a new parent. Through her early years, Olympia maintained contact with Ruth and her mother, although they lived some distance from one another. Both families eventually moved to the same eastern U.S. city. The mother divorced and entered school, and Olympia became a central figure in her niece's life.

From fifth through eighth grade, they "talked on the phone every day, often at length" and saw each other frequently. Just before entering high school, Ruth's mother remarried, and the family moved to California. During the niece's years in high school, college, law school, and early professional life, they spoke and visited less often. Olympia and Ruth now live within a 5-hour drive of one another, and even with their commitments to children and careers, they manage to talk on the phone monthly, e-mail more often, and visit once or twice per year. Their relationship is close, and Olympia clearly admires her niece. They talk about common family members, their similar careers, their experiences of parenting, and the many things friends can share. Their relationship is unusual in the number of significant life events that occurred for Ruth, her mother, and her aunt. Throughout these periods of change, the relationship of Olympia and Ruth was affected in terms of the time they had available for one another and the ease with which they could visit, and yet they have maintained their commitment and remain close.

Often changes in the degree of contact between aunts and nieces, uncles and nephews were occasioned by the development of new relationships and the obligations that ensued. Raymond, age 26, describes a unique relationship with his uncle, age 46, who is his mother's brother. Raymond's parents divorced when he was 2, and he speaks of his current relationship with his dad as "like two adults sitting in a bar talking about the weather." At times Raymond and his uncle Les lived in neighboring communities, at times more distant. Throughout Raymond's life, his uncle has been an important source of support and companionship. Raymond consults his uncle about his career, his friendships, and nearly all of what he does. He describes frequent occasions of support and advice. They visited often during his adolescence when Uncle Les was the only important male figure in his life. In his words, his uncle "provided direction." A highlight of their relationship is their mutual interest in music and playing guitars together. Recently Uncle Les married for the first time. Raymond understands his uncle's new relationship has reduced the time they can spend with one another.

> I haven't seen him for a month and a half and I used to see him 2 or 3 times a week. That's because he got married and I'm in school.... With him working two jobs there is just no time for us. It doesn't bother me because every time I pick up my guitar he is right there.

More typically it is nieces or nephews who marry or become parents, and as a result their relationships with aunts and uncles change. In Raymond's case, it was his uncle who married and changed careers, and at the same time Raymond entered the university. He reflects on these events and the changes they have wrought on their relationship later in the interview. Regardless of what happens to their relationship in the future, the many contributions of his uncle are evident.

> One of the things we do is sort of a philosophy. We call it the *Lost Chord*. . . . In [learning a new] song you're missing a chord and trying to find it, but then once you find that missing chord it puts the whole song in harmony and we realized we could apply that to life. So one of the biggest things he taught me about life is always searching for that something to put in my life to make it a little bit smoother sounding. Eventually when you get 80 or 90 years old you can look back and find that you've had a lot of good music.

Several aunts and uncles mentioned age-related changes in their relationships with nieces and nephews, and especially as children entered adolescence and young adulthood. Aunts and uncles seemed to understand that as their nieces and nephews became older, they would see less of one another. An uncle describes a relationship with his brother-in-law's son as once quite active but less so as the nephew entered high school. A recent visit seems to capture the spirit present in many of my conversations with aunts and uncles who had adolescent nieces and nephews. "He visited last week. He called first. We fed him" (Uncle Jimmy).

Aunt Sandy shared details on her relationship with her 16-year-old niece, Mimi, with whom she visits once or twice a week. Sandy comments on how a developmental change in her niece led to a change in their relationship. During a recent visit, Mimi seemed to have disappeared, occasioning some anxiety for her aunt, a call to neighbors, and to the police.

> Anyway, before the police got there, she came down. She had been up a tree listening to her CD player and her batteries went dead, that's why she came down, but to my knowledge she'd never climbed a tree before in her life and it never occurred to me to look up a tree because she's an urban girl, and it's something I would do, but not her, and she's usually so thoughtful of everyone that I can't imagine that she didn't know that I was going to be worried about her, but she really needed that space and to make a statement that she had changed, that things were changing. You know, I really took notice of that and realized she was changing. She was going through some different things and she wasn't a child any longer.

I asked Sandy what she thought Mimi was trying to communicate in the arboreal incident. She replied that she thought Mimi was saying,

> "I can take care of myself. I'm resourceful in ways that you never knew I was." You know, that kind of stuff. So I was pissed, but I was secretly surprised and I think pleased that she was able to fool us, or whatever, you know, make a statement and climb the tree.

Occasionally teens add a bit of drama just to try and get our attention, and they do.

Individual Circumstance: Childlessness

Childlessness influences the relationships of aunts and uncles with their nieces and nephews with some regularity. Half of the uncles and slightly more of the aunts reported they were childless.[1] These figures are higher than the general population, in which approximately 18% of women aged 40 to 44 (i.e., women of similar age to the aunts interviewed here) remain childless, including those who elect not to have children and those who are unable to do so.[2] Quite possibly, childless adults experience greater involvement with nieces and nephews, relative to those who become parents, and this may account for their overrepresentation here.

Several factors seem to influence the involvement of childless aunts and uncles. Aunts often mention that they had the time, and consequently the opportunity, to become involved with their nieces, as well as the inclination to do so. Aunt Sandy states: "I have more time to give to my nephews and nieces and the desire to do that, to incorporate them into my life." She goes on to observe how busy life can be, especially for parents: "I know how stressed out and busy parents are. It's just a whole different world. . . . So yeah, I have a busy life, but I don't have that 24/7 demand they do, and I have the time and the desire."

Of the 17 childless aunts, 6 explicitly mentioned the availability of time as an influential factor, and for others it is implied. Nieces occasionally mentioned this issue about their childless aunts as well, whom they perceived as having more time. Curiously the issue of having more time for children does not appear overtly in the interviews with uncles. Perhaps fathers, and men in general, have more discretion regarding the amount of time they spend with children, and consequently the issue is not as relevant for them

[1] Ten uncles and seventeen aunts were childless.
[2] Downs, 2003.

as it is for women. Typically fathers spend considerably less time engaged in direct child care relative to women, and proportionally more of that time is spent in discretionary activity such as play.[3] Although the involvement of fathers in child care and household labor is steadily increasing, women still perform about three times as much as men.[4] For women, the issue of available time is more salient regardless of personal preferences, and childless aunts have more time for children. As Aunt Theriza says, "I'm not distracted by doing these things [child-centered activities] with my own children." For men any involvement with children, one's own or those of another, is more discretionary.

For some the opportunity to be with children and to participate in their upbringing was clearly significant, and this was true for both aunts and uncles. In these cases, the children of siblings were eagerly anticipated, and relationships with them began in infancy and were often highly developed. Uncle Nick enthusiastically recounts being present at the birth of his nephew. Nick is 28 and lives with his female partner. Much of their social life revolves around activities with his sister, her husband, and their three children. They visit on Saturdays and stop by one another's home during the week for coffee, and occasionally he and his nephew "have a kick around the local school" (i.e., play soccer). The nephew's biological father has been largely absent for most of his life. Encouraged by his sister[5] and his own interest, Nick maintains a consistent and frequent influence in his nephew's daily life. He adds, "Yeah basically I want a bigger part in my nephew's life, because apart from my immediate family I didn't really know my relatives."

Two of the aunts were present at the birth of their nieces, and several have maintained relationships with nieces throughout their infancy, childhood, and young adulthood. Aunt Connie is a 50-year-old administrative assistant, married, and childless. She has four sisters with whom she speaks several times per week. They visit often, and because of the number of children in their respective families, they have monthly birthday parties as a matter of routine. She says, "I am probably as close to my sisters as I am to my husband." Connie was present at the birth of her niece Brice, who is now a college student, and in fact at the time of the interview, they were enrolled together in a college class, Human Sexuality. The sisters arrange occasional weekend trips to distant cities – New York, Montreal, Boston – where they shop, visit museums, or attend evening performances. As a young adult

---

[3] Marsiglio et al., 2000.　　　　[4] Coltrane, 2000.
[5] Incidentally, Nick's sister first saw an article describing the "Uncles Project" in a local newspaper and subsequently encouraged his participation.

and the oldest niece, Brice is now invited to participate in their adventures. For Connie, the importance of her niece, her own love of children, and the depth of her relationship with her sister, Brice's mother, is illustrated in a story she shared toward the end of our interview. Some years ago, Brice's mother offered to have a baby for Connie. Connie relates the story:

> After having her last child my sister said, "I would like to have a baby for you."
>
> RM: *And what did you decide to do?*
>
> I would have loved to, but my husband said no. If I could turn back time, I would have. So that's love, and that's Brice's mother.

Connie's story speaks volumes of her devotion to her family, and a community of women who freely share their intimate lives and their children. What childless aunts and uncles occasionally share is a sincere need to parent, and their nieces and nephews can serve as surrogate children with the full knowledge and cooperation of parents.

Uncle Robert, a catholic priest, and Uncle John, a single gay man, both commented on the importance of their respective nephews, and sometimes their nieces. Robert comments, "Having really good relationships with my nephews and nieces satisfied a lot of my need for generativity and seems to nullify my own need for children." John expresses a similar sentiment about his nephew: "He is about the closest thing I've got to a son so that is why I take it so seriously," he says.

Parents recognize the significance of their siblings in the lives of their children, and they certainly recognize the importance of their children to aunts and uncles. Aunt Sandy says of her sister and her husband, "They've been really good with their kids, sharing their children. Instead of babysitting, they call it *child opportunities*. They call up and say, 'Here's a child opportunity for you.'" Aunt Roslyn considers her nieces and nephews "a real gift for me" and continues, "I'm just so grateful to my brother and sister for having children." The gift of children reverberates across households. When families work well, everyone benefits.

Sharing Interests and Having Fun

RM: *Would you consider your uncle a role model?*

Definitely! I definitely admire his attributes. He has got a family and I see his hard working skills and I've always thought that was pretty neat.

RM: *Are there other qualities you admire?*

Yeah, he is a big kid. Like when we get together we kick around a ball or arm wrestle. I've always interpreted him as a hard worker, but he still knew how to enjoy himself. He's a fun guy. (Nephew Brig)

With my aunt Julie it was really a relationship where we just played around [and] had fun. She was very playful, and very young. [Aunt Julie and her partner] used to pick me up on Fridays and we would go [to] the laundromat and they would sit me down on the washing machine and I would sing songs in French the whole time. (Aunt Elena)

Whether we are listening to the voices of aunts or uncles, nieces or nephews, having fun is an important and common ingredient in their relationships. Aunts and uncles describe their delight in playing with their young charges, and they easily draw up memories of playing with their own favored elders. Fun is typically associated with play or recreation, and aunts and uncles clearly recognize their special privilege in this regard. As Aunt Elena describes, "if [my nieces] make a mess it doesn't matter because they don't live here. It's not like you're building a behavior; you're just happy to see them. Whereas, if you're a parent and you are the one always cleaning up the mess and you're tired of playing servant to your child, that behavior irritates you."

Uncles and aunts create experiences that are fun for children, and often they join right in. Uncle Michael comments on a recent visit with his young nephew, "We went to see Monster Trucks. It's fun. It's not something you see every day," he says.

Nieces and nephews often described *being fun* or *fun loving* as personal attributes or qualities they admired in their favored aunts and uncles. In this way, they are viewed as distinct from parents, often unconditional in their love and support, relatively unconcerned with discipline and setting boundaries, and as a result more *fun*. "I tell my aunt what I am going to do and she says great, or whatever. She can be more fun than my mom," says Angela.

At other times, having fun is cast in the context of being together as a family. Jamie remembers his first communion, an important event in his childhood, and his absolute delight with his uncle's unexpected attendance. He says: "spending that day with my family was actually a lot of fun because I had lots of cousins that came over and it just kind of turned into a family reunion type day. It was good seeing the whole family. That is some of my favorite time."

Fun can also represent a means rather than an end in itself. Uncle Stephen described the recent death of his teenaged nephew's mother and his contested relationship with his father. "We just go out and have some fun.

Kind of get his mind off things," he says. Other aunts and uncles understood that they provide a playful contrast to routine family life unencumbered by the necessary house rules of parents.

Aunts and uncles may be somewhat unique relative to older grandparents, who are less apt to engage in play.[6] To the extent that aunts and uncles are young and in good health, they appear to be more apt to engage in spontaneous play and recreational activities and to be regarded as more playful, a highly desirable attribute, by nieces and nephews. This pattern of findings is consistent with previous research.[7] In these regards, play and recreational activities serve to build affectional solidarity.

In the later adult relationships of aunts and uncles with nieces and nephews, fun can be one of the features that helps fuel their friendships. Uncle Chris describes his 43-year-old nephew as "a lot of fun," and "easy to be around." They share similar interests, visit frequently, and spend occasional vacation time together. We consider the issue of friendships among adults and the importance of having common interests in Chapter 7.

Activities regarded as fun (or persons so regarded) share a common attribute. They are occasions when attention is transformed from routine events with predictable outcomes (or parents with anticipated demands) to occasions with novel and unexpected qualities. The importance of aunts and uncles as a means to transform the attention of their nieces and nephews is evidenced through the activities in which they engage their nieces and nephews, in the ways they themselves describe such activities, and in the way nieces and nephews perceive such activities. Their stories are suggestive of how transformations of attention are highly valued – central features of their relationships and, more generally, of friendship. Transformations of attention are occasions in which the obligations, duties, responsibilities, daily hassles, and all the worries they bring to bear are momentarily cast away from conscious attention, replaced with the novelty of new experience and the more playful qualities of a companion. As we shall see in the chapters that follow, the transformation of attention is a recurring effect of aunts and uncles on siblings as well as their children, and for this they are unique and highly valued.

Family Values and Traditions

Aunts and uncles are often drawn into relationships with their nieces and nephews because of their family values and traditions. Aunt Beatrice

---

[6] Cherlin & Furstenberg, 1986.　　[7] Ellingson & Sotirin, 2006; Hansen, 2005.

described distant relationships with her own aunts and uncles as a child and a memory of a holiday visit gone awry, an experience she never wanted to see repeated in her own life. At age 12, she insisted on a family pact with her siblings. She recounted a day in the family car when the pact was made.

> [I said to my brother and sisters], "no matter what we're sticking together and no matter what when we have kids, our kids will know each other and they will be cousins together, and we will be part of each other's kids' lives." And everybody remembers it, even my youngest sister remembers that moment in the car when we kind of made this solemn pledge.

I asked if she had talked about this pledge recently. She replied they had, "because we all missed having cousins. We all missed having close uncles and aunts." Currently Beatrice maintains a close relationship with her nieces and nephews and particularly her sister's oldest child, whom she sees nearly monthly and shares e-mail with weekly. She says of her niece, "I know a lot more about her inner life than I do about my own sons." She recounts how one of her sons and her brother's son are best friends. And she speaks of how she and her siblings value their roles of aunt and uncle. "It is a feature of all of our lives that we really value."

Aunts and uncles maintain a variety of other family traditions that encourage and support relationships with nieces and nephews. They develop traditions around the celebration of birthdays, holidays, vacations, and special events, sometimes to mark important milestones, a sixteenth birthday for example, or even how they spend an ordinary Friday night. "In my family it was fudge night. When my maternal grandmother was around, all of her children, and their spouses, and their children would get together at her house for Friday night fudge and that's where everything was decided. Who people would vote for and how they felt about certain issues" (Aunt Alexandra). Aunt Connie recounts how in the previous month, there were seven family birthdays. In this large extended family, the opportunity for a get-together and celebration is ever present. Because the number of cousins is so great, aunts and uncles simply designate one day a month for a family birthday party to which everyone is invited.

For some families, the traditions that develop between extended family members are unique to each relationship; for others, traditions are passed across generations. Aunt Ilse and her niece plan camping trips each summer. Uncle Michael continues a long-standing family tradition of providing enriching activities for his nephew as his mother once did for the entire family. At other times, the tradition is entirely direct and straightforward.

"Having an uncle was important for me, and being an uncle is an important role. Family is important, very important" (Uncle Ricky).

Ethnicity

For many aunts and uncles, nieces and nephews, ethnic backgrounds played an important role in the way their relationships emerged. As we noted earlier in Chapter 2, families with a Franco-American heritage comprise a substantial portion of the population of Maine, where most of the respondents resided. Eleven of the participants self-identified as Franco-American, and they often, although not always, considered this a significant feature in defining their family relationships. They spoke about the closeness of their communities bounded by a common language (French) and customs, which were often described in terms of religious values based in Catholicism and those revolving around food and holidays. "We have a big family that is really close," said Fiona, "and Catholic." Fiona reflects on her college friends and their differences as she recounts the importance of her family and, by implication, their greater centrality relative to her friends. "My parents are the people I go to for advice whereas my friends go to their friends."

Some aunts and uncles were clearly aware of the intersections of ethnicity and class backgrounds and how these features colored their experience. Elena spoke of her understanding of being Franco and growing up in a Franco community and how these experiences represented a "social handicap," viewing her background as undervalued in the larger community, an understanding she has shared with her niece. Other Franco aunts spoke of the importance of renewing their connections to Franco communities and their language. Maya says: "it hasn't been that long that being French is important to me. I just never thought about it much, but in the past years I've been very involved with different Franco-American groups. . . . I wanted [my nieces] to know that they were French and some of the traditions that go along with [being French]. . . . I said to my niece, 'You are a little Franco fem.'"

Two of the aunts, Raye and Addie, and one niece, Tess, self-identified as Native Americans. All expressed the importance of "being part of a community," although they were reluctant to judge how their experiences might differ from non-natives. "I can't not be a Penobscot'" said Addie. "I mean it's just who we are." Tess identified as an Eskimo and as such saw her family in a different light, readily identifying how her experience might differ from others. "My mother's family, being Eskimo, is not very loquacious and there is not a lot of keeping in touch if they are distant from one another."

In Tess's ancestral community, long separations were once an accepted part of life as families left on solitary hunting forays. She goes on to illustrate other differences such as the importance in her community of gifts of fuel oil for Christmas, differences in conversational styles in which long silences are acceptable, differences in the literal use of language, and differences in the importance of community.

Still others commented on their mix of ethnic backgrounds, all of which contribute to their experience. Addie recounts: "Actually I think I'm a woman first, then I'm Native, then I'm Italian." At times participants embraced their origins and saw in them unique qualities and traditions. At other times, they seemed to minimize the influence of ethnic identities. Fiona, Elena, and Maya are unique in their awareness of their Franco backgrounds and the importance they attach to it. Raye, Addie, and Tess easily articulated their connections to their native communities and heritage. Whether this awareness of heritage colors the nature of the relationships with family members, how they interact, or the closeness that develops among aunts and nieces and uncles and nephews is not entirely clear. Certainly close relationships appear among Franco and non-Franco, Native and non-Native alike.

CONCLUSION

Uncles and aunts vary widely in the depth of their relationships with nieces and nephews. Some maintain close and long-standing relationships, and some do not. A variety of factors seem to be especially important in influencing their relationships. Geographic distance is important for some and can limit the development of their relationships; on the other hand, living in close proximity can encourage such developments. But such simplistic equations are not terribly insightful or predictive of the course of personal relationships among kin. Contemporary mediums like cell phones and the Internet can and do ameliorate the challenges of maintaining long-distance relationships by offering a convenient means through which family members can observe frequent contact and keep informed of one another's daily lives. Rather than detract from time spent in face-to-face interaction, a concern in earlier theorizing about computer-mediated activities and communication, these new mediums seem to represent important ways in which the range of family relationships are expanded and existing relationships are maintained.[8] The structure of communications by e-mail likely parallels

[8] America Online, 2000; Boase et al., 2006; Katz & Rice, 2002.

more traditional forms of communication in some ways in that messages pass through complex chains of relationships. People routinely communicate to and about each other through face-to-face interaction, phone, and e-mail. An aunt learns of her niece's activities through the aunt's sister, and parent, who is in direct contact with her child. E-mail serves as a convenient means by which such chains of communication are realized.

Our findings contrast with recent diary studies of Internet use that suggest little association between Internet use and family interaction,[9] or positions that suggest e-mail is best suited for developing friendships rather than family relationships.[10] Quite the contrary, aunts, uncles, nieces, nephews, parents, and grandparents seem routinely to use computer-mediated communications to maintain and enrich their relationships. Recent surveys find e-mail among the most popular Internet activities, and more than 50% of users report routinely sending e-mail to a sibling or extended family member.[11] Partners supplement face-to-face interaction with phone and asynchronous communication mediums (e.g., e-mail and text messaging) when direct contact is limited because of time constraints or geographical distance. Then, too, computer-based mediums provide new ways in which families can communicate across households through the use of personal or shared Web pages that host news items, photos, or memoirs (aka blogs). Uncle Pat shared, for example, that he occasionally visits his nephew's Web site as a means to learn of his nephew's activities, in addition to direct but infrequent exchanges of e-mail with his nephew and more frequent communications with his sister (the nephew's mother).

One question that remains is whether computer-mediated communications replace or interfere with face-to-face interaction and ultimately limit affectional solidarity or closeness. Two views have emerged in the literature.[12] A *Dystopian perspective* argues that Internet use limits access, involvement, and expression, for instance, by limiting the full range of discourse available in more personal communications, and thereby isolating family members. A *Utopian perspective* argues that Internet use effectively enhances access, involvement, and expression, for instance, by overcoming the deleterious effects of geographic distance, social distance (e.g., difference in class, age, or gender), and temporal constraints while adding new mediums of communication that complement traditional forms of expression. Judging from the aunts, uncles, nieces, and nephews in this study, new mediums of communication seem to be an asset and instrumental in

---

[9] Shklovski, Kiesler, & Kraut, 2006. [10] Boase & Wellman, 2006, p. 715.
[11] Katz & Rice, 2002, chap. 11. [12] Katz & Rice, 2002.

supporting affectional solidarity, a position that contemporary research clearly supports.

In a mass survey of the impact of Internet use on the daily lives of Americans, researchers at the Pew Internet and American Life Project tracked current use by querying volunteer participants about what they have ever done online, as well as what they did in the previous day, and in this way captured a snapshot of online activity.[13] The use of e-mail, rather than replace rich in-person communications, seems to encourage more frequent communications of all forms and closer relationships, a finding supported by a growing body of research.[14] Online Americans report that their use of e-mail has increased the amount of contact they have with family members and friends, and for a significant proportion, it has brought them closer to their families, improved their family relationships, led to new insights about family members, and restored formally dormant relationships (e.g., with a sister, brother, aunt, uncle, or cousin). This work is also suggestive of how e-mail offers communication opportunities that might not occur otherwise. Respondents note, for instance, that it is often easier to say frank or unpleasant things in an e-mail than in direct conversations, and most agree that this is good for their relationships.

E-mail transfers, however brief, are suggestive of how this medium may enhance the knowledge family members have about one another, and consequently the closeness of their relationships. A 41-year-old woman shared that "Little funny things that my nieces and nephews do that wouldn't be worth a long distance phone call I get to hear about through e-mail."[15] Her comment is consistent with Aunts Theriza and Beatrice, and Uncles Pat and Al, who routinely communicate online with their nieces, nephews, and siblings about routine daily life. It may well be that e-mail, text messaging, and the like facilitate the transfer of slight detail, the "little funny things" that few others know but nonetheless serve to ground intimate relationships.

A variety of additional questions emerge from our brief foray into the role of new communication mediums. Certainly e-mail, cell phones, and other Web-based technologies have the potential to support – and in some cases deepen – existing relationships. What is not entirely clear is how conflicts that emerge over e-mail, for instance, are interpreted and resolved. On the other hand, new mediums of communication may encourage the revitalization of dormant relationships or encourage relationships that might

---

[13] Rainie et al., 2000.
[14] Boase & Wellman, 2006; Katz & Rice, 2002, chap. 10.
[15] Rainie et al., 2000, p. 24.

not have otherwise emerged because of a variety of factors, not the least of which are time constraints and geographic separation.

Yet another feature that appears to be important and influential in determining the tenor of relationships among aunts and uncles and their nieces and nephews is the character of relationships between adult siblings. When adult siblings experience close relationships, they tend to maintain closer relationships with each other's children, and when their relationships are estranged, the relationships of uncles and aunts with nieces and nephews are limited. Lateral solidarity fuels intergenerational solidarity. In similar ways, relationships among grandparents and grandchild are facilitated when older generations and parents embrace close ties.[16]

Other factors such as careers, family obligations, and marital discord can additionally influence relationships. Aunts and uncles were quick to point out how their careers and obligations to their own children limited the time available for other family members. Childless aunts and uncles, on the other hand, acknowledged how their status provided greater opportunity to nurture relationships with nieces and nephews and provide support in the form of child care to their siblings. Whether childless aunts and uncles, relative to those who are parents, are more apt to activate relationships with nieces and nephews is unknown, but they are clearly poised to do so. For some, like Uncle Nick who was present at the birth of his nephew, and Aunt Connie who was present at the birth of her niece, the status of being childless adults was consequential in inspiring their motivations to develop relationships with children. Their relationships have the potential to be lifelong bonds, important for their own development as well as their nieces and nephews. From the outset, their participation in birth highlights the importance of close ties among siblings with implications for all family members.

The experience of parental separation and divorce complicates relationships. Aunts and uncles were clearly aware of this and in many cases served as confidents for both parents and children. Francesca regards her 11-year-old niece as "part of my life [and] every aspect of it," and she shared her concern about how her niece's parents and their ongoing marital struggles might affect her relationship with her niece, a concern she shared with her brother and niece's father. Francesca is unmarried and childless, and like many aunts and uncles in similar circumstance, her relationship with her niece is singular in her life, considered irreplaceable, and multiplex in that it blends elements of parenting or mentoring a young girl with elements of

---

[16] Goodman, 2007; Monserud, 2008; Ruiz & Silverstein, 2007.

friendship and recreation. The relationship speaks of a strong bond emerging from Francesca's personal commitment to her niece and brother, her strong sense of family values, and a fortuitous match of interests on the part of aunt and child. Close relationships among aunts and nieces, uncles and nephews emerge when adult siblings are engaged in one another's lives, when they share similar values that emphasize maintaining family relationships, when aunts and uncles experience a sense of personal commitment to their young charges, and when they simply like one another because of similar disposition and interests. If they happen to live near one another, all the better, but it is neither necessary nor essential. Of the many dimensions of intergenerational solidarity, structural solidarity, evidenced by physical proximity, is arguably the least important.

What can we conclude from this chapter? Families are composed of core relationships developed, lived, and maintained across multiple households and best viewed as social configurations of interdependencies rather than *free radical* dyads existing apart from and independent of their relational context.[17] To be sure, a certain degree of personal discretion characterizes the relationships of uncles, aunts, nieces, and nephews. All are relatively free to pursue their relationships with one another, or to forgo doing so. Normative solidarity, evidenced by a sense of obligation to develop ties with kin, likely is influential but less so than other core elements of solidarity, including affectional dispositions and similarities of interests, beliefs, and attitudes. Families, as social configurations, are built on cascading intersections of personal relationships that are simultaneously dependent on personal dispositions – each member's normative beliefs and each member's liking for another – individual statuses as parents or not, as well as solidarities that reach within and across generations.

---

[17] For similar perspectives see Widmer, Castren, Jallinoja, & Ketokivi, 2008; Widmer, LeGoff, & Levy, 2006.

4

Essential Aunting and Uncling

Aunts and uncles viewed their roles in a variety of ways, some quite distinct, often seeing themselves as adjuncts to parents, as third parties with unique perspectives, or, in a surprising number of cases, as surrogate parents. Each of these roles is illustrated throughout the interviews. Aunts and uncles freely discussed how they viewed themselves and their relationships with favored nieces and nephews, and they just as importantly talked about their siblings. In turn, nieces and nephews shared their views of a favored aunt or uncle and the ways in which they were influential and, in many cases, continue to be so. The three primary roles of adjunct, third-party, and surrogate parent are not necessarily mutually exclusive. Relationships change over time, and perhaps one of the more important attributes of the ties linking family members is their resiliency, their long histories, and the expectation that relationships will continue well into the future. This expectation of continuity is consistent in many of the interviews and represents an important context for the relationships that develop. I consider each of these issues in the pages that follow, considering first how aunts and uncles viewed the importance of their relationships in general terms and how such relationships change over time. I then consider how aunts and uncles supplement parents, acting as objective third parties or surrogate parents, often when biological parents are unavailable or entirely absent.

AUNTS AND UNCLES IN THE MIX OF PARENTING

I don't worry so much about shaping Mimi's character, or all that other kind of stuff that a parent is supposed to worry about. That's not my job. My job is to be a friend, a mentor, a support person. I'm really big on: "Good job, Mimi!" or "Aren't you wonderful!" (Aunt Sandy)

Like many of the participants, Aunt Sandy readily identifies some essential components of her role, that of aunts in general, and, by extension, that of uncles. Themes that appear consistently throughout the interviews include providing unconditional support, acting as a confidant and sounding board, fostering interests, modeling good family citizenship, or simply acting as a playmate and recreational partner. Most often these essential themes are paired with the understanding that continuity is important. As one aunt said: "The important thing is to be there if they need you" (Aunt Stella).

Aunt Olympia discusses the importance of continuity and what this has meant to her niece, Ruth, whose mother had divorced when she was 12. Olympia describes a series of transitions that her sister underwent, including a separation and eventual divorce, a change of careers, returning to school, and developing a new relationship. Olympia says:

> When Ruth was living in Boston she needed to just have someone she could be with [to understand her situation]. You know: what's it going to be like, what does it mean, what should I think, what can I do? And she could do that with me. She could just relax and not worry about things. She was in the situation where she almost had to be the grown-up in the family and it was just too hard for her. So [with me] she was allowed to be a kid. Her parents had been separated for a few years and her mother had changed careers and was going back to school. And you know I was predictable. She didn't always know where her mother was, but she always knew where she could find me. She knew what frame of mind she'd find me in because things in my life were very consistent. It was kind of peaceful, predictable and often fun. A good place to be. I tried to make sure I was available.
>
> *RM: Is being available an important part of being an aunt?*
>
> Yes, I think it is important. I think it's important for kids to know that there's someone within the family who loves them without all the sets of expectations that go along with parental love, can love them for who they are and see possibilities that maybe their parents don't see, and be there for them.

In the early years of this relationship, Aunt Olympia was herself childless (although she later married and had children), and, through some fortunate circumstance, both families moved from different states in the midwestern United States to the same eastern community. For a relatively short, but highly significant, period of 4 years, and while Ruth was in fifth through eighth grades, the two families lived within a "15-minute bus ride." Aunt

Olympia visited with her niece weekly, and they talked on the phone every day, sometimes at length. Undoubtedly Olympia was an important adult at a critical period in the life of her niece. She supplemented the work of Ruth's mother and in some ways acted as a second mother. She acted as caregiver and confidant for both mother and child. In this instance, personal needs and circumstance collided, yielding some far-reaching outcomes for all concerned. The needs of her niece and sister for a supportive confidant, her own circumstance as a childless young professional, and their joint relocation all helped fuel their relationships. Ruth is now 35 and married with an infant daughter; like her aunt, she is a faculty member at a major university. They continue to talk monthly, or more often, by phone and e-mail, and by virtue of some common experience as mothers and professors, they have much to share. They commiserate on the challenges, frustrations, and occasional joys of faculty life, of teaching and writing, of balancing professional commitments and mothering, of working in departments with few senior faculty who are women and fewer still with children. As they grow old together, and share in family, personal, and professional realms, virtually all of their major life experiences are held in common. Aunt Olympia is uniquely positioned, perhaps like no other person in Ruth's life.

By referring to Aunt Olympia's role initially as a supplement to the work of Ruth's mother, we should not infer that such work is secondary. It is richly textured, valued, and influential, perhaps as much for Olympia as her niece. A relationship that began with the needs of a young child for a confidant and caregiver and of a mother for help in her parenting has transformed into that of a lifelong mentor, with elements of a peer-based friendship.

This essential supplemental parenting is a common experience for both aunts and uncles and often served as the grounding for their future relationships. With infants and young children, their activities center on providing child care and parental relief efforts. For instance, Francesca often includes her 11-year-old niece in her weekend activities because her niece's mother works and her father is involved in coaching on weekends. Aunt Denise, who is single and childless, provided additional care for her twin nieces, especially when they were infants, simply because their parents were exhausted. The infants had irregular sleeping hours, and as Denise says, "somebody would have to get some sleep in that house. So I would go over for a few hours. It was kind of a changing of the guard."

Denise's nieces are older now, age 7, and their relationship has matured. Denise serves as a confident for her nieces and in many ways buttresses the work of her brother and sister-in-law. On a rare sleepover night, occasioned because the parents were away for the weekend, one of the twins shared that she had "kissed a boy on the bus" earlier in the week. "I could tell something was kind of on her mind," Denise said. "She was tired and then kind of brought it up to get my reaction. So I didn't react, I just said: 'I think that's against the rules and you know better. Maybe you should talk to mom and dad about it, that's up to you.'" The incident demonstrates how aunts serve important functions for children by helping them negotiate their concerns and learn respect for the boundaries parents have established, while doing so in a comforting atmosphere. Denise says: "I tell them all the time, 'it doesn't matter what you do, what mistake you make, I'll still love you.'"

Aunts and uncles supplemented parents by providing alternate sources of information and acting as confidants, particularly with regard to sensitive topics, issues for which nieces and nephews considered their parents too judgmental. Drugs and sex seem to top the list of sensitive topics, and aunts and uncles are sought out for their counsel. Elspeth considers her aunt a second mom, "like my best friend mom," she says, and one she has turned to when her friends were experimenting with drugs. Greco maintains a strong relationship with his nephew, who recently expressed his interest in experimenting with psilocybin and other psychedelic drugs. Greco shared his own experiences, good and bad, which he felt was more important than being too judgmental. He welcomed the confidence and trust his nephew placed in their relationship.

At times nieces and nephews seemed to use their aunts and uncles as sounding boards for issues that they eventually shared with parents, and in some cases, parents gladly accepted the help. A mother, for instance, called and thanked her sister for intervening and having an intimate chat with her daughter on mom's least successful topic, the daughter's sexual activity. Similarly, an uncle relates how his brother encourages the relationship of uncle and nephew. Jessie says of his brother and father to his nephew: "His dad knows that we have a close relationship. There are some times [his dad] will bring up a subject in the hopes that I will bring it up with [my nephew]."

Aunt Harriett, who is herself a mother of two children, comments on a similar theme, her appreciation of and understanding of the importance of aunts and uncles for children. She says, "It is nice for a mother to know that her daughters or sons can have these other adult supportive relationships."

The positions of aunts and uncles sometimes amplify those of parents, and at other times they are distinctly complementary, particularly when they enact a partisan support for nieces and nephews or advocate on their behalf.

Aunt Isabella spoke about her experiences as a child and her relationship with her own aunt.

> I was an early adolescent and wanted nylons. And my father was just not hearing that. [My parents] were just not even responding. And one day [my aunt] walked in the house and laid down a package on the table and she said: "Here are your stockings. I know you've been asking for them." And she gave me three pairs of stockings. I was 11. I was thrilled.

At other times conflicts between parents and children severely limit their communication, and aunts and uncles become important family confidants or at least alternate parental figures. An 11-year-old niece tells her Aunt Francesca things she would not share with her mother because, as Francesca explains, her niece doesn't "want to disappoint [her mother], or maybe is a little fearful of her reaction." Francesca adds that sometimes her niece's mother "kind of flies off the handle." For her young niece, Francesca represents a stable, consistent, and trusted adult figure, and conveniently they live next door to one another.

Patricia found it easier to get along with her aunt than her mother. Her aunt served as a buffer between mother and daughter. Patricia says of her mother, "she has never been somebody that I can share things with, and mostly my aunt has always been very understanding and always on my side." Later in the interview she adds: "My aunt was more of a confidant than my mother could ever be." Patricia is now a professional in her mid-50s; her aunt is 86. They visit monthly and talk on the phone nearly daily.

All families are challenged on occasion, and one of the most difficult challenges is the death of a child. Julie's brother died when she was in her early 20s, and although she had always had a close relationship with her mother, in this circumstance her aunt became a critical person in her life as she tried to understand her loss at a time when her mother was not entirely available to her. Aunt Rosemary described how she intervened with the family initially by making all the funeral arrangements and later by supporting both mother and her daughter. Rosemary describes how she lost her first husband when she was younger and that experience helped her understand her sister's and niece's grief, as well as her own. The experience is a poignant example of how aunts and uncles can be important sources of support for families, and especially for children, when parents understandably are occupied by the sometimes overwhelming exigencies of life.

In cases in which mothers are raising children as single parents, aunts and uncles can complement and add a measure of balance. Nicole's parents were divorced when she was an infant, and throughout her childhood, she spent a considerable amount of time with her aunt; during summer vacations, she lived with her aunt and grandmother. Estella relates that she is closer to her aunt since her parents divorced, and when she returns home over semester breaks in her graduate study, she inevitably elects to stay with her aunt. "In a way," she says, "it's sort of a neutral ground so my Mom doesn't feel hurt by me staying with my Dad and vice versa. I just enjoy staying with my aunt anyway."

Aunt Susan was single when her niece and nephews were young, and her sister "worked constantly."

> My sister struggled and had to work and work just to take care of Nika and her two brothers. Nika used to beg me to come and take them out and have fun. And that's what I did when they were little. We'd go camping, and shopping. When she was about 10, she went through a hairspray stage, and she'd call me up and beg me to buy her hairspray.

Susan goes on to say that because she was young and single, she had the time, and inclination, to become involved with her sister's children. She understood that her sister was overwhelmed with providing for and raising her three young children. In this way, the family work of aunts parallels that of grandparents, and especially grandmothers, in the provision of child-care support for single parents.

During her adolescence, Nika experienced an escalation of conflict with her mother and, according to her aunt, some difficulty in getting along with her mom's boyfriend. As is often the case, Aunt Susan intervened and provided housing. For her last year in high school, Nika lived with her aunt, who continues to intervene in conflicts between mother and daughter. Adolescence can be a difficult time for parents and children; aunts and uncles are at times clearly aware of this and provide welcome interventions that help ease family conflicts. In some cases like Aunt Susan's, they provided a safe haven in the form of temporary housing.

Sunshine experienced some difficulties with drugs and alcohol during her early adolescence, a circumstance that eventually led to an encounter with law enforcement officials. Her father, with whom she was living, was unwilling to let the situation continue. Sunshine went to live with her mother and the mother's boyfriend but got along with neither very well. Aunt Ray describes her niece as "a very strong-willed, independent person." Ray took in her niece while she completed high school. "I had her come [and] stay with me and we talked a lot about what she was going through."

In the family stories recounted by Aunts Susan and Ray, the conflict between parents and children were fairly severe. More often aunts and uncles intervened in less intense conflicts between adolescents and parents, and more important, they understood such conflict to be normal parts of adolescent and parent development. Many commented on the issue. Patricia describes how her aunt came to teach her to drive. "My mother didn't drive," she says, "and my father had no patience with me. He would get so annoyed at me that he would say, 'Forget it!' My aunt was the one who came to the rescue. She taught me how to tie my shoe. She taught me how to tell time. She taught me now to drive the car. My father made me nervous 'cause I felt like I had to get it all right the first time and [my aunt] would just laugh." The circumstance is perhaps ordinary, for who hasn't been in the situation of occasionally being impatient with a child?

Uncle Michael, a college librarian, understood that the relationship between parents and adolescents was quite different from his own. "Teenage boys are notoriously difficult, in my experience, in terms of sharing things with parents," he says. "They are often secretive, or [believe] parents are jerks." Michael describes how in his experience uncles don't "carry the same baggage as parents" and therefore are able to establish unique relationships with nephews. He describes his unique position as being "on the inside because you are a family member, yet you are on the outside because you're not in a tight family circle."

Both aunts and uncles were aware of the special needs of adolescents to differentiate from their parents in order to develop their own unique identities, and they understood how these developmental tasks colored their relationships. Aunt Lena described her relationship with her niece as similar to a mother's in terms of the mutual concern and desire to nurture, but different in the sense that nieces are not struggling with "how do I separate from my aunt to become who I am." Several aunts mentioned that they can be more "objective" than mothers because of this difference between mothers and aunts, as did uncles with regard to their greater objectivity relative to fathers.

Aunt Theriza described a week spent with her niece driving across country. She understood that her niece, Liz, "was constantly in a snit about something" usually regarding her mother's expectations. Theriza shared the story of their return home and her subsequent conversation with her sister.

> I told my sister, "we had a good time together." And my sister said: "She didn't get into any of her moods?" And I said: "No we get along great. She doesn't have to get into moods with me, I'm not her mother." And we both laughed about that, you know, and she said: "Yes that was exactly what I was going to say. It's not because you were so wonderful and I'm not, it's because you're not her mother."

Theriza continued the conversation, saying to her sister: "You know we don't have the same kinds of issues and she doesn't have to assert independence from me." In this way, both sisters shared their understandings of how the relationship of mother and daughter differed from that of aunt and niece, differences that appear to be significant and commonplace.

Perhaps as Aunt Olympia opined, "it's important for kids to have someone that they can trust and feel safe with and nurtured and loved. A family member does all those things, but you can also break loose of those things. I think that's really really important. It's one way you experiment with who you are and still stay safe." In this instance, Olympia was actually referring to her own daughter and her relationship with Olympia's sister, a relationship that she encourages and her sister welcomes. From Olympia's point of view, "breaking loose" is an important part of growing up and discovering, or creating, a sense of self. In this way, aunts and uncles figure in important ways in the developmental pathways of their nieces and nephews. They may in time develop relationships that mirror friendships, but in some ways their responsibility continues even among young adult nieces and nephews.

> The thing about an aunt that is special that is not the same as a friend is that an aunt can be a safe person when you're an adult and you still want to be a child. (Aunt Roxy)

Aunts and uncles provided experiences and knowledge that directly supplemented parents and occasionally provided experiences that parents could not provide. John speaks of his understanding of uncling:

> His parents have to teach him how to get through life and I like to think I'm teaching how to find the good things in life. You know I get to talk about stuff that his parents wouldn't. Like art.

Similarly, Marty describes her aunt's contributions as they complement her parents: "I'm glad I have [my aunt's] inputs besides my parents. Because I love my parents and I respect them a lot but they don't have all the experiences that she has."

A nephew, Jamie, describes being introduced to athletics by his dad, an interest the nephew continues as a high school football coach. He describes a different and complementary influence of his uncle. "Getting into outdoors, fishing, four-wheeling, snowmobiling and stuff like that was more my uncle's influence."

Aunts and uncles frequently spoke of being role models for the children in their lives, or as Aunt Susan offered, "to live well in front of them." They routinely defined their role as "just being there" with core elements of friendship, mentoring, and support. For some, the act of role modeling is perhaps not entirely conscious. Natalie describes her aunt as a fun person: "you always come [away] from meeting with her with a good feeling altogether." Her aunt lives and works in Paris, and to Natalie she represents a different lifestyle from that of her parents.

Addie views her role in terms of "providing information about life in general" and is a bit more conscious about being a role model for her 20-year-old niece Heather. Addie lives with her daughter and sister, Heather's mom. Heather visits often. "She'll come over to say hi, take a shower, or wash her laundry." Although her relationship with her aunt is close and comfortable, her relationship with her mom is often contentious.

Heather has some difficulty finding her way, has started college classes several times, but unsuccessfully, and seems to lack direction. Addie recounts how her niece "shared with me that she feels like a loser." Heather's dad was abusive of her mom, her siblings, and Heather, and he continues to experiences difficulties with substance abuse. Given the circumstances, it is perhaps not surprising that Heather is at times adrift, unsure of her place and purpose in life. Addie tries to be supportive, to be there to listen, to encourage her niece to work through her problems, and to be "a bit of a role model for what she can do and be in her life as a woman." Addie shares with her niece her own experiences, the importance of being independent and of not putting up with abusive men. "I think what I try to give her is the knowledge that it's okay not to put up with [abusive men], and that if it means being alone for a while [because] you want to just figure out who you are without having someone else in the mix, then that's okay too." Addie is clearly a strong, consistent, and positive voice in her niece's life, and perhaps a much-needed mentor. When the relationships of aunts and uncles were at their best, role modeling – the sharing directly or vicariously of how to manage personal situations, people, and relationships – merges with a more active, purposeful mentoring.

Aunt Sandy, like many other aunts, viewed her role in these terms, emphasizing the importance of taking an interest in her niece's life and, in her words, "promoting her interests, being a cheerleader, and offering alternatives to her parents' view on life." Nonetheless, Sandy was clear to distinguish her role from that of her niece's parents. "My job is to be a friend, mentor, and support person. . . . It's not my job to make sure the kids turn out to be valuable human beings. That's the job of their parents."

Aunts and uncles provide enrichment experiences that supplement the activities, interests, and skills of parents or at times complement them. This complementarity is demonstrated in the variety of ways aunts and uncles provide enrichment opportunities, including visits to libraries, concerts, museums, sporting events, outdoor activities, or any activity that complements what parents ordinarily provide. They can offer technical information or advice in areas in which their knowledge and experience exceeds that of parents. For instance, Leigh is a college senior. Her aunt is the only other person in her family with a college degree, and she appreciates "the fact that she is someone older that I can talk to if I have questions." Michele describes learning about photography from her aunt, who is a professional photographer and artist. "I just like seeing her in action," she says. "I've watched her have a passion for something she loves and not be afraid to try something new and different." This is an instance of role modeling in its simplest and perhaps most effective form.

Michael's nephew elected to complete a project on the ecology of a local river and enlisted the help of his uncle. Being a university librarian, Michael was all too happy to send along a package of educational material and then arrange for him and his nephew to visit the local expert on water quality in a state environmental protection agency. In a similar fashion, Carla Lyn invited her niece to visit her office and then shared the initial page proofs of her latest publication, something her niece had not seen before. Of course, it is difficult to say whether the experience had any lasting impression on her niece. The interests of adolescents can sometimes be mercurial. Carla Lyn's niece was initially interested in engineering, then medicine, but lately a career in business seems to be winning out because she "wants to make money without working so hard," which at some level is rather a universal sentiment.

This kind of enrichment opportunity derivative of the professional expertise and contacts of aunts and uncles extends the range of experiences parents can provide for children, and they are most often fairly routine outcomes of a phone call or visit. More demonstrative are the longer enrichment opportunities that occasionally develop. Rosemary is currently planning a trip to the Bay of Fundy and eastern Canada with her 25-year-old niece. In this way, they will continue a tradition of spending significant time with one another, a tradition that began when her niece was 11 and Rosemary took her on a trip to London. I asked Rosemary how she came to take her niece on extended vacations. She replied: "Well because I love her to pieces. She is the crown jewel of my life. So I just do a lot of things with [her], and just help her grow up. I feel like I've had the opportunity to teach her little things, and if there are different crises in her life, I want to be part of those."

In other circumstances, aunts and uncles complement parents because of their distance from the "hot zones" of adolescence. Lena arranged for her niece's summer job because "My sister has been backing off [the issue of a summer job] because it would be the kiss of death to have your parent recommend something to you when you're sixteen." In this instance, Lena's knowledge derived from the positive experiences her son had working in a similar position the previous summer.

Aunts and uncles, by virtue of their professional expertise, can complement the knowledge of parents and advise them directly. Beatrice, as a former director of a special education program, was able to help her brother and sister-in-law understand the battery of tests and technical reports generated when their child underwent a series of diagnostic tests for learning disabilities.

In summary, common themes in the family work of aunts and uncles include providing support and companionship, acting as confidants, and modeling alternative family or career choices. Aunts and uncles supplement the work of parents in virtually all areas of the lives of their nieces and nephews, and this may be especially important for single parents.

The relationships of aunts and uncles change and adapt with the development of children and the needs of parents. During the labor-intensive years of infancy and early childhood, they provide parents with direct child-care relief. During adolescence, when issues of identity development are primary, they can ease or mediate conflicts between parents and teens, serve as testing grounds for the identity development of nieces and nephews, and, just as important, provide support for parents and act as their confidants. Aunts and uncles often become critical sources of support in times of special need, such as the death of a family member or cases of separation and divorce.

THIRD-PARTY PERSPECTIVES

The unique contributions of aunts and uncles are in part derivative of their third-party perspective. Uncle Benny, a New Zealander, captured the essence of this viewpoint when he likened his role to that of a "camera four perspective," a reference to a car-racing video game in which one camera resides with the driver, one in the passenger seat, one on the race track, and the forth from above has a view of the entire track – the widest possible perspective. This distinction between the responsibilities and perspectives of parents relative to aunts or uncles was common.

Olympia expressed a similar sentiment: "well I just think it's that you are a member of the family circle but you're not limited by the constraints of that circle. You're a place where [nieces] can go and you know the context of everything. You know how the rules operate, and you know what the expectations are, and yet you're not limited by them. You're kind of outside that."

Aunts and uncles saw themselves as independent and occasionally less prone to judgment, relative to parents, and nieces and nephews agreed. For instance Jerry, an 18-year-old student from New Zealand, says, "I can talk about girls and stuff like that [with my uncle, and] some of the stupid stuff I've done that I couldn't tell my dad."

Buddy is 19 and visits with his uncle monthly. I asked him if his uncle ever gave him advice, and he replied: "Not really. He's more like someone that would listen and talk to you. I suppose he really doesn't judge you."

Most often the opinions of aunts and uncles are highly valued. Elspeth described introducing her new boyfriend to her aunt, which for her was a significant event. "I don't know," Elspeth says, but "her approval means a lot to me." Bruce shared how his uncle "influences me in the sense that I always want to impress him. I never want to disappoint him. If I did something that he was going to hear about or see, I would put in a lot of effort."

In each of these examples, aunts and uncles serve to augment the work of parents, sometimes by directly mentoring their nieces and nephews, sometimes by directly mentoring parents. Their unique perspective is in many ways derivative of their simultaneous distance from the interior of families – the relationships of parents and children – and their knowledge and lifelong experience with family members. As Aunt Lena says, "I just get to do fun things and I don't have to set any limits." This later theme is shared by several aunts and uncles. "You get a lot of the joys," says Aunt Theriza, "but almost none of the pains." She goes on to explain how her relationship to her niece differs from that of a parent and child.

> I might help financially but I'm not ultimately responsible for college tuition or new shoes or whatever it is that kids need. You know my sister had to worry about feeding and planning. I had to buy [my niece] gifts and breeze in from out of town, be fun to be with and go away and let my sister deal with making them do their homework and all that boring stuff that parents have to deal with.

Uncle Michael expressed a similar theme when reflecting on his role relative to that of his nephew's parents.

> There is less responsibility and direct involvement. I'm sort of a satel-lite... outside of things.... I certainly enjoy the relationship but at the same time I recognize I'm not getting the tuition bills right now. And so I am not the one directly responsible but sort of the next tier out I guess. I don't have kids so I certainly enjoy uncling. But I'd be the first to say they are pretty radically different. [He laughs.]

Aunts and uncles who viewed their roles in these ways were quick to point out how they benefited from having greater emotional distance from the immediate and daily responsibility for raising children while still maintaining their involvement. "There is a little distance, a little less emotion involved," says Aunt Harriett. "The love is there, but you're not in each other's face. You can just accept that person as a whole and not worry about the little stuff at all." Curiously she went on to add how her relationship with her niece influenced her thoughts about her own children. "Being an aunt helps you realize the role you could be playing with your own [children]." Or as Aunt Olympia offered, "I really enjoy all the different personalities of my nieces and I like that we can do all the fun things but then I don't have the burden of being the bad cop." She laughed and then added: "We can have a good time and talk about things like what's right in a given situation and what isn't and how to do things, but its fun. And [my nieces] can be a little more relaxed than they might be with a parent."

The third-party perspective of aunts and uncles allows them to offer nieces and nephews alternative ways of living, of developing relationships, careers, and personal interests. As Aunt Roxy described when I asked how her relationship with her niece differed from that of her parents: "Part of the way I see my role in her life is to invite her to think about things in a way that I would like her to think about them regardless of what her parents would like. I have the luxury of tossing out 'what ifs' and they can be way out."

In a variety of ways, aunts and uncles enrich the lives of their nieces and nephews. Their contributions are often highly valued, considered irreplaceable and unique, and derive from the longevity of their relationships, knowledge of family members, and third-party status. At the same time, they are often deeply affected by their experience. Their relationships with nieces and nephews spill over and affect their understanding of their own parenting and their relationships with their own children.

SECOND MOMS AND SECOND DADS

Under some circumstances, aunts and uncles replaced absent parents or otherwise enacted significant parental roles, and they were treated as such by their nieces and nephews. Aunts and uncles became surrogate parents for one of three reasons. Those aunts who lived in extended family units sharing one home or neighboring homes in the presence of a sibling, perhaps a sibling's spouse and children, often acted as surrogate parents for the children. Grandparents were occasionally present in the same households. In other circumstances, aunts and uncles served as parental figures when the father of a niece or nephew was absent, typically because of a divorce or problems related to substance abuse. Finally, some aunts, uncles, nieces, and nephews described close relationships that seemed to be based on opportunity (they saw each other often and easily) and personal preference in that they simply liked one another. For many of these nieces and nephews, their favored kin relation supplements strong, positive relationships with parents, and they describe such kin as *like a dad*, or *like a second mom*. For others, a conflict-habituated relationship with a parent is paired with an intimate relationship with an aunt or uncle who is considered in ways similar to a parent. In all of these cases, aunts and uncles intervened at times to provide housing for their nieces or nephews, sometimes temporary and sometimes on a more permanent basis. We consider each of these arrangements in greater depth in the pages that follow.

Extended Family Households

One of the aunts and three of the nieces described living in extended families during significant periods of their childhood or adolescence. Although several of the nephews and uncles lived in the same communities or even in the same neighborhoods, only one nephew, Sherman, a Native American, described living in the same household, and that was a recent development. Sherman's uncle moved into the home of Sherman's mother and grandfather as a result of the uncle's separation from his wife. Sherman is a 20-year-old university student, and from his point of view, he and his uncle have a modest relationship and talk only infrequently. "When I was younger, I was a lot closer to him than I am now, but now that I'm grown up I don't really talk to him as much." Sherman admits that his uncle does ask him about how he is doing in school. "He is like real proud of me," he says with a smile.

In contrast to Sherman's experience, Raymond lived next door to his uncle during his childhood and adolescence. Raymond's uncle recently married and moved to a neighboring community. Their relationship was introduced in the previous chapter. In many ways, his uncle acted as a father figure for Raymond. His mother divorced when he was an infant, and he now visits with his biological father only occasionally. A remarriage also ended in divorce when he was 13 or 14. Raymond was closer to his stepdad while growing up, and they still keep in touch, although their relationship seems restricted to talking about sports. Of his stepdad, Raymond says: "Baseball is our thing" and "something we connect most about." In contrast, Raymond clearly depends on his uncle for all manners of advice regarding family, personal relationships, and career; there seems to be little they don't discuss. During his youth, Raymond spent his summers crisscrossing the country with his uncle, who at that time was a long-distance trucker. When I asked if he thinks of his uncle like a father, Raymond replied: "In a lot of ways yes. We do have that but I don't think most father and sons would go to the lengths him and I go . . . he is always teaching me something whether it's changing a tire, learning to use a computer, or playing guitars." From Raymond's perspective and experience, relationships with fathers are restricted, whereas his relationship with his uncle is not so limited. Our interview is littered with examples of wisdom and wit. Raymond described how "a lot of the stuff [my uncle] taught me is more about life itself" and followed this statement with an example from his late teens.

> I drank a lot. I was having fun. My uncle said, "respect alcohol and the alcohol will respect you."
>
> *RM: Did he tell you not to drink too much?*
>
> No, he said: "Everything in moderation. You don't have to go overboard. Enjoy life; just be careful how far you go." That's how he is.

Raymond's uncle recently changed careers, and Raymond encouraged him to do so. On his uncle's most recent birthday, Raymond sent a card and enclosed a song he had written, a "satire of a truck driver turned insurance salesman."

Elena is now 46 and lives with her partner and two children. As a young child, she lived in her mother's household. Elena's two favored aunts lived in a neighboring household that included Roberta, who was her mother's sister, and Jackie her aunt's partner and lover. Elena's grandmother, another aunt, and Elena's husband and their two children lived in the same building. She referred to her aunt and her aunt's partner as *Ma Tante*, an endearing phrase used in the Franco community in which she was raised, and now thinks of them as her "two other mothers" – and for good reason. Elena says, "I think that for [my mother] it was very helpful to have her sisters nearby that could be part of the family and could help her raise her own children." Elena had three siblings and described many instances of her aunts' parenting activity. When Elena was 12, a series of events, including her father's death a year earlier, her mother's illnesses that required a series of operations, and a catastrophic disaster had the effect of deepening her connection to her aunts.

> A year after my father died, [my aunts' home] had one of those big massive gas explosions. It was a really traumatic event, two people died and three escaped. My Aunt Jackie was upstairs, and she turned on the hot water, and the sink flew right past her, if she had been leaned over, it would have taken her head off. Gas collected in the basement, it ignited, one wall of the house blew out and the house basically collapsed. She managed to get down stairs, on a broken stairway, in a house on fire, get through the hallway which was full of glass, and break her way through. She was a really tough lady. She got into the bedroom where my grandmother and my other aunt were, and she got them. She said, 'I'll clear a path for us, follow me.' The door was blocked so she made it to a window and the firefighters were there and they pulled her out. She turned around and [my grandmother and other aunt] weren't following her. She fought with the firefighters to go back in to get them, but before she had turned around, the building had collapsed. The whole family fell apart. My grandmother was dead. My Aunt Roberta was dead. It was never the same after this, there was no place to go to, there was no center for the family, but these people who were in the explosion came to live at our house and my mother took care of them.

During this recovery period Elena reported some conflict between her aunt and mother, perhaps in part due to their different views on parenting Elena, differences in values, and perhaps some jealousy on the part of Elena's mother regarding Elena's growing closeness with her aunt. Eventually Elena's aunt Jackie moved into her own apartment, Elena entered adolescence and high school, and in time she moved out of the community to pursue a university education and career. It is clear her aunt was an important influence in her life, and in some ways, although Aunt Jackie is deceased, she continues to be an influence. Elena now maintains a relationship with her own niece, who is married with children and living in a distant state. They visit several times per year and often share their experiences as parents of young children, or experiences in their professional lives because they both are teachers. As Elena reflects on this, she comments on her own relationships with her aunt and what this means about aunts more generally.

> I feel like I've been a fairly good role model and a fairly good friend [with my niece], but I'm not sure I've been very good about being emotionally close. I had a physical closeness with my Aunt Jackie that I don't think has

been replicated. Sometimes those things are not about talking. Talking is one thing, but I think [closeness is] really about just spending time with somebody, just being with them the way that you just are with children. I think that with most of my nieces, we haven't been in the same town, we only see each other during holidays, so the entire relationship is based on three or four meetings a year.

Yeah, I think just being there without any reason, just to be there and be with somebody and enjoy that time. That's what my Aunt Jackie did so well with me. Just being there, being with me, wanting to be there.

Elena goes on to describe how her relationship with her Aunt Jackie influences her relationships with her own children. For her, Tante Jackie was "a good role model for what I can do for my own children. It's not about teaching them," she says, "it's not about being a role model. It's about just being there... with them." I asked Elena if her mother gave her similar lessons, or if she thought about her mother in similar ways. She replied: "I'm not saying she never felt that way, but I didn't get that feeling. Maybe, as far as I was concerned, aunts are for teaching you about love."

In this family, an aunt became a central figure in the life of her niece. Their relationship was hallmarked by frequent contact and some periods of living in the same household; a diversity of activities common to that between parents and children, and occasionally between aunts and children; and a measure of intensity that is perhaps not common and brought on by the intersection of personal dispositions and catastrophic circumstance. It would not be entirely correct to refer to Aunt Jackie as a substitute parent; Elena maintained an important and influential relationship with her own mother and continues to do so. Yet, in many ways Jackie and Elena were like a mother and daughter, and not surprisingly Elena refers to her aunt as a "second mother."

Patricia is a successful professional in her mid-50s, single and childless. When she was born, her parents moved into the home of her aunt and maternal grandmother, where she lived throughout her childhood and early adolescence. She describes her aunt as a second mother and, like so many nieces, regards her aunt as a fun person. "My aunt provided kind of a comic side to life," she says. "She was the one who wanted to do fun things. My mother and I never did those fun kid things together, and my father definitely never did stuff with me." At the same time, her aunt was her confidant and mentor and served as a buffer between the inevitable struggles that can occur between mother and daughter. Patricia says of her mother, "she has never been somebody that I can share things with."

Here again mother and aunt experienced some conflict, and Patricia recounts instances of her mother attempting to establish her parental authority. "My mother would say to my aunt, 'well she's my daughter and I will tell her what to do.'" Patricia went on to say, "there has always been that strife between them, my mother feeling very jealous of the fact that I would go to my aunt, or that she would know certain things, or that I would talk to my aunt more than I would to talk to her." Although we cannot know with any certainty, the conflict between mother and sister seems to be in part some residual sibling rivalry and in part due to a jealousy regarding the closeness of a daughter and her aunt. Mother and aunt are now elderly women, living together, and their rivalry continues, much to Patricia's dismay. "I realized that there were so many old tapes that were playing between the two of them. They could push each other's buttons and it would get them going and I think that actually I come to my mother's defense, which I never thought I would do, and I think my aunt is sometimes unfair with my mother."

Although her father was present in the household, Patricia does not present a very close relationship with him. "He worked a lot" she says, and nothing more. Patricia's aunt and mother were in many ways jointly parenting her. Both encouraged her to develop her interests, to be the first in her family to attend college, to develop a career, and while she was unable to talk to her mother about the intimate details of her life, she did so with her aunt. "She would always be there for me," Patricia says of her aunt. At the time of our interview, Patricia's aunt and mother were well into their 80s and again living in the same household. Patricia lives within a half-day drive, visits monthly, talks with her mom daily and her aunt several times per week. In addition, her aunt writes weekly. She has spent every Christmas for over a half century with her aunt and mother, as well as most other holidays and all birthdays. Toward the end of our visit, Patricia added: "My aunt is old, and has been with me since birth." I left with the feeling she meant more than a simple physical presence, rather the intimacy born of growing old together, of personal biographies that are cowritten.

Diana's story of her early years shares some similarities with Patricia. Diana is in her mid-50s; she and her husband are retired and live in a retirement community. Diana lived with her aunt, whom she refers to as a second mother, and her uncle from birth until she was about 6. Her parents divorced when she was young, and her mother eventually moved into the same household. In her middle childhood, Diana and her mother eventually moved into a separate residence in an urban area, although Diana continued to spend her summers with her aunt, her uncle, and their children on the mid-Atlantic coast. Her father was nearly absent from her life, and she reported seeing him on only three occasions before her own marriage. I asked her what she thought was most memorable about her aunt. She replied: "Acceptance more than anything else. The love she had was not dependent on anything, it was just there and it wasn't that you were being good or anything, it was just there." Like Patricia, Diana describes her aunt as more fun, and less judgmental and controlling, compared to her mother. From Diana's perspective, her mother and aunt were not terribly close and had "different lifestyles." However, her mother and aunt shared some similar interests and values regarding homemaking, and both were avid readers, a complement of interests Diana shares. Diana's marriage, her children, and her eventual career as a teacher led to some distance in her relationship with her aunt. Although they maintained contact over the following decades, it was largely occasioned by holidays and important family events.

Estella is a 28-year-old graduate student from the southwestern United States. Her aunt moved into her mother's home when she was a freshman in high school. She describes their early years living in the same household: "At the beginning our relationship wasn't that close. She was kind of somebody new but as time went on, it was easier for me to speak to my aunt. My aunt was a lot more open than my mom." She went on to describe what she particularly liked about her aunt. "She is just a very patient woman and very easygoing. She just makes you feel very comfortable around her. [I can] talk to her about anything, completely the opposite from my mom." Throughout her adolescence, she was an important source of advice and encouragement and she continues in this role.

Estella experiences some conflict with her mom, although there are clearly instances of support as well. Her parents were initially reserved about her going away to college and moving away from the family's rural home to a large urban university in the midwestern United States, although her mom ultimately bought her a plane ticket, which for Estella was an important sign of her mother's eventual acceptance, approval, and support. Estella talks with her mom "a couple of times" per month and her aunt less often. "I probably do talk with my mom more often but usually she'll call and say I'm sending you this or just kind of general chitchat." Her mother often sends packages of food or reports on the activity of Estella's sister, her aunt, or other family members. Even so, she reports being closer to her aunt. "I'm not really sure why that is," she says, "I can just talk to my aunt a lot easier. I think we're a lot more similar in personalities." Her aunt is an electrical engineer, and Estella is now working on a graduate degree in mechanical engineering. She credits both her mom and aunt for

Table 4.1. *Nieces and nephews living in extended and near-extended families*

Participant	Age	Mother divorced	Aunt or uncle mother's sibling	Aunt or uncle single	Aunt or uncle childless	Mother and aunt/ uncle conflict	Niece/Nephew closer to aunt/uncle than to parent
Aunt Elena	46	Yes	Yes	Yes	Yes	Yes	Yes
Niece Patricia	53	No	Yes	Yes	Yes	Yes	Yes
Niece Diana	54	Yes	Yes	No	No	Yes	No
Niece Estella	28	Yes	Yes	Yes	Yes	Yes	Yes
Nephew Sherman	20	Yes	Yes	Yes	No	No	No
Nephew Raymond	26	Yes	Yes	Yes	Yes	No	Yes

encouraging her to do something nontraditional for a Hispanic female, to be strong and independent financially, and to "marry not because you have to but because you want to."

Estella's mother and aunt continue to maintain close contact, and although there were occasions when they did not entirely agree on parenting Estella, in large part, they are both supportive in their sometimes unique ways. When Estella visits her family, she stays with her aunt rather than the homes of either of her parents, because it represents a neutral ground, favors neither of her parents, and avoids any potential jealousies and ill feelings; she also does so simply because she enjoys her aunt's company.

The stories of Elena, Diana, Patricia, and Estella share several similarities (see Table 4.1). All lived with their mothers and aunts (mothers' sisters) for a significant period of their childhood or adolescence. In three of the four cases, their mothers were divorced, and all of them developed strong bonds with their aunts, who in some ways seemed to complement their sisters in skills and temperament. Nieces consistently reported some conflict with mothers, and relatively little with their aunts. They uniformly describe aunts as easier to get along with or more understanding and less judgmental, and their aunts were typically single and childless for much of the time they lived in the same households, with the exception of Diana's aunt who was married with children. It is not surprising that nieces reported some conflict between mothers and aunts, particularly when nieces reported favoring aunts over mothers. In all of these families, men were sometimes present but, in the eyes of nieces, not terribly engaged.

The stories of Sherman and Raymond share some similarities in that matrilineal kin ties seemed strongest – both lived with their mothers and their mothers' brothers. Their mothers were divorced when they were young, and for much of their childhood and adolescence, their uncles were single. However, in only one of these cases (Raymond's) is the uncle acting as a surrogate father and intimate. Sherman has a rather cavalier approach to his relationship with his uncle, perhaps in part due to his own need for independence and his uncle's only recent move into the same household.

Absentee Parents

Five of the uncles described relationships with nephews whose fathers had been absent since the nephews were very young, and similarly three nephews described minimal, if any, relationship with their biological fathers (see Table 4.2). I asked uncles whether they served as substitute fathers or thought of themselves in this way. One uncle, Nick, was present at his nephew's birth: "I actually cut the umbilical cord, which was quite fun." This uncle was particularly close to his sister (who recommended his participation in the study) and her 11-year-old son, whose father is entirely absent. Nick visits his nephew weekly or more often. He went on to describe his relationship: "I just kind of understand that I should be a friend and kind of an adult role model. Like a parent but not so close perhaps."

Freddie visited with his 27-year-old nephew weekly and described his nephew as "like a son." When I asked him if he considered his nephew a friend, he paused thoughtfully and then replied: "I consider him a friend but also someone that is closer than a friend. He does fit almost into the son category." In some ways his response is not surprising because their relationship was clearly intimate, and their contact frequent and multiplex. If, however, the relationship was more paternal, I wondered if it would be less reciprocal, and if largely fraternal and more friend-like, I expected greater reciprocity. So, I asked.

RM: Would he give you advice?

That's an interesting question. There again it is mostly approval. I've got this truck sitting in the garage that is mostly in pieces right now. When I bought [the truck] it was kind of like well I bought this. "Did I really get taken to the cleaners on this?" [He laughs.]

In this case, Freddie shares his ambivalence over a recent purchase and in so doing seeks his nephew's approval, which in the uncle's eyes he receives. This defines a relationship characterized by reciprocal support. The nephew is like both a son and a friend to his uncle. The exchange also raises the question of whether the nephew's support for his uncle is an instance of

Table 4.2. *The relationships of aunts and uncles with nieces and nephews with an absent parent*

Participant	Niece's/ nephew's parents divorced	Reason for niece or nephew's absent parent	Closeness of aunt/uncle and niece/nephew
Aunt Susan	Yes	Parents divorced when niece was very young. Minimal contact with father.	High
Aunt Olympia	Yes	Parents divorced when niece was young. Father not active on day-to-day basis.	High
Aunt Rosemary	Yes	Parents divorced when niece was young. Minimal contact with father since age 11.	High
Niece Janice	Yes	Father minimally involved during childhood; parents divorce when niece was 18. Niece visits with father annually or less.	High
Niece Diana	Yes	Parents divorced when niece was an infant. Little or no contact with father until niece's adulthood.	Moderate
Niece Nicole	Yes	Parents divorced when niece was an infant. Mother remarried when niece was 8.	High
Niece Fiona	Yes	Parents divorced when niece was 2. Little contact with biological father. Niece has relationship with stepdad whom she regards as her father.	High
Uncle Robert	No	Father died when nephew was 12. He is now 17.	High
Uncle Nick	Yes	Father absent since childhood.	High
Uncle Billy	Yes	Twin nephews' alcoholic father absent since birth.	High
Uncle Stephen	No	Nephew's mother recently died.	High
Uncle Evin	Yes	Mother alcoholic and absent since early childhood.	Low
Uncle Sammy	Yes	No contact with father since childhood; unknown if living. Maintains relationship with stepdad, now divorced from mother.	Low
Uncle Freddie	Yes	Father alcoholic, absent since early childhood.	High
Nephew Brig	Yes	Father absent since early childhood, visits less than annually.	Low
Nephew Heath	Yes	Father absent since early childhood, nephew hasn't seen father in 8 years. Mother remarried four times.	High
Nephew Mario	Yes	Father absent since early childhood; visits less than annually and lives abroad.	Moderate

generativity. Must generativity be cast forward as a concern for a future generation, or is it best viewed as a concern for others, regardless of generation? We return to this question in Chapter 5.

The mix of paternal mentoring appeared in many of the interviews. Another uncle, Robert, spoke fondly of his relationship with his sister's 17-year-old son, whose father had died when he was 12. Robert's nephew lives with his mother, 4 or 5 hours away from his uncle. They visit several times per year and had done so recently. "We just hung out together," says Robert. "I find I just like talking with him. He needs to express his ideas... and I think anything that develops companionship really I don't mind.... It is sort of a more paternal thing I think." Robert is a Catholic priest and ministers to a large, urban university campus in New Zealand. He recently offered to share his home with his nephew should he decide to begin his university studies.

Although he lives with a disability that limits his activity, Billy maintains a relationship with his 13-year-old twin nephews, whose alcoholic father has been entirely absent since their birth. The families visit monthly, and every other month the twins stay over with their uncle for a weekend. I asked Billy if having lesbians as parents was significant for the children or for his relationship with them.

> Perhaps it is for this particular pair of lesbian parents. They've both been very strong. Basically they have taught their kids to do a lot of thinking for themselves. And not to accept other people's say so, just because they say so, just because they're who they are. That sort of thing. I've seen other kids growing up in heterosexual families that don't seem to be getting that kind of leadership. Because it is not as strongly emphasized I guess.

Billy went on to describe how his sister and her partner encourage his active involvement in the lives of their sons.

> They are actually very pleased that I am involved and they are happy to let me have as much involvement as I can, especially as my nephews actually described me as their favorite uncle. And they have borrowed me a book in the past about male relationships with children and stuff like that. My sister said: "You know you don't have to read this, but if you want to [here it is]." I've got to admire the way they are looking after their kids.

I asked Billy if the boys ever complain about their parents. They do. Lately the conversation is about where they can and cannot ride their bikes and being sent to bed too early. Such are the concerns of young boys.

Three of the nephews indicated having little or no relationship with their biological fathers, and one of these maintained a close relationship with his uncle. "It's like all my uncles have picked up the job that my dad didn't do. They are like dads," says Heath. Heath speaks with his favored uncle several times per week and talks to him about "work, uni [university], stresses, what's going on, or anything that pops into my head." He does occasionally talk to his uncle about his mom but laments that "both of us are more than mystified by women." Heath clearly admires his uncle and particularly "his ability to cut through the crap and get straight to the point." Heath admires his uncle's determination and his ability to get along with people. "His whole attitude toward life is what I want to adopt into mine," he says. Heath is now planning to get another tattoo just like his uncle's.

Three of the aunts described relationships with nieces whose parents divorced when they were children, and although fathers were not entirely absent, contact with them was minimal. Aunts in these cases provided considerable help to mothers and nieces, and although it would be a stretch to think of them as replacing an absent parent, they do supplement mothers, sometimes in significant ways for relatively long periods of time. When Olympia's niece was a young child, her parents divorced. Olympia's sister-in-law and daughter moved to a community where Olympia was living with her husband. During this period, Olympia visited her niece frequently and spoke daily by phone, often at length. Olympia says: "I spend a lot of time with her. She was kind of a latchkey child so I was sort of the other grown up in her life. . . . I was a person she talked to when she wanted to chat." Later in the interview she says, "She had an array of issues with [her parents] throughout her life, you know like little kid type issues. And when [her parents] split up that was really hard on her. So I was kind of an inside/outside person that could be available." Eventually Olympia's sister-in-law remarried and moved to a different state. Nonetheless, aunt and niece continued to maintain a close relationship by sharing in their experiences as professional women and mothers.

Rosemary maintains a close relationship with her sister and sister's daughter. Both mother and daughter call on Rosemary for her counsel, support, and companionship. When Rosemary's niece Katie was 3 years old, her parents divorced. Although her father maintained some involvement with his children when they were young, this essentially ended before Katie's adolescence. Her father, for instance, failed to acknowledge her high school graduation in any way. Not surprisingly, the relationship of Katie, who is now 25, and her father is estranged with no current contact. Rosemary is married and childless and treats her niece with great sensitivity and affection. In Rosemary's words, they often "just hang out for the day." Of their relationship, Rosemary says, "I'm more like a motherly type with her. I mean I'm really watchful and I still give her those little bits of advice." Recently Katie sent her aunt a mother's day card, much to Rosemary's delight.

A remarkable element of this family is the closeness of aunt, sister, and daughter. I asked Rosemary if her sister ever called on her for advice about Katie. She replied, "just the other day actually. She saw Katie's boyfriend in a kind of compromising situation . . . and she asked me if she should [talk about this] with Katie." Both aunt and mother share a common concern about Katie's new boyfriend, and yet at the same time they seem to respect Katie's privacy and in this case decided to let Katie raise the issue in her own time. Each seems to rely on the other, and they do so with a kind of ordinary intimacy. Rosemary describes a recent visit, one that followed the mother's discovery of the "compromising situation."

> Last year [my niece] graduated from the school of nursing and I could feel that I had to let go a little bit more. She didn't need my advice as much. She has a special chair in my kitchen and she sits on that chair and there's this whole scenario that goes along with this chair. I can tell if she's upset because [if] she rocks a certain way I know she's upset [and] something's going to come up. But I don't ask her. I don't say, "Oh what's wrong or what's bothering you?" because it will come up naturally and it's better that way. Her mom said that to me recently: "I'm really learning about how to approach her. If I don't say anything to her, she'll bring it up on her own."

The story illustrates several issues. Both aunt and mother are concerned about Katie, and they share advice about how best to parent her, which fortunately, and wisely, they agree on. But in this moment of our conversation, Rosemary also shares some regret that Katie seems to need less of her, has completed her university studies, and is developing her own career. She laments, "I had to let go a little bit more" and in this way suggests a kind of separation and healthy identity development that is common among parents and young adult children. Rosemary's comment hints at how her relationship with Katie is like that between a parent and child.

I asked Rosemary if her niece ever gave her advice. She laughed and then replied: "I ask her about fashion. And hair advice." Oddly enough, this is a rather common response. Aunts often seek out the fashion advice of their nieces. Uncles and nephews left sartorial issues unmentioned, which suggests that the uncles' interest in hair and such things is negligible.

Four of the nieces described relationships with their biological fathers that were estranged and relationships with aunts that were in many regards like a parent. Janice is 27 and working in a homeless shelter while she completes her second novel. She coaches a hockey team in her spare time. Janice feels strongly about her aunt, Audrey, and visits with her weekly. Of her aunt she says, "She was always my substitute mother, my second mom, and I love having that tie with her, even as an adult." Janice's parents were divorced when she was 18, although it seemed her father was minimally involved throughout her childhood. "Audrey," she says, "did a lot of nurturing for me that my father didn't do. [She provided] a different perspective than my mother. We were always at each other's throats and my aunt was neutral and she helped me get through some tough times." Janice provides an example from her adolescence: "If my mother and I were fighting about something I could talk to my aunt and hash it out and I didn't have the same aggravation talking to her about things as I did with my mom. My aunt helped me look at the problem through her eyes as an adult female and a mother. [She would say] 'you really shouldn't be going out with boys until 2 in the morning.'" In this case, Janice sees her aunt as someone who replaced her absent father as well as someone who buffered a tempestuous relationship with her mom and was able to recast her mom's "unreasonable" requests as reasonable.

Aunt Audrey was important for her sister and niece; this was especially true during her sister's divorce, when Audrey counseled both. Janice described this period. "I was going through a gray area when my parents were getting a divorce and my mother was constantly bad mouthing my father. That was a real sore point. You can only take so much of that.... But my aunt would often step in and say, 'you can't put your daughter in the middle. It's not fair.'" Later in the interview, Janice reflects on her relationship with Audrey. "Even sitting and watching TV with her is nice. It's a feeling very similar to being with my mom, nurturing and protective like when you're with your family."

Having an absent parent does not necessarily guarantee a close relationship between an aunt or uncle and their niece or nephew. Evan visits irregularly with his 16-year-old nephew, whose mother is an alcoholic and has been absent since his early childhood. In this case, the relationship of Evan and his brother is strained, and their children also do not seem to get along well. This combination of circumstances limits Evan's contact with his nephew.

Mario thinks highly of his uncle and visits him with his father "once every couple of years." Before entering the university, Mario visited with his uncle several times per month; they now visit on holidays. He describes the relationship: "I'm probably closer to my uncle than I am to my father because he has kind of moved away and I haven't heard from him." When I asked Mario if his uncle has had an influence on him, he replied, "Not to a great extent." In fact, the entire interview is decidedly taciturn.

> *RM: Does he very give you career advice?*
> Probably not.
> *Does he ask you about school?*
> I'd talk to him just to make conversation.
> *How about more general advice?*
> I can't remember a specific time.
> *Was he ever critical of anything you did?*
> No.
> *How close would you say you are to your uncle?*
> Fairly, not extremely close.

Although Mario's father is absent and he feels closer to his uncle, all things are relative, and their relationship is limited in emotional depth and complexity.

For other nieces and nephews, although their biological fathers were largely absent, relationships with stepfathers were strong. In three cases, one involving an uncle (Sammy) and his nephew and two involving nieces (Nicole and Fiona) and aunts, the relationships with kin are important supplements to the work of parents and stepparents.

Compatibility and Conflict

Some nieces and nephews become highly involved with their aunts or uncles because of their mutual compatibility and liking for each other, and this may or may not be paired with conflict-habituated relationships with parents. Sabina described a close relationship with both of her parents and especially her mom. "I talk to my mom about anything and everything and my mom and I will go out and do things and stuff like that," she says. Sabina describes her aunt as "like my other mother figure. . . . She knows everything that's going on with me as well as my mom does. . . . No matter what time of day or night it is, if I need anything I know I can count on [my aunt] too. She is always there for me." Later in the interview Sabina comments on the longevity of her relationship with her aunt: "I can't remember a day from when I was young that she wasn't around."

Sabina views her mother and her aunt as close but very different people. Her mother is described as outgoing and free-spirited and her aunt as very organized and less spontaneous. In describing herself, Sabina says, "It's funny I think I'm a combination of both." Her comments illustrate how

Sabina's relationship with both women influences her in essential ways and provides her with a broader base of support and friendship readily available throughout her childhood and adolescence, and continuing into her young adulthood.

Shenna describes a very different circumstance and says she is closer to her aunt than her mother. She also speaks with her aunt more frequently. She says of her mom: "I don't really get along with my mom. We have completely different views of things." Shenna is a 23-year-old university student and single parent of a 5-year-old daughter. She tries to have more contact with her mother so that she can get to know her granddaughter. Shenna's parents have each experienced problems with substance abuse, for which her father was once incarcerated. During her childhood, her parents separated and divorced, and her mom refused to let her visit with her father, a situation that Shenna saw as unnecessary. Shenna believes she has little in common with her mother, which she contrasts with her aunt, with whom she shares an abundance of common interests. "We like the same kind of music, the same movies. We like to do similar things, and games, and we like to socialize, visit, go shopping and just hang out. My mom doesn't like to shop, she doesn't like to talk, she doesn't like to play games, she doesn't like to watch movies, she doesn't like to watch TV, and doesn't like the kind of music I like." Shenna admires much about her aunt and considers her a close friend. They share interests and details about each other's daily concerns, and they visit often. I asked if there were qualities she didn't admire in her aunt. Shenna regards her aunt as sometimes selfish or hypocritical and sometimes indecisive, but yet she describes her aunt as someone she loves regardless of the qualities she doesn't like or agree with. Of their occasional disagreements, she says: "I'm mad at her for a couple of days and then I'm good again." Given the difficulties Shenna's parents experienced individually and in their marriage, and the difficulties Shenna has in maintaining a positive relationship with her mother, it is fortunate her aunt was available; she represents an important and meaningful positive adult role model in her life.

CONCLUSION

The family work of aunts and uncles both supplements and complements parents. The involvement of aunts and uncles range from occasional visits and relatively distant or superficial contacts, to daily involvement and relationships that are complex, consistent, and consequential. The primary roles of aunts and uncles span a variety of activities and include supplementing or complementing parents, acting as third parties with unique perspectives, and acting as surrogate parents, themes that extend reports identified in earlier work on aunts and uncles.[1] Parents and their sons and daughters draw on their nearby kin – aunts and uncles – for support, counsel, and companionship. Aunts and uncles actively nurture their relationships with nieces and nephews, whom they sometimes regard as like daughters or sons. Undoubtedly there are many who remain uninvolved, and yet there are clearly instances of long-standing involvements that are highly valued. At times aunts and uncles act as second mothers or fathers and are regarded as such by their nieces and nephews. Aunts and uncles may do so in families where children are actively involved with both of their parents, in which case aunts and uncles add to the mix of family intimates, and the responsibility for raising children spans multiple households. In other cases, when a birth parent is absent through premature death, problems associated with substance abuse, or, more frequently, desertion and divorce, aunts and uncles act as surrogate parents. The interviews reflect the demographics of contemporary families, in which divorce is relatively common and the custody and responsibility for raising children falls on mothers. The impact of divorce on relationships among grandparents and grandchildren is similar in that divorce is one of the more common proximal causes for grandparents becoming primary caregivers for their grandchildren,[2] and they do so commonly.[3] For example, among grandparents aged 65 and older, 17.7% are living in households with grandchildren, and of those 42% are primarily responsible for raising their grandchild.[4] Like grandparents, aunts and uncles can be especially important sources of support for single parents. In many cases, they provided counsel to a recently divorced sibling, typically a sister, as well as to nieces, and they are highly regarded for their emotional and instrumental support.

Although aunts and uncles occasionally become permanent guardians of their nieces and nephews,[5] for many becoming a primary or coprimary caregiver is a temporary adaptation that results from the needs or personal preferences of family members. At times, nieces and nephews turn to aunts and uncles because of conflicts that emerge with parents. Aunts, for instance, provided their nieces with housing, especially during the turbulent periods of adolescence. In other instances, nieces and nephews recalled instances in which they lived with their aunts and uncles for significant periods of time, not because of conflicts with parents but because they simply liked one another, and in these cases, parents encouraged such relationships. Sabina,

---

[1] Chebra, 1991; Ellingson & Sotirin, 2006.   [2] Hanks, 2001; Roberto et al., 2001.
[3] Caputo, 2001; Dunifon & Kowaleski-Jones, 2007; Hanks, 2001; Silverstein & Marenco, 2001.
[4] Blieszner, 2006.   [5] Davidson, 1997.

for instance, was quick to point out that she had a close relationship with her parents but enjoyed being with her aunt and as a result occasionally chose to live in her aunt's household. In other instances, the close relationships between adult siblings drew them together, perhaps coupled with a measure of financial need on the part of a young aunt or older sister and parent. These instances of mutual support and caregiving further demonstrate both how aunts and uncles can become critically important in the lives of parents and children as well as how families are organized across multiple households.

One question that remains is how aunts and uncles compare with grandparents in the nature of their relationships with children and parents, as well as how the two generations are likely to differ in the care they provide to children and the character of relationships that ensue. The distinguishing features that characterize the impact of grandparents relative to aunts and uncles may be largely rooted in the experiences that define their relationships and the widely shared expectations, or norms, that define their roles. By virtue of their status as siblings, and often as peers, aunts and uncles share a distinct developmental history that likely influences their interaction as adults and understanding of one another's needs. They have the potential to have shared nearly all important developmental milestones – childhoods, graduations and early relationships, marriages, parenthood, divorces, the aging of their parents – and to understand these events in similar ways. Siblings share a unique relationship history, and they are apt to be at similar stages of life. They are often relatively similar in age because Western families typically experience a shorter duration of child rearing because the number of children per family averages no more than 2, and the interval between the birth of the first and last child is relatively narrow.[6] Their relationships are among the most long-lasting, relatively voluntary, egalitarian, and typically active.[7] In a large and representative sample of U.S. families, 66% of respondents considered a sibling to be a close friend, 50% had monthly contact, and 33% said they would rely on a sibling in an emergency.[8] More recent inquiries find that nearly 70% of siblings with Internet access contact a brother or sister by e-mail at least once per week.[9] Siblings are often practically present in each others lives, especially sisters who exchange help in routine household labor and child care.[10]

Adult siblings create and extend the reach of family relationships by expanding family configurations, creating the positions of uncle, aunt, niece, nephew, cousin, and in-laws.[11] By virtue of their personal friendships with

---

[6] Connidis, 2001.
[8] White & Riedman, 1992.
[10] Eriksen & Gerstel, 2002.

[7] Eriksen & Gerstel, 2002.
[9] Rainie et al., 2000.
[11] Matthews, 2005.

nonkin, coworkers, professional colleagues, and neighbors, they broaden the array of social contacts available to one another and in this way build the social capital available to families. Uncle Michael, for instance, was able to call on a professional colleague to meet with his nephew for the purpose of completing a school report. In this way, aunts and uncles add resources derivative of their personal relationships and thereby potentially available to parents and their children. Taken together, current research on adult siblings and the frequency of their contact are suggestive of just how common active relationships among aunts and uncles with their nieces and nephews might be. The range of their influence on contemporary families is illustrated in the mix of ways in which they complement the work of parents, act as third parties with their unique perspectives, and, on occasion, become regarded as second parents. In the following chapters, I continue the inquiry into the essentials of aunting and uncling and look more closely at the contributions and influence of aunts and uncles.

5

Mentoring

In this and the next two chapters, I explore the appearance of generativity in the relationships of aunts and uncles with nieces and nephews. Mentoring and intergenerational buffering are two primary requirements of generative cultures,[1] and in this chapter, I examine how and when they emerge in families. Although generativity is often viewed as an individual attribute appearing in the midlife development of adults,[2] as we shall see, it is enacted in a relational context involving parents, their children, and extended kin. Viewed in this way, mentoring and intergenerational buffering are akin to active thoroughfares with a good deal of bus traffic passing within and across generations, rather than individual conveyances passing along one-way avenues. To be sure, aunts and uncles actively mentor their nieces and nephews. In addition, they actively mentor parents and in this way further secure their importance in building generative family cultures. Then again, relationships are negotiated enterprises, even those involving older adults and younger children. Just as offspring can influence the development of their parents, nieces and nephews influence the development of their kinfolk, and they do so by actively mentoring their aunts and uncles. These generative thoroughfares have been largely unexplored to date, although they are clearly central and active.

Aunts and uncles actively mentor nieces and nephews in a variety of ways. They are valued for their support, counsel, and occasional criticism in matters of school and career, spirituality and moral values, and relations with parents, siblings, and other family members. Although the mentoring of aunts and uncles is similar in many ways, they differ with regard to important areas of intimate relationships with peers. As we will uncover here, aunts know more about the relational lives of their nieces than uncles

---

[1] Kotre, 2004.　　　　　　　　　[2] McAdams & Logan, 2004.

do of their nephews. We begin the exploration of mentoring by first visiting the more general ways in which mentoring appears and how and why it is valued by nieces and nephews.

Aunts and uncles varied in terms of their manner of giving advice or offering support of their nieces and nephews. Although most did so and considered such activities important,[3] some were reluctant to be very direct in either regard and preferred to listen commiseratively while commenting only indirectly, if at all.

> I just listen to him. Although we don't see each other that often, I think I have a good understanding of some of the dynamics that he has in his life and so I just listen to him, and he asks about what I am doing and that sort of thing. (Uncle Robert)

Aunts as well as uncles were apt to provide supportive listening and regard such exchanges as important elements of their relationships. Connie maintains a close relationship with her 22-year-old niece Brice. She occasionally gives Brice direct advice but does so with care and respect. Connie says, "It's very important to do more listening than preaching. [Brice] is an adult, a very bright mature adult. I like to listen to what she has to say, and if I'm asked my opinion, I'll give it." Ilse also regards supportive listening as important in her relationship with her 16-year-old niece but does so with some trepidation. "It's interesting," she says, "because I've really had to learn what works. [My niece] is an only child and she has good boundaries, and I really like that about her." Recently Ilse's niece became involved with an older boy, a development that concerns Ilse. "I got a little worried about [her new relationship] and just how physically intense they were together, so I wasn't sure what I should do. I'd call and check on her and ask how they were doing and she'd say that they were fine. I didn't want to be too pushy about it, but then I worried." Ilse respects her niece's privacy, while maintaining open communication by calling at regular intervals. Yet she does so with a bit of apprehension – will her niece weather the storm of late adolescence wiser and unharmed?

Nephews and nieces also reported this style of supportive listening without the exchange of direct advice or criticism. Janice, a 27-year-old niece,

---

[3] Instances of mentoring, support, and supportive listening occur in all of the interviews with aunts and 81% of the interviews with uncles and in nearly all of the interviews with nieces (100%) and nephews (84%).

remarks about her aunt: "You can talk with her about anything and she will commiserate, and just sort of be very reassuring, or if she knows anything about [the topic], she will try and offer some insight."

In these ways, aunts and uncles mentor their nieces and nephews by listening and acknowledging their concerns, encouraging their confidence, and doing so in a largely nonjudgmental context. Aunts and uncles value these opportunities in which nieces and nephews share important elements of their personal lives, their relationships with friends and lovers, their negotiation of parental demands, and their experiences at school and work. In large part, effective mentoring is often nothing more than communicating understanding.

COMMUNICATING SUPPORT

More direct mentoring of nieces and nephews, a cornerstone of generative action, occurs in nearly all areas of personal and relational life. Aunts and uncles are sought out for their advice concerning schooling, careers, personal relationships, family matters, spirituality, and virtually all activities of their nieces and nephews. For Aunt Francesca and her 12-year-old niece Maria, it's off to the hot tub for a soak and warm chat. "It's a quiet place," Francesca says, "and there is usually no one around. It's out in a gazebo in the backyard. We soak, we talk, and she brings up some things. It's always a nice time for us. She brings up things that are happening at school or relationships with her friends."

At times aunts and uncles were encouraging some lesson without being terribly proscriptive, and their mentoring took on a more general tone, a prescription for healthy living.

> Advice is an interesting area. I never say to them, "Do it this way." No matter what it is. I'll try and let them know I appreciate what they are doing, and the reasons they are doing it. And if they ask for advice, I'll say I can't do that, you have to do what you would do and not what I would do.... I try as much as possible to maintain their independence the same way their parents do. (Uncle John)

Similarly Uncle Jimmy is reluctant to give direct advice to his nephew Loni, "but if he asks me what I think about things, I'll tell him," he says. I asked Jimmy if he could think of a recent example. He replied: "Loni wanted to know what kind of tattoo he should get. It is coming up on his 18th birthday and he told his mom and dad he was going to get a tattoo and he wanted to know what I thought he should get. So I told him it would probably hurt, so something small." Sage advice, I thought.

Aunts and uncles often layered their conversations with generic lessons encouraging the developing interests and aspirations of their nieces and nephews in matters of school and career, their confidence to try new things, or simply trusting in their own intuitions. Aunt Ilse says, "We've had this ongoing talk about intuition for years and how it's a really valid skill to have."

Aunt Theriza encouraged her niece to take a more active role in designing her career interests. She recounts a conversation with her niece Liz. Graduation was a few weeks away, and Liz seemed tentative about her plans for the future and what would happen. "Good things don't [just] happen," Theriza advised, "if you want something to happen you have to make it happen."

Nieces and nephews often characterized their favored aunts and uncles as supportive and encouraging, but even the most demonstratively instrumental support was occasionally laced with a distinctly intimate, loving intention. Several recalled how their aunts and uncles sent greeting cards on special occasions, and one uncle sent cards to his nephew before his university examination periods, a simple but significant way to express generativity as the following nephew illustrates.

> Most of his advice is more [like] encouragement. "It's good what you are doing, keep up the grades," stuff like that. If I am having exams, sometimes he'll send me a card and say, "Good luck." And if I did well, "Congratulations, you did well." Just encouragement and stuff like that.
>
> *RM: Can you think of the last time he did that?*
>
> Um, bursary [i.e., university entrance exams].
>
> *RM: Was that helpful to you?*
>
> Yes, it was actually. It helped me work harder . . . and, the more support you have, the better you do. (Nephew Art)

Van visits with his uncle routinely, often in the afternoon on his way home from work. "I just see if he needs a hand with anything," he says. I asked Van if his uncle ever gave him advice. "It's quite subtle, bits and pieces. . . . If we are sitting at a table he might tell a story and I can tell he has an ulterior meaning, almost like a story with a moral." Van describes his uncle thus: "He is like always happy to see me. Always has a good yarn and cracks a few jokes. He's a very funny person, very rude. Never a sentence without a swear word. It's ridiculous but it is just him." Van describes two incidents involving his uncle. Both demonstrate their strong, if masculine, bond. On one occasion, Van suffered an injury while playing rugby, the national sport of New Zealand.

> I remember seeing him in the hospital. When he saw the x-ray and my leg, I could just see in his face that he knew I would never be able to play rugby again. Everyone else is being real positive saying that "you can get back in the game." He grabbed my hand and he ran his hand through my hair. Just the look of sadness in his face. Coming from a sportsman's point of view it was tough.

On another occasion, Van was preparing to leave his home on the North Island (of New Zealand) for the first time to work in the agricultural fields of the South Island. Again his uncle was there with his own brand of simple, direct, and honest support tinted with a bit of wisdom.

> Last year I left to go to work in the vineyards for a few months and he actually, totally out of the blue, gave me a hundred dollars, which is really odd from him. He said, "Take this," and "Look you are going away, just keep your eyes open, work hard, do what they say and you'll find your feet as you go." I took that on board. I valued it because he'd taken the time to say it.

Van's uncle had provided a ride to the ferry terminal where Van was to leave for an indeterminate length of time working in the vineyards of the South Island and had given him a sum of money for the journey. Both acts could be characterized as instances of instrumental social support, but it seems unlikely that the uncle's intention was purely instrumental, and most certainly it wasn't received in that way.

The advice of aunts and uncles was not always influential even when given, and especially when their relationship with a niece or nephew was relatively distant, visits infrequent, or interests too divergent. Nicole says of her aunt that they have "definitely had some conversations [but] nothing like life changing." Uncle Tom doesn't believe he gives his nephew much advice, "just saying be good, behave yourself as much as you can." Ian describes his uncle as "into surfing, snowboarding, [and] meditation." Although Ian admires his uncle in some ways, he shares a different set of interests, values, and life goals.

On rare occasions, nieces and nephews were critical of their aunts and uncles, particularly in regard to overindulgence in alcohol, problems with anger management, or because they simply seemed to lack direction in their lives. Dirk enjoys his uncle's company and considers him like a friend but, at the same time, has some concerns that his uncle "doesn't know what he is doing in life," which is a reasonable conclusion given that Dirk's uncle has three children by two mothers, one of whom was the family's babysitter. Dirk also believes his uncle drinks excessively. As these examples illustrate, it is important to recognize that not all relationships with aunts and uncles work well, not all aunts and uncles share close relationships with their nieces and nephews, not all counsel is well received or regarded as useful, and not all qualities are admired.

MENTORING RELATIONSHIPS

Aunts and uncles differed in the focus of their mentoring in one area. Aunts and nieces were more likely to discuss relationships with romantic partners as well as issues regarding sexual activity, and they did so in greater depth, than uncles and nephews. Nineteen percent of uncles and nephews discussed relationships issues (10 of 52 participants), whereas 48% of aunts and nieces did so (25 of 52 participants). Sentiments like Uncle Freddie's were common: "That's not something I'd really want to get involved with. How somebody selects a person [romantic partner] is pretty much their own taste." Freddie visits with his 27-year-old nephew weekly, they share a variety of common interests, and, later in the interview, Freddie characterizes their relationship as like that between a father and son. They are clearly close, but talk about romantic relationships is not part of the mix.

When uncles and nephews do talk about such relationships, it is often relatively superficial. I asked Uncle Michael whether he ever spoke to his 19-year-old nephew about girlfriends. He laughed and replied, "Well with kids that age it seems to be sensitive stuff. He doesn't really volunteer that [information]. He'll mention that he went to the prom with so-and-so and that it was a friendship. It's not a topic of great or lengthy discussion, but neither is it avoided." Michael's comments suggest that although he is willing to discuss the topic and on occasion queries his nephew, his nephew is recalcitrant with regard to this issue. Perhaps this is typical of adolescent males, and it certainly contrasts with adolescent females, who talk more about their relationships and involve aunts in this talk. One exception is Uncle Jessie, who related: "Other than his high school buddies I would say I'm the [only other person he talks with] because he says, 'I can't talk to anyone else about Suzie Q.' I've tried to steer him in the direction of building strong friendships in high school." Uncle Jessie's relationship with his nephew is unusual in this regard because his nephew seems to share some detail regarding his romantic interests and seeks out the guidance of his uncle. They were the only uncle and nephew pair to do so.

Aunts and nieces were much freer in their conversations about boy-friends, sexuality, marriages, and breakups, even if aunts were on occasion a bit overzealous. Aunt Rebecca describes an *accidental* encounter with her niece.

[My niece] did have a rather long-term relationship, and I remember, just by accident, on their first date we ended up at the same movie. I was with my three friends and I said [to my niece and her boyfriend] "we'll sit here with you," but my friends sort of dragged me to the other side of theater. They helped me realize that maybe that wasn't appropriate.

Entirely unlike their male counterparts, aunts were actively concerned with potentially abusive relationships, and at times they shared their con-cerns with nieces. Aunt Rebecca is an attorney and very familiar with abu-sive relationships. In this context, her concern about her niece is under-standable. Later in the interview, she describes her niece as "very attrac-tive, very outgoing, and innocently naïve" and expressed her desire that her niece develop a healthy, respectful relationship. Rebecca's concern for her niece is certainly shared by other aunts who voiced similar themes, especially concerns about controlling and potentially abusive men. Connie drew from her own experience when speaking to her niece Brice about her boyfriend.

I saw her coming up with what I have now [in my marriage] and I wouldn't want it for her. Brice's boyfriend was much too controlling and unless he goes and gets professional help, I don't see how it's ever going to change.

RM: Was he ever violent?

No, not violent, but in the time they dated, she rarely got to spend any time with her friends or family because he always wanted her right under his thumb.

Connie was ambivalent about Brice's boyfriend. She expressed liking him, attended his college graduation, and invited him to family gatherings, but at the same time, she thought the courtship was unhealthy for her niece and unlikely to lead to a healthy marriage. Relative to the relationship talk of uncles and nephews, Connie's knowledge of her niece's relational life and partner is remarkable. It speaks to a high level of intimacy, trust, and respect – qualities that certainly appear among uncles and nephews but not typically with regard to relational partners.

Aunt Stella told a similar story regarding her niece, who asked for her opinion on the niece's relationship with her boyfriend and how Stella felt she was being treated. Stella shared her response: "I would tell her things that we saw. I remember my daughter growing up had a relationship with a guy, and we could see that there was verbal and emotional abuse, but she couldn't at the time. The same thing was happening with [my niece]. . . . I think she felt comfortable in thinking 'is this really the way it should be?'" In this instance, Stella was able to share her observations and in part validate the concerns of her niece.

Aunts also shared their concerns about their nieces' level of sexual activity and their use of appropriate protection. Aunt Ilse tells of such a conversation occasioned as her niece was applying for a position working in peer education within a family planning office. Ilse recounted how she found it difficult to talk with her parents about sexuality when she was young, to which her niece replied, "Oh god, mine too." Ilse continued, "So we just sort of entered that water . . . and I just tried to normalize [the topic]." At the time, Ilse's niece was involved with a boyfriend but indicated to her aunt she was not ready to become sexually active, much to her aunt's relief. Similarly, Aunt Dorthea says, "I talk with [my niece] about what it means to be having sex at a young age. I don't think that she is yet, but I know that is on the horizon at some point. So I talked with her about safe sex." Here again aunts and uncles seemed to differ. Aunts raise the issue of sexuality with their nieces because they are concerned about issues of health and unintended pregnancies. Such issues did not appear in my conversations with uncles.

At times nieces shared concerns regarding their partners with their aunts, perhaps seeking their advice, and at other times they simply sought their aunt's validation and support of their relationships. Elspeth recalls introducing her partner to her family and especially her favored aunt. "I brought my boyfriend down from Connecticut with me, and I remember being kind of like well I like him a lot and my aunt was like 'he's awesome!'" Elspeth continues enthusiastically, "and now we've been together for like two years, and I talk to her about him all the time." For Elspeth, as for other nieces, the blessing of a favored aunt was important, a confirmation of her choice of partners and the relationship's viability.

Aunts were also involved in helping nieces to make decisions about discontinuing relationships or, at other times, deepening commitments. Susan recounted instances of both, each with a different niece. For instance, an adolescent niece called her because, in Susan's words, she was having this "big, major boy problem. [My niece] said 'he was being weird,' and I said, 'dump him and move on.'" In another instance, an older niece shared with Susan her concerns about marrying a man who was ten years older.

Susan is uniquely experienced in this regard because she is married to an older man. Susan wisely shared some of the difficulties of doing so based on her own experience but at the same time encouraged her niece to trust her own feelings. Again, both the depth and routine of relationship talk is remarkable.

Relationship talk is an important arena in which aunts, and at times uncles, mentor their young charges by offering to share their experiences and their observations. Certainly nieces and nephews also draw on the counsel of their parents. Aunts and uncles add to this mix, and they are advantaged simply because of their experience and personal knowledge of all parties and because they are often viewed as more objective than parents. This does not mean that nieces always embrace the council of their aunts, at least at the time it is given. For instance, Janice recounts how her aunt encouraged her to separate somewhat from a now former partner, suggesting she "needed to work on herself first." At the time, Janice "had no idea what she meant and definitely wasn't ready to give up on the relationship." Aunts shared their concerns, sometimes with great diplomacy, as well as their blessings, but in the end respected the need for their nieces to make decisions for themselves. When they work well, the relationships of aunts and nieces are routinely intimate, resourceful, and trusting, as are the relationships of uncles and nephews, although the latter are not typically so in terms of relational talk because it does not appear to occur with any depth or regularity.

SPIRITUALITY AND RELIGION

In many of the interviews, aunts, and occasionally uncles, recounted conversations regarding issues of religious beliefs, spirituality, and moral development.[4] Their conversations ranged from directly encouraging nieces to attend religious services to more reflective stances on issues of core beliefs, although rarely were aunts dogmatic. Francesca encourages her niece to reflect on her belief in God and the importance of community. She recounts, "We've had lots of conversations about God and what I believe. I try to impress on her that people have a lot of different beliefs about God and you will have to find your own way in that." She encourages her niece to

---

[4] The importance of this area and the ways uncles participated in the moral development of their nephews was not entirely anticipated, and consequently in the early interviews with uncles and nephews, I neglected to inquire about this important area. Later interviews with aunts and nieces routinely included questions about religious beliefs, spirituality, and moral development. Aunts appear more inclined to indicate that they discussed such issues with nieces (75%) compared with nieces who do so with aunts (53%).

participant in Sunday services because, as she says, "I believe in community spirit. Even if you don't believe in the whole message, it's good to sing the songs, be with people, and have a donut after [the service]. I think that it's healthy for kids, to sit quietly for an hour, think and hear the stories."

Susan recalls how her niece, Nika, began to doubt whether God was real and in any way important in her life. Susan shared her own strong belief in God but at the same time encouraged Nika to consider the issue carefully and "figure it out for herself." She questions her niece about essential values and further encourages her to consider "what you are going to do in life, what you believe in. Like does it matter if you ever get married, or does it not matter?" The conversation was fueled in part by activities Nika engaged in while away at college. From her aunt's perspective, Nika was promiscuous and "doing stuff I did not agree with." Susan considered her niece's conduct and questioning normal, and yet their subsequent conversations were heated, direct, and intense. Nika thought her aunt was "ignorant," and Susan thought her niece had "lost her way." Perhaps more important, the conversations occurred. Nika was able to share her experiences with her aunt, knowing Susan did not approve of them. In turn Susan was able to encourage her niece to consider her actions carefully and to think about their meaning in the broader perspective of essential values. In this way, aunts serve as a sort of moral compass for their nieces by encouraging them to develop individual standards of conduct and to live by them. As Susan said, "To me my beliefs are who I am. They are not just over here and I have a few little beliefs. I kind of marry them."

Stephen maintains a close relationship with his nephew, and in some ways, they are more like brothers than uncle and nephew. Stephen is 22; his nephew Paul is 17 and recently entered college. I asked Stephen if he ever gave his nephew advice. "I give him advice all the time," he says. "We talk about things in the Bible." He encourages his nephew not to smoke or abuse alcohol as his friends might. Stephen has strong religious values and readily applies them to this own life; he encourages his nephew to do the same. I asked him what he liked about being an uncle, and he replied: "Just giving him advice about [my] experience ... giving him values."

For many of the aunts, their appointed role as godmother of their nieces influenced how they regarded their role as an aunt.[5] Godmothers are especially significant in Catholic communities, where parents select siblings or other intimates to buttress religious and cultural practices.[6] At times aunts

---

[5] Six of the aunts indicated that they were godmothers.
[6] di Leonardo, 1984; Falicov, 1999; Sault, 2001.

viewed their status as godmother as a commitment to raise a child within a particular faith, but for many it was interpreted as a lifelong commitment to the child's welfare. Comments such as "I took it as a commitment that I would always look out for [my niece]" (Aunt Barbara) and "It is a promise that I will always protect [my niece's] well-being throughout her life" (Aunt Beatrice) were typical. In this way, the moral and religious beliefs of aunts influence how they regarded their position in their families and their responsibilities to younger generations.

Then, too, conversations about spirituality were not always cast within a strictly religious context. Aunt Ilse encourages her niece to develop her "own sense of connectedness to the world" and to "celebrate that spiritual, intuitive wise part of herself." In this way, Ilse sought to encourage her niece's sense of social responsibility, wisdom, and intuitive sensibilities.

For the Native Americans I interviewed, the issue of reconciling Christian practice with native traditions was paramount. Aunt Addie, a Native American, recalled talking with her niece about Christianity and Native American practices, how they differ but can be blended. Similarly, Tess considers her Native American heritage important. Her mother and aunt were required when young to give up their native language, speak English, and enroll in a missionary school. Tess recalls asking her aunt about traditional native practices, which she considers "a huge issue" and one not easily reconciled with the experiences of her elders.

In each of these examples, aunts were important moral beacons for their nieces. They sometimes encouraged direct engagement in religious practices, suggesting that their nieces consider their actions in the context of essential convictions and develop their own sense of values to live by. Aunts and uncles alike can and do act as spiritual mentors, actively engaged in the all-important moral development of their nieces and nephews.

MENTORING PARENTS

Aunts, and occasionally uncles, also mentored parents. They did so by simply providing opportunities for parents "to vent, to share information about their side of parenting and get confirmation, feedback, or a second opinion" (Aunt Ilse). At other times, mentoring parents involved providing support to parents who were dealing with sensitive issues regarding their children. Aunt Maya's sister shared her concerns about raising a child with Down's syndrome. Maya said of her sister, "She shares with me when she is worried [about] him. She wants him to fit right in." Maya's response was to tell her sister, "You know, I saw him at that concert and he was so cute." Maya's sister shares her worries and concerns about her son, and in response Maya provides confirmation of her sister's parenting.

The sexual activity and relationships of adolescents are common topics of concern. Aunts and uncles mentored parents directly by providing alternative points of view or information that was unknown or unavailable to parents, or simply by listening to a parent's concerns. Everyone needs a muse, parents included.

Parents also relied on their siblings to communicate with their children. As Aunt Beatrice remarked, "it takes a little pressure off my sister to have someone a step removed saying the same things [to my niece] in a different way." At other times, siblings simply commiserate in common experiences. Aunt Maya relates a conversation with her sister about their sons. "Just last week [my sister] said to me, 'my son gives me these one-word answers.' I told her that was going to happen because my son was the same way." As a son, I could relate to the story in a personal way.

INTERGENERATIONAL BUFFERS

We can usefully think of two forms of intergenerational buffering. One form centers on interrupting the transfer of dysfunctional behaviors across generations (e.g., alcohol and substance abuse), largely through mentoring. A second form of buffering commonly involves intervening directly or indirectly in the relationships and daily hassles of family members (e.g., a parent and child). Here we consider how aunts and uncles focus their mentoring by encouraging the civil behavior and healthy life choices of nieces and nephews and thereby interrupting the replication of dysfunctional behaviors enacted by parents or other family members. In the next chapter, we consider the second form of intergenerational buffering, in which aunts and uncles serve as partisan supporters or critics of parents and children or otherwise mediate in routine family conflicts.

Aunts and uncles shared their own experiences with the hope that their nieces and nephews would benefit from them, and they shared their misgivings and hardships in the hope their nieces and nephews would have better lives. Aunt Elena recalls her own wish for mentoring when she was young, an experience that motivates her in her relationship with her niece. "I feel like nobody did that for me, like I didn't have a role model for most of the things I did in my life." Elena was among the first in her family to attend college. She became an international athlete and later earned a doctorate in her chosen field. She continued, "it is so valuable to have someone who is interested and who cares." Although Aunt Elena regretted her own lack of a role model, a muse to encourage her aspirations, other aunts and uncles actively sought to guide their nieces and nephews away from errors they might have made or dysfunctional family behaviors, often involving drug or alcohol abuse. Aunt Addie is a 46-year-old single mother who maintains an active role in the life of her 20-year-old niece. Addie shared that her niece lacked direction and was unable to continue with school. "We talk about where she is going in her life," Addie said. "She came from a pretty dysfunctional family and I came from a dysfunctional family. So I talk to her about things that she needs to do that would maybe help her get direction in her life." Addie is determined to help her niece understand her background and that of her family, and to sever a cycle of substance abuse.

Aunt Sandy shared a similar story. As a recovering alcoholic, she is clear about the importance of sharing her experience with her niece Mimi. I asked if she ever talked with her niece about alcohol or drugs and whether Mimi had ever asked for her advice.

> It's not as simple as that because her parents drink and she knows how I feel. So I make it really clear, you know, that I don't think it's a positive life-enhancing experience, but it's part of life. There is really no way to escape it in our society and it's a natural thing for kids to be curious.

Later in the interview, Sandy returned to this theme and shared the kind of advice she provides her niece.

> The take home message is: "Life isn't fair and you need to learn to be responsible for yourself, set healthy limits and boundaries, say 'no' when you don't want to do something, and be responsible for your own happiness. Don't depend on your parents. You already have a history with them and they have other interests. In other words, besides complaining about it you need to start learning how to deal with it because it's not going to change."

Uncle Greco had a lifelong history of substance abuse, of which his nephew was in part aware. He described his teenage nephew's recent interest in drugs. Greco's narrative illustrates a close relationship with his nephew, a distinct level of trust, and the unique way in which uncles (and aunts) can supplement parents.

> He likes to ask a lot about drugs. Last Thanksgiving he hit me with a bomb. He was asking me a lot of questions about psychedelics and psilocybin. He felt he could talk to me about stuff that he couldn't talk to his mother about.

RM: And what did you tell him?

I tried to say if you are determined to do this stuff, if you are determined to go with your peers, you have to try and have as much of a controlled environment as possible, try and keep your initial purpose in mind, and don't over do it.

RM: You wouldn't say, "Don't do it"?

Well I gave him a couple of stories that might have scared him. I told him what a bad trip was like. There is a greater leeway there to be a buddy, which you really can't do with your own children, as much. You start going into the wrong area with your own children. With my nephew it's the opposite. It would feel wrong to try and dictate anything to him. All I could do was feel glad that there was a confidence between us that he could trust.

In each of these cases, Addie, Sandy, and Greco, in their mentoring, act as intergenerational buffers as they attempt to provide their nieces and nephew with candid advice based on their own experience. We cannot know with certainty whether they were successful in their influence, although their comments are certainly measured and thoughtful. The circumstances of Aunt Sandy and Aunt Addie are complicated because each recounts the story of a niece whose home life is marred by substance abuse. The fact that Sandy, Addie, and Greco continue to maintain strong relationships with their nieces and nephew speaks to their potential influence. They are positive voices in the lives of their nieces and nephew, highly invested – each visited with their niece or nephew at least monthly if not more often – and each is actively sought out for companionship and counsel.

MENTORING GENDER

Uncles engaged with their nephews in traditionally masculine activities such as attending or participating in sporting events, woodworking and mechanics, fishing and hunting, and the occasional shopping expedition. "A lot of guys when they are going overseas get a silver fern tattoo. The one I'm getting is my coming-of-age tattoo. [My uncle and I] are going to price it up this weekend. . . . He designed it and it's got lots of colors and stuff" (Heath).[7]

---

[7] The silver tree fern (ponga) is a native plant of New Zealand and is commonly used as a national symbol.

Then of course there is preparation for the annual gift-giving enterprise in its distinctly masculine egression.

> Annually we try to go out shopping Christmas Eve. Of course, at that time of the year everything is pretty well gone and picked over. We'll plan on meeting up around 11:30 at night and we'll be out until one or two in the morning. We both pick stuff up. It's kind of the opportunity to get away from the womenfolk. (Uncle Freddie)

The issue of relationships with women occasionally took on a less than feminist character in the conversations of uncles and nephews. For instance, 24-year-old nephew Heath explained: "I think both of us are more than mystified by women in general." His experience seems to justify the mystification, at least in regard to establishing relationships with longevity. Heath's uncle has been divorced twice, his grandmother is divorced, and his biological father and mother have both been married three times. Heath goes on to say, "One thing I don't want to do is get married heaps."

Occasionally nephews embraced traditional masculine values, as Heath's relationship with his uncle illustrates.

> I think that [what's important] is the fact that I've been brought up with my mom for most of my life, and when I go to my uncle's place – because he is a beer-drinking, hard man you know. He's got tattoos and that sort of stuff and I see that masculine male image, and that's how I want to be.... My girlfriend found him uncomfortable [intimidating] at first but now she loves him. He calls her "pantyhose" cuz she has got nice legs.... He makes her feel welcome.

Yet again the socialization of nephews goes much further than traditional depictions of masculinity allow. This same nephew (Heath) goes on to say about his uncle and aunt:

> Hard work is the number one thing I respect him for. There's also the love he shows to my auntie because number one he loves her a lot. I respect that because it is totally unconditional. I respect his ways and view on life, which is totally different than mine.... I respect his sporting sense, knowledge of football. He likes good food and good wine.... And I respect that because he's taught me a lot to do with those things. Like nice wines and nice foods and what goes with what.... He has taken the time to show me how to cook good food on the barbecue.

In the midst of the masculinity are lessons regarding valuing family members, demonstrating love for one's partner, and developing homemaking skills. This juxtaposition of traditional masculine values with a less stereo-typical and diffuse gender is present in the following relationship:

> We talk about cartoons. We draw principles from that because those kinds of [TV] programs are filled with men who have got power. Sometimes when you watch that you feel that you've got power, you feel that you can do that. So it's the way you got to be. You've got to be strong in a lot of things. Things will come and get you, but if they do you rise up to the occasion. (Uncle Stephen)

In contrast, when I asked this uncle if he ever talked with his nephew about what it means to be a man, he replied:

> I think I might have mentioned it once or twice, but not really. When I talk to him mainly we talk about other youth. Like when he goes to town, I just say look around you, look at the people your age and be glad you're not doing that kind of stuff, like partying or drinking too much. I want him to be able to govern himself.

In this way, uncles were involved in teaching traditional masculine values, although they often seemed flexible in their approach to their nephews, relying on the wisdom of experience as they broached issues of personal development, family, intimate relationships, and friends. One uncle, Danny, actively nurtured his 14-year-old nephew's more artistic interests and abilities. "He is not a child who is really robust, or fits the normal tough Kiwi mold. He is more creative and expressive and that's something I've consciously fostered."

Another uncle, a father of three young daughters, expressed his appreciation for having time with his teenage nephew.

> We have a lot of fun together. Having three daughters, it is kind of nice having a young man to spend time with. I spend a lot of time with my daughters, but there are some things that girls [aren't interested in]. "Oh, that's gross. I don't want to fish; I don't want to touch slimy worms" and whatever else.
> *RM: Would you go fishing with [your nephew]?*
> Oh yes, we have been fishing and hunting.
> *RM: And your girls aren't interested?*
> Less so. They will go with me. They like rock climbing with me. We have a cottage on the coast and when the tide is out there are some good cliffs to rock climb. They will do that with me but some of the gross things, that's not their forte. (Uncle Jessie)

Here again traditional male interests are shared, but the line separating masculine from feminine interests is blurred.

The character of gender talk among aunts and nieces differed from that of their male counterparts. Women often talked about careers, mothering, balancing work and family lives, all in the context of establishing independent lives, an essential efficacy based on personal needs and interests. Elena speaks eloquently from her own experience in response to my question about whether she ever talks with her niece about what it means to be a woman. "Certainly," she replied, "although it is a bit troubling. I feel a lot of ambivalence about that particular term, 'to be a woman,' because on the one hand it is true, there are all these things that you go through as a woman, as a mother. I think that I spent so much of my life trying not to be defined by that space. [I talk] to her about what it's like to not be limited to the space of what people would call the space of women." The theme of not being limited by traditional definitions of women's roles appeared often in conversations I had with aunts, and often they drew on their own experience in full recognition of the tension for young women that exists in trying to establish balanced identities.

Susan recounts a similar theme and does so by reflecting on her own mother. "My mother stayed home and took care of us, but let's face it, my generation can't do that. It isn't that I wouldn't want to and if [my niece] could that would be great, but you've got to do what you've got to do." There are two elements of Susan's commentary that are important to distinguish. First is the notion that, for, woman working is required; dual-earner families are a necessity. In fact, Susan and her husband own several businesses, and Susan is a well-known professional in her field who travels widely. They are, relative to their rural neighbors, wealthy with an annual income of more than $100,000 in an area where annual household incomes average less than half that amount.[8] Certainly for some women, working is an economic necessity, but in this particular case, we could reasonably question whether income is the sole motive. The second theme in Susan's comment suggests yet another reason women elect to work. "You've got to do what you've got to do." This comment suggests the motivation for work is centered in the value placed on personal development and the realization of individual aptitudes, knowledge, skills, and interest.

---

[8] At the time of our interview in 2004, median family incomes in Maine averaged approximately $45,180, and less than 10% of households had annual incomes greater than $100,000 (U.S. Census, 2000).

Francesca says of her 11-year-old niece, "what I don't want her to do is just settle on something without exploring all the options out there for women. There are so many things that you can be and have every right to explore. Those options weren't there for women years ago." Denise speaks of her 7-year-old niece: "It's not a traditional message. I tell [my nieces], and I know their mom does, and I hope all women in their lives [tell them] that you can do anything you want and be anything you want."

In their conversations with nieces, aunts encourage personal efficacy, and they seem to engage such conversations more often and in greater detail than uncles. Certainly uncles encourage their nephews' aspirations and celebrate their achievements, but they do so in the context of traditional conventions and traditional expectations. They rarely, if ever, discuss having children, parenting, or balancing career and family interests. Simply put, the relationships of aunts and nieces reflect change in how women regard themselves and their relationships. Aunts occasionally reflect on this change, and in their own ways, they are vanguards of enlightenment. Francesca brings her personal experience into her mentoring with her niece.

> We've had this conversation that when you cry or show your emotions, that's an okay thing to do. I've told [my niece] about the time we had an administrative team meeting and this man said something very hurtful and I started crying. I was very embarrassed that I cried, and then I thought no, he should know that I was upset by his comment and I'm okay with that. Some women would say you can never cry or show a man you're upset, you can't cry at the workplace, and I don't believe [in] that caving or giving in. I've told her that she should believe in what she believes in, and if your friend doesn't, they should respect you. We do those little life lessons. Very often we'll do it through my own story and that seems to help her; she likes that. She likes to hear where my struggles are and that I've had to work through some things.

Theriza shared with her niece her own experience as a young college student and in doing so illustrated changing values regarding sexuality.

> One issue that I've talked to both Emily and her sister about is how sexuality has changed since I was their age. I can't remember how it came up, but when I was a college student, it was illegal in the state of Maine for birth control to be prescribed to minors, and the campus doctor would only prescribe the birth control pill if you were engaged. So if there was a girl on the floor who had a diamond ring she'd loan it to her friends. [The doctor] must have wondered why every girl on campus had identical engagement rings.... I went through I don't know how many

different pregnancy scares with my friends, you know, "oh, god, what am I going to do?" and probably most of them waited for their periods with fear. . . . it became this huge thing in our lives, which modern women don't have to deal with anymore; they can make decisions in different ways.

Sylvia shares her experience following a divorce and discusses the financial inequities that women once had to negotiate, and to a certain extent still do.

When I got divorced, I had been the breadwinner for a while, I was making more than my husband by a tiny amount, but I could not get credit in my own name for two years after that breakup, because it was assumed that he was the breadwinner. . . . He closed all of our charge accounts and I went to go open one, and I could not for two years. It was pathetic.

The experiences recounted by Francesca, Theriza, and Sylvia illustrate changing values, standards of conduct, and opportunities regarding the role of women in families and communities, issues that directly affected the lives of these aunts and will likely affect the lives of their nieces.

On other occasions, aunts and nieces talked about another fundamental element of the experience of many women – beauty and makeup. Ilse shared a story in which her niece wanted a new makeup kit and a willing model on which to try it. Ilse volunteered but not without reservations.

I was really struggling about the whole beauty myth, and I didn't want her to feel that she had to wear makeup. We've had this understanding that she could ask me for whatever she wanted for Christmas, and we would have this dialogue about it. So, she wanted a makeup kit, and I struggled over it, and I asked friends about it, and finally I decided that I wasn't going to make a big deal about it. If she wants a makeup kit, I'm going to get her a makeup kit. So, I did, and I went to visit them, and she made me up, and we went to the mall. It was so hard, because I could see myself in shop windows and I just did not look like myself.

We've talked a lot about it, and I found this great book which we both read about women needing to look a certain way and be a certain size, it's really not just makeup, it's the whole [issue of], 'You aren't beautiful unless you fit this particular image,' and we've talked about that and how that is with her friends and how she feels about it.

In these ways, aunts drew on their own experience, cognizant of the many cultural fault lines that exist for all women – and especially young women – in the midst of developing balanced identities. In large part, their conversations focused on building healthy relationships and healthy personal lives, as well as developing career interests that are unlimited by convention and instead speak to a mix of individual and relational interests. At times aunts were deeply involved in mentoring their nieces, as were uncles with their nephews, but the tenor of their conversations differed in important ways. Aunts and nieces share more detail regarding their relationships, and they recognize the peril of limiting women to traditional family models. Aunts shared their experiences with divorce and its aftermath, with abusive or disrespectful men, with working in nontraditional occupations and positions of authority, and with child rearing – all of which touch on issues of gender identity. In some ways, uncles were equally sensitive and concerned about the welfare of their nephews, but they did not seem to consider actively how working with and relating to women in nontraditional spheres might challenge conventional definitions of masculinity for their nephews. They most certainly encouraged their nephews, but they did not seem to address issues of balancing personal interests and work with fathering and family life. For men, there is apparently no pressing need to do so. The difference in the gender mentoring of uncles and aunts is sometimes subtle but far reaching. Perhaps the essence is captured in Addie's comment regarding her niece and young women in general: "I like to help young women to have the confidence in themselves as women." It is a comment that could just as well be made by an uncle, with an important exception: the lack of recognition that traditional definitions of masculinity limit men's balance of individual and relational lives.

CRITICISM AS SUPPORT

Aunts and uncles were of two minds with regard to criticizing their nieces and nephews: some were reluctant to do so, and some were not. At times, aunts and uncles were reluctant to be critical for fear of distancing their young charges. Uncle Robert is an example of such a position. When I asked if he was ever critical of his 17-year-old nephew, he replied: "I'm inclined not to be. I'm just relieved that he's got someone to talk to, and that he feels he can talk to me." At the time, Robert's nephew was experiencing some difficulties in adjusting to the recent death of his father and considerable conflict with his mother. In this context, Robert's sensitivity toward his nephew is understandable. Similarly, Aunt Raye was concerned about her 17-year-old niece and her troubled relationships with her parents, who are divorced, as well as her misuse of marijuana and alcohol. Their relationship had only begun to develop over the previous year. Raye emphasized maintaining a close relationship without confronting her niece. "I wouldn't want to put any distance between her and I," she says. "She knows you should not be smoking, but what am I going to do? I don't want her to do that and to get to that goal I've got to be [patient]."

Other aunts and uncles were more directly critical of their nieces and nephews, often regarding civil behavior or, in the case of aunts, the relational choices of their nieces. Uncle Benny is an example of the former. When I asked if he is ever critical of his nephew, he immediately replied:

> I told him to shape up. I lectured; he listened about the responsibility of becoming an adult. He was just being a typical 19 year old. You know "I've got a spare dollar in my pocket. I think I'll spend it," rather than getting his car fixed. [So I tell him to] apply himself more, to buckle down. He is not a child anymore, [but] an adult in the real world. . . . He threw a sneaker at his father and I said: "Maybe you shouldn't have done that." Mostly it is just "life lessons" rather than specific advice.

Similarly aunts often engaged in this brand of life-lessons talk when transgressions of civil behavior occurred, typically in reference to their nieces' childhood or adolescence. Olympia shared a story about her young niece, who was in a snit regarding a homework assignment that wasn't quite perfect.

> [My niece] was a big perfectionist and she didn't have whatever she needed to make her homework perfect. My brother and his family had been living in Saudi Arabia and had just returned. They had this saying that "only Allah is perfect." So I was trying to make my niece understand this. And there was a story from my mother's past that I remember telling her. My mother worked for the Secretary of the Navy during World War II and she made some dreadful mistake in a report and she actually cried in the Secretary's office. And he said to her: "my dear why do you think they call them erasers?"

In another instance, Aunt Dorthea recounted an episode in which her young niece was using inappropriate and harmful language in reference to her friends as faggots and her sister as a slut. "I talked to her about the meaning [of those terms] . . . and that it is okay to not like someone, or how they act. . . . It's okay to be angry but [it's important to] think about how we channel that anger." In these instances, aunts and uncles supplement the work of parents by encouraging civil behavior regarding personal conduct, school friends, or family members, particularly siblings.

When the relationship between uncles and nephews took on the character of a friendship, advice or criticism took more of an immediate tone in reference to a particular event rather than an intended lesson. Uncle Chris and his lifelong partner often invite his nephew on trips abroad. On one occasion, they were preparing for a trip to Australia and encountered a bit of late adolescent obstinance.

> He is a real neat guy. I'm not critical. . . . There is nothing to be critical of. Once he got uptight and he came over to see us. I remember we asked him not to wear jeans on the plane because we thought we could get him upgraded. We said: "Look, don't wear your jeans and we'll probably get you upgraded." [Well, he said:] "No one tells me what to wear." Immediately I said: "Look! Don't be such a bloody fool." I remember that time. [He laughs.]

Nephews accepted this kind of criticism from their uncles without negative sentiment, and they distinguished between criticism from uncles and that from fathers, the latter of which they often viewed as more judgmental. The distinction supports the significance of uncles as third parties who are concerned about their nephews but not entirely responsible for them, and their strength and importance to nephews and their parents is in part derivative of their third-party status.

Nieces also voiced an appreciation of their aunts' perspective, although it was not always entirely neutral. Janice shared a story of what in her words amounted to "making a poor choice" when she left her job "in the middle of the night" without notice to her employer, who was a friend of the family, or to her mother on an extemporary trip to Florida with her boyfriend. Janice says of her aunt: "She was angry because I ruined my relationship with the family [I worked for], and put myself in danger, and I was driving an uninsured car." I asked how her aunt knew of the episode. Janice replied, "She knows everything. I don't hold back. I tell her everything." The relationship she describes is one built on closeness, respect, and a high degree of trust. Janice now realizes it wasn't the wisest of decisions, and her aunt certainly agrees, but their relationship continues and has the resilience to do so.

Heath's uncle is critical of how Heath spends his limited funds, a criticism Heath understands. "I spend money like it's going out of fashion," he says. "[My uncle] is a bit critical of that. He tries to point me in the right direction." When the relationships of aunts and uncles with nieces and nephews are at their best, the flow of communication is open. Transgressions in the form of unacceptable behavior or lapses in judgment are accepted as such but not necessarily approved. The zephyr of adolescent digression is weathered.

Much of the critical commentary of aunts and uncles is directed at encouraging civil behavior or about making responsible decisions regarding school or work. In this way, aunts and uncles are similar. In one domain they differ: aunts are more likely to evaluate critically their nieces' choice of friends and romantic partners, whereas uncles did not voice similar concerns about their nephews. Aunts expressed concerns about boyfriends who were viewed as disrespectful of nieces, overly jealous, controlling, or potentially abusive. Aunt Erma reflected on her niece's current involvement, an opinion that mom (Erma's sister) shared. "We love her. We want to be supportive, but we really think this guy is a mistake." Uncles, in contrast, never seem to discuss issues of respect, jealousy, or control with their nephews.

Aunts seemed to take a more direct interest in their nieces' relational lives, including their nieces' nonromantic friendships, and in doing so encouraged discussion of the appropriate treatment of friends. In short, aunts have more knowledge of their nieces' relationships with peers, and they more freely share their observations and expectations; in this way, they encourage a brand of relationship literacy that is apparently limited in the mentoring of nephews by uncles.

REVERSE MENTORING

Just as aunts and uncles were influential in the lives of their nieces and nephews, they were in turn influenced. Nieces and nephews mentor their aunts and uncles in a variety of ways. Nieces often provide fashion advice for their older aunts, an arena in which uncles and nephews never seem to visit but aunts welcomed.[9] Aunt Rebecca recounted how her niece worked at a large department store and on occasion would purchase clothes for her because "she thinks I need little skirts and stuff." However, when her niece suggested a tattoo, Rebecca declined. These instances of *reverse mentoring*, however superficial at the outset, can serve as ways for nieces to express their affection and concern for their aunts. They are very much instances of care giving functioning to confirm, enrich, and sometimes deepen relationships.

Instances of reciprocal influence and reverse mentoring appeared in a number of other areas. At times aunts and uncles reported simply learning from their younger relatives through observation, admiring at a distance their proficiencies at home as parents, or at work as professionals. Aunt

---

[9] Nieces provided advice on fashion in 12% of the interviews with aunts and nieces (6 of 52), and not surprisingly the topic was absent in the interviews with men with the exception of designing and shopping for tattoos.

Harriett views her adult niece as "an extremely creative person who has had to make some tough decisions careerwise." Harriett expressed how observing her niece manage her family, parenting, and developing her career has helped her reach a similar balance in her own life and "make different decisions for my life."

As aunts and uncles were valued as intimates who listened well and provided support in matters of schooling, careers, and relationships, adult nieces and nephews reciprocated the support. Shenna is 23, a single mother and full-time college student in her senior year. Her aunt is 41 and also a single mother with two young children. She has an interest in returning to school to become a physical therapist. Shenna speaks from experience when she counsels her aunt, encouraging her aspirations. "I keep telling her," she says, "just because you have two kids doesn't mean anything. There are a lot of resources out there to help. I just say, 'You can do it!'" In another instance, Janice shared a story about her aunt who was concerned about the work she was being asked to perform in her position as an office manager, which she thought was inappropriate. Since Janice also worked in an office, Aunt Audrey valued her niece's opinion. In both cases, aunts actively sought the advice of their nieces, and nieces in turn mentored their aunts.

Nieces and nephews occasionally provided welcome advice regarding personal relationships, including relations with other family members, advice regarding children and especially adolescents, and advice regarding the romantic partners or spouses of aunts and uncles. Mark recounts how he offers his uncle advice regarding family members because, from Mark's perspective, his uncle "tends to do things that are slightly incendiary with other members of the family."

This kind of *family work* in which partners discuss how best to understand or communicate with other kin appeared regularly in our conversations. Uncles and aunts alike rely on their older nephews and nieces for their perspectives, and at times they provide direct advice, as Mark did in dealing with family members, or they act more indirectly as sounding boards. Active listening to the concerns of aunts and uncles regarding family members or simply acknowledging their experiences without judgment are valued responses in much the same way nieces and nephews valued nonjudgmental responses to their own concerns.

Nieces and nephews demonstrate a brand of caregiving and mutual connection by offering suggestions for planning family events or recommendations for appropriate gifts; and their counsel in these matters is actively sought. Mark's uncle, for instance, sought his advice on selecting presents for his wife as well as suggestions for weekend getaways.

For aunts and uncles with young children or adolescents, older nieces and nephews were at times relied on for their perspectives in matters of child care, policing adolescents, and understanding young adults. Addie recounts how her niece, who is 20, "talks to me about my 11-year-old daughter, and I guess she tries to help me understand that I can be a little more lenient with her." This simple comment underscores the potentially reciprocal, and uniquely parallel, nature of such relationships. As aunts and uncles are often valued for their objectivity by parents and their children, aunts and uncles seem equally to value the perspectives of their older nieces and nephews. In another instance, Janice shared how her aunt was deeply concerned that her daughter Ellen was engaged "so young," not ready for marriage, and perhaps not selecting the best of partners. Janice says, "We had these long talks about him and about whether he was good for Ellen." Although we cannot know with certainty the response of Janice's aunt, or precisely why she turned to her niece in this circumstance, it seems likely that aunts value the perspectives of their nieces, who bring to bear their unique and immediate familiarity with young adulthood, a certain degree of objectivity, and knowledge of all parties and their interrelationships. As an impetuous young adult whom we met earlier in this chapter, Janice once ran off with a boyfriend, quitting her job without warning and leaving the Northeast where she and her family resided for sunny Florida. She is no stranger to impulsive and improvident decision making. Her aunt was very well aware of this experience and at the time none too pleased with her niece's brash action. Nonetheless, Janice's experiences as a young adult gave her a certain expertise that her aunt readily drew on in seeking advice about her own daughter.

On rare occasions, nieces and nephews shared their advice regarding the dating partners of aunts and uncles. Yvette's aunt shared some concerns about her own boyfriend, who in their view acted inappropriately at a family gathering. Yvette's response: "Just dump him. It's not worth the hassle." In another case, Nat, in his own laconic way, describes his friendship with his uncle. I asked Nat if his uncle ever talks to him about his marriage. He replied: "Yeah, he tells me things that happened, things that bother him. Stuff like that."

Then again nieces and nephews were sometimes simply valued as companions, very much like good friends. Uncle Chris regards his relationship with his adult nephew as "very special," and in some ways their relationship is unique within their family context. Both uncle and nephew are gay men. Chris says, "[Our relationship] means a lot to me in many ways. I think it means a lot to him. He's got someone he feels is family that is okay [with his sexual orientation], and I've got someone in the family who has got a better comprehension of me."

In some instances, nieces became the primary caretaker for an ailing aunt, as in the case of Elena, whose aunt suffered third degree burns over her back and shoulders as the result of an accident that was traumatic for the entire family. During this time, Elena, a young girl, nursed her aunt back to health.

> I remember nursing her wounds, and I remember that I would put salve on them and it was traumatic for me because burns are very painful. This was somebody very close to me, and it was really traumatic and emotional. . . . I had a room downstairs with my aunt and we slept together. I was a 12-year-old girl, sleeping with a woman who was 50. We slept together like we did when I was young, when we used to snuggle and take naps together. I think that was a moment of emotional connection and healing.

In this case, Elena was called on to care for her aunt during her long recovery, and in doing so she undoubtedly participated in the family's recovery from a significant tragedy. In the accident, several family members died, including Elena's aunt's partner. Both niece and aunt had lost a significant person in their lives. The "moment of emotional connection and healing" of which Elena speaks was likely important for both niece and aunt.

Other nieces spoke of close childhood relationships with aunts that continued into adulthood. As their aunts became frail, they were called on to care for the very adults who had once cared for them. Patricia lived with her aunt and mother for most of her childhood, and she describes her aunt as a second mother. Patricia is now 53 and visits monthly with her elderly mother and aunt, who after a period of living near each other but in separate households now live together. In addition to her regular visits, Patricia calls daily. Because she is an only child and her aunt never had children, Patricia is an important caregiver for both aunt and mother, sometimes intervening in their occasional sisterly disputes.

> My aunt would say, "your mother drives me crazy." At first it was kind of funny, but after a while I realized that there were so many old tapes that were playing between the two of them that they could push each other's buttons. It would get them going and I think that actually sometimes I come to my mother's defense, which I never thought I would do. I think my aunt is sometimes unfair with my mother. . . . I say to them: "This is old stuff, you've got to let it go."

Whether young or old, nieces and nephews actively mentored their aunts and uncles, and each seemed to value the same essential qualities, and perhaps each benefited in the same essential ways.

CONCLUSION

The generative concerns of aunts and uncles are demonstrated throughout their relationships with nieces and nephews as they recounted instances of providing advice regarding school, careers, relationships, values, and virtually all areas of life, as well as the occasional criticism. They did so directly and indirectly, often with great sensitivity. Their support took the form of information, instrumental aid, and advice but just as often was an expression of their caring. Throughout the literatures on parenting,[10] friendship,[11] and kinship,[12] there is a consistent finding that women's relationships are more expressive, relative to men. As is often the case in gender-based comparisons, the distributions are overlapping. Aunts and uncles shared many similarities in their styles of mentoring and the subjects of their concerns. Then, too, nieces and nephews valued similar features in their favored aunts and uncles, with displays of support and active listening with minimal judgment being chief among the most valued qualities. Differences in the mentoring styles of aunts and uncles appear, but often they are rather flexible and do not adhere to traditional definitions of gender. For instance, women are generally viewed as kin keepers and largely responsible for maintaining ties with kin.[13] One way in which they do so is by sending holiday greeting cards to family members,[14] which in itself is a generative activity. Nonetheless, uncles occasionally do so as our interviews illustrate, and with important results for nephews. Mean comparisons of intimacy obscure the lived experience of some men – albeit a minority – who are intimate, the intimacy of men who are so indirectly, and the all-important interpretations of relational partners – in this case nephews – to exchanges of instrumental supports. An uncle's gift of a relatively small amount of money on the occasion of a move away from home was interpreted by a nephew as a significant demonstration of caregiving. The enactment of gender is flexible in the service of generativity and socially constructed in a relational context.

In two areas, aunts and uncles differ in important ways. Aunts and nieces talk more about relationship issues, particularly the intimate relationships

[10] Hosley & Montemayor, 1997.
[11] Wood, 2000.
[12] C. L. Johnson, 2000.
[13] Leach & Braithwaite, 1996.
[14] di Leonardo, 1987.

of nieces. In this regard, aunts seem to know more about their nieces' relational lives than uncles do of nephews. Aunts offer their evaluations of the relational partners of nieces, they voice concerns about sexual activity, safety, health, and unplanned pregnancies. They share their concerns about controlling and potentially abusive partners, often relating their personal experiences with such men. This does not mean that uncles were unaware or unconcerned with the developing relationships of their nephews, but their concerns were of a different metal and largely unspoken. On no occasion did uncles express concerns about the potentially abusive behavior of men, nor did they directly address the responsibilities associated with being sexually active. On the other hand, uncles did serve as role models, sometimes modeling positive relational stances and sometimes rather negative stances. Heath, for instance, was clear to mention how much he appreciated and admired how his uncle acted toward his aunt. His uncle may not speak to him directly about maintaining healthy relationships, but his actions are not silent. In another instance, Heath mentions the many divorces in his family, a circumstance he does not wish to repeat in his own life. "One thing I don't want to do is get married heaps," he said. Whether intentional or not, uncles, like aunts, acted as role models and in this way mentored their nieces and nephews. Aunts simply did so more directly with regard to nieces' intimate relationships, and they expressed more concerns about issues of health and safety.

Aunts and uncles also differed in their perspectives on issues of personal development and the balance of work and family life. For aunts and nieces, the issue is critically important and often discussed. Aunts freely shared their experiences of having children while maintaining a career or of working in fields typically dominated by men, as well as the challenges that face women in seeking a balance among personal, professional, and family lives. Uncles and nephews did not seem to discuss such issues, or at least did not do so as directly. The challenge of balancing fathering with developing a career was never directly approached, and neither was the issue of what it might mean for a young father to be partnered with a career-oriented wife and mother, a rather typical scenario for contemporary families. Here again, although the subject was not broached directly in conversation, uncles did model active fathering for some nephews and absent fathering for others.

As aunts and uncles actively engage in the lives of their nieces and nephews, they also actively mentor parents. They do so by sharing their perspectives, their experiences, or otherwise serving as counselors, advisors, or supportive friends who are uniquely positioned because of their insider's knowledge and long-standing relationships with all family members. Parents at times actively sought out the support or counsel of aunts and uncles in dealing with a particularly thorny issue regarding a child, often an adolescent. Aunts and uncles act as mediators or conciliators in the relationships of parents and children, similar to the way that grandparents can mediate disputes among parents and children.[15]

It is perhaps not surprising that aunts and uncles act as intergenerational buffers by intervening in the relationships of parents and children. Aunt Sandy, for example, encourages her niece to make wise decisions in her life, to establish healthy limits and be responsible for her own happiness and not to depend on her parents who have a history of substance abuse. Whether aunts and uncles act as partisan supporters of parents or children, they can be uniquely influential and central players in families. In the following chapter, I explore further the issue of buffering as aunts and uncles act as relational mediators in the affairs of parents and children.

Although I began this inquiry thinking of generativity as "a concern for future generations" as it is typically defined,[16] in fact generative actions are frequently lived and expressed between all generations. As aunts and uncles mentored nieces and nephews, they were in turn mentored. Nieces and nephews provided advice to their aunts and uncles regarding relational partners, dealing with other family members, personal development, future schooling, and careers, and they routinely acted like good friends commiserating with uncles and aunts about common experiences and interests. For Aunt Francesca and her 11-year-old niece Maria, their talks often occurred in the family's hot tub. Francesca said, "we soak, we talk, and she brings up some things." In this comfortable environment, Francesca learns about her young niece and her concerns. To be sure, Francesca is an effective mentor, but she also uses the opportunity to be mentored and wisely listens to and values the perspectives of this young woman and the insights she is able to share.

Instances of mentoring by nieces and nephews appeared throughout the interviews, and aunts and uncles valued their advice and experience in a variety of arenas. In this domain, the findings differ from earlier research. Communications scholars Laura Ellingson and Patricia Sotirin reported no instances of reciprocal support or reverse mentoring in their study of aunting: "Nieces and nephews told of learning skills from their aunts but not teaching their aunts, confiding in their aunts but not being confidants

---

[15] Goodman, 2007. [16] de St. Aubin, McAdams, & Kim, 2004.

for them, receiving gifts and encouragement from aunts, but not giving to them." They go on to note: "From college-age nieces' and nephews' perspective, the role of aunt is that of a giver rather than a receiver of care and support."[17] This is a very different portrait of the relationships among aunts and nieces or nephews, as well as those with uncles, than reported here. I suspect the difference comes from the limited nature of the query put to the nieces in the Ellingson and Sotirin study, who were simply asked to write an essay about their aunts without further instruction or specific questions. In other regards, their work and that of others is similar in that instances of mentoring by aunts and uncles of their nieces and nephews are commonplace.[18] This issue is important because when queried in some detail, aunts, uncles, nieces, and nephews are quick to locate the bidirectional nature of their relationships – relationships that are decidedly interdependent, with each party being influenced by the other. Key features such as generativity and intergenerational solidarity are best viewed from this perspective. The family relationships of siblings and their children span decades and often include sharing all significant developmental milestones of childhood, adolescence, and adulthood. Several aunts and uncles were present at the births of their nieces and nephews, some of whom are now young adults. Some nieces and nephews were present at the marriages of their aunts and uncles. It should not be surprising that they are mutually influential in each others' lives. Traffic in exchanges of gifts, encouragement, skills and knowledge, and all manners of instrumental and expressive support is two-way. Family relationships are bidirectional and interdependent and differ largely in terms of the degrees of interdependence. In some families, there is more traffic and the bus is more regular in routing between households.

[17] Ellingson & Sotirin, 2006, p. 497.
[18] Chebra, 1991; Ellingson & Sotirin, 2006; Sotirin & Ellingson, 2006.

6

Family Work

The family work of aunts and uncles takes on a variety of forms but shares some common characteristics as aunts and uncles, as well as nieces and nephews, exchange knowledge about family members, mediate occasional family disputes, or act as partisan supporters or critics. Aunts and uncles talk with nieces and nephews about their parents, siblings, grandparents, and other kinfolk. They tell and retell stories of family members. They share significant events, developmental milestones, and news of current activities. In so doing, they create a family's unique biography and secure the place of each individual within a continuity of generations and relationships. In this chapter, we consider each of the realms of family work as they illustrate how uncles and aunts enact generativity throughout their relationships with family members, particularly nephews and nieces. At the same time, the conduct of family work further illustrates how families are composed of interdependent relationships organized across multiple households. Of course families vary in their permeability, in the knowledge members have of one another, the frequency with which they communicate, and the unique family norms that govern their conversations or the lack of them. Some aunts and uncles have little contact with their siblings or other kin; others have considerable contact. Our task in these pages is to illustrate this diversity and in particular to illustrate how aunts, uncles, parents, and their children often rely on one another in a variety of significant ways.

In general, *family work* is routine thought and conversation about family members and includes elements of direct symbolic expression (e.g., exchanging gifts) and rather indirect or certainly less visible expressions (e.g., planning a holiday gathering). As we will see from the perspectives of aunts and uncles, nieces and nephews, it can take a number of forms

and function to sustain relationships and the interdependence of family
members, as well as at times interfere in the conduct of family relationships,
appropriately or not. It is similar in some respects to the notion of marriage
work in which friends discuss their primary partners (e.g., spouses) with
the consequence of influencing their relationships (e.g., marriages).[1]

Not all families reported significant engagements in family work, but
most did. Ninety-five of 103 participants reported talking about family
members, typically parents, siblings, or grandparents. Some reported limitations in the nature or depth of their conversations. "My family, um, has a
general philosophy, which works better in some situations than others, that
almost any difficulty can be dealt with if you just don't talk about it" (Aunt
Theriza). In this particular family, the niece's father was an alcoholic. Aunt
Theriza found the father's behavior toward his daughter unacceptable, and
yet she was reluctant to raise the issue with her niece, to be in her words
"confrontational" about the father's actions, fearing that this would only
distance her niece. In this instance, the lack of talk is ironically an expression
of caregiving. Yet in other families, there seem to be few limitations. Mothers and sisters talk about their daily lives, their children, and their partners,
all of which keep family members informed of one another's circumstance,
activities, and emotional dispositions. Uncles learn about their nephews
directly by talking with them or indirectly through a parent or another
aunt or uncle. Parents learn about their children through aunts and uncles
and rely on them for their counsel and occasional interventions. Aunts and
uncles chat with nieces and nephews because they are genuinely interested,
because they regard doing so as their responsibility, and because parents
and other family members expect them to do so. All of this is kin work.
Although Aunt Theriza's communications are restricted in some regards, in
others she routinely advises her niece, and perhaps her guidance is welcome.
This is not always the case.

We consider four social locations or forms of kin work in this chapter:
talk of nieces and nephews about parents initiated by either aunts and
uncles or nieces and nephews; talk about other kin – for instance siblings,
grandparents, and other aunts and uncles; instances of intergenerational
buffering – for instance when aunts act as partisan supporters or critics of
nieces; and finally instances of family storytelling in which individual and
family biographies are cast.

---

[1] For a discussion of marriage work, see Helms et al., 2003; Oliker, 1989; Proulx, Helms, &
Payne, 2004.

PARENT WORK

Nieces and nephews routinely talk about their parents to their aunts and
uncles; 81 of 103 participants reported doing so.[2] Conversations about
parents served to help nieces and nephews understand their parents' perspectives, gain insight into their parents as individuals, or suggest ways to
manage difficult situations. Their conversations range from discussions of
particular events to understanding long-standing and often troublesome
conditions.

Lana shared with her aunt her frustration at not being able to see her dad
as often as she liked. Her dad was experiencing a long commute to work,
limiting the time he was able to spend at home. Aunt Ilse says:

> There was a point when [Lana] never got to see her dad, and when he
> came home on the weekends all she wanted to do was hang out with him,
> and I could tell that it was really hard for her. So we did a little problem
> solving: Could she be in touch with him? Could she call him during the
> week?

In another instance of supportive problem solving, Aunt Susan advised
her niece in managing her wedding plans. Among the many fault lines in
planning the wedding was the issue of where to sit her parents, who were
divorced and rarely spoke, her father's new wife, and her mother's fiancé.
Susan clearly relates that conversations with her niece about her parents and
siblings occurred throughout her childhood and continue to this day. At
times it is simply a matter of listening to her niece's concerns, and at other
times it is a matter of offering suggestions for managing relationships with
cantankerous family members, including where to sit them at gatherings
with sedative effect.

Conversations about parents are not always directed at specific problems or issues. Lee does not ask his uncle for specific advice regarding his
mother, but he does value learning about her relationships with her siblings
when they were younger. He says, "it allows me to understand where my
mom is coming from. A little deeper understanding of the present without asking, 'I'm having a problem with my mom. How should I deal with
it?'" Often aunts and uncles who have relatively close and long-standing
relationships with their siblings and their siblings' children are uniquely
positioned to counsel by offering suggestions for managing relationships,

[2] Aunt Debbie was not included in this line of questioning because her niece was an infant
at the time of our interview.

offering personal insights about family members, or simply listening to another's concerns.

In some instances, aunts and uncles are critically important, especially in understanding cases of parental divorce or chronic illness. Of her 11-year-old niece, Francesca says, "We have some pretty serious talks. Pillow talk. When her parents were having some hard times last year, she point blank asked me if they were going to get divorced." Although Francesca could not answer her niece's question, because her brother and sister-in-law had made no decision to separate, she could offer an all-important venue for her niece to voice her concerns.

Parental divorce can be difficult for older children as well, and the effects of divorce can linger. As a college student, Bess was deeply concerned about her parent's recent divorce and her father's deteriorating health resulting from diabetes and alcohol abuse. Bess took responsibility for her father's health care by arranging doctor's appointments and finding services when he lost his eyesight. Bess's aunt provided her emotional support when she most needed it. Of this time, her aunt says, "[Bess and I] talked quite a bit. I don't know if it was advice [that I gave her] or if I was just consoling her."

Chronic illnesses and substance abuse by parents are frequent problems about which nieces and nephews speak with their elders. In one poignant story, Jamie shares his concerns about his ailing father with this uncle.

> My father is very ill. He has lost his vision and part of his feet and it's very hard for him to walk. Sometimes it is very discouraging and he gets down and depressed and I just don't want to be around him. My uncle very much understands and we talk about that very often. It's his brother and he cares about [him] a lot. He's always there for him and I would always be there for my father, but sometimes it's really kind of a downer to see him this way because my father has always been such an upbeat and outgoing guy.

In this case, as is true in many of the conversations we had, it is not always important that aunts or uncles provide direct advice, and perhaps it is not always possible to do so; rather it is important to have someone who can listen to your concerns. Jamie's uncle does so, and he does so from the perspective of an uncle and father's brother, a dual perspective that Jamie appreciates. Jamie's uncle provides a place where Jamie can share his feelings in much of their complexity and feel he is understood, which may be all he needed at that particular moment. Perhaps Jamie's uncle has experienced a similar reaction – and emotions – to his brother's deteriorating health. The essential conduct of a relationship is often seated in emotion work.[3]

Sharing emotions and concerns as well as frustrations about parents are fairly routine matters of conversation. Lee talks to his uncle often and shares his frustration when he has a disagreement with his parents. "He always asks me to be more considerate," Lee says of his uncle. Ilse describes how her niece can "rant and rave" about her parents, her brother, and a host of other issues in her life. "I think she just needs to let off steam," Ilse says. In each case, an uncle and an aunt can act as rather neutral but informed parties with whom nieces and nephews can share their feelings about their parents, siblings, friends, and other family members without censorship, with minimal judgment, and knowing full well that they will be understood. Incidentally, it is often a two-way street. Occasionally, aunts and uncles spin a rant. Aunt Dorthea visits with her niece often. Dorthea shares concerns about her aging mother and father, as well as about her husband and her daily hassles. I asked Dorthea how her niece responds: "She listens. Laughs. Let's me know when I am being a bit much." The emotion work of aunts and nieces, uncles and nephews is reciprocal.

On rare occasion, a niece or nephew may engage in marriage work with an aunt or uncle. As we noted earlier, aunts, unlike uncles, are well informed of their nieces' intimate relationships and often share their concerns or offer support. Then, too, aunts may seek out the opinions of the nieces regarding a new intimate partner. Rarely, however, do aunts seem to talk openly about their primary partners with nieces and engage in what we might call marriage work in much the same way good friends may talk about daily events and matters important to them, including their partners.[4] There is one interesting exception, however. Dorthea is 28 and married without children. She spoke of her own aunt and the character of their relationship at length. I asked her if she spoke to her aunt about her marriage and husband. "Oh yea," she replied, "all the time. She tells me to go easier on him. And then we laugh." In return, Dorthea's aunt talks about her own husband, which suggests a peerlike friendship between aunt and adult niece. This was the only clear example of marriage work to appear in my interviews in which an aunt discussed her intimate partnership with a niece. Occasionally an uncle might ask a nephew to suggest a possible holiday gift for his wife, and more often nieces comment on aunts' romantic partnerships, but neither aunts nor uncles seem to share routine experiences concerning their partners or

---

[3] Hochschild, 1979.

[4] See Helms et al., 2004; Oliker, 1989.

spouses with nieces or nephews. Given the relatively young age of the nieces and nephews in this study (half were aged 21 years or younger) and the fact that about 80% were unmarried and not living with a partner, perhaps this is not so surprising. With an older sample and as the relationships of aunts, uncles, nieces, and nephews mature, we might find more examples of reciprocal marriage work or sharing in personal and relational experience.

Aunts and especially uncles often encourage their nieces and nephews to be more considerate of parents. Lee relies on his uncle to get a more objective, informed picture of his family, because as Lee notes, his uncle "is the one that knows about my family the best." Perhaps uncharacteristic of uncles and nephews, their private conversational time together often occurs when they go out shopping together.

Van recalls how his uncle "says a bit about my mom" and encourages him to "look after her and stuff like that." Van's story is similar to Dirk's in some ways; both experience some difficulties in their relationships with their mothers and both are encouraged to be a bit more emphathetic by their uncles, but Dirk's story includes two additional themes – one concerns how information about family members is transmitted across multiple house-holds, or family units, and one concerns the reciprocal nature of family work. Dirk recounts how his uncle chastises him for his lack of contact with his mom. "Sometimes [my uncle] will say: 'why haven't you emailed your mom?' He says it with a bit of shittiness in his voice sometimes, [and] I know that his brother has [talked to] my mom [and] might have heard a line about me not getting in contact." Van says he now e-mails his mom weekly. "So that's enough," he says. His uncle has an influence and in this case encour-ages his nephew to be more considerate. Family relationships are sustained through his uncle's efforts. One curious element of this instance of family work is the routing of communications. Apparently one brother (and uncle) speaks directly with Van's mother, this brother speaks with Van's favored uncle, who then speaks with Van. The routing of messages is typical in that it involves multiple households and relationships and is a signature element of how family work is conducted. Perhaps Van's mother speaks directly with him regarding her concerns, but it is not inconsequential that her brothers also share in communicating those concerns. The routing of information across multiple households, family units, and individuals suggests that the direct effects of an uncle on a nephew and his relationship with his mother are only part of the story. When aunts and uncles share their experiences and reflect the views of a mother and her relationship with her son, the wider tracings of kin are linked to one another in a web of common knowledge, common concern, and common expectations. In this way, the conduct of personal relationships is dependent on the social configuration of ties with kin.

Like many families, Van's is complicated by a divorce and the relatively recent remarriage of his father. Van shared how he talks with his uncle about his stepmom – but not for his own benefit necessarily, but rather because his uncle "was trying to get a better picture of her." The conduct of family work is often reciprocal, with uncles and nephews influencing each other and likely being dependent on each other for information, advice, and reflection. In this case, Van seems to have mentored his uncle or at least encouraged a developing relationship between his uncle and stepmom. Van says, "He has grown to like her a lot to the point where the other night my stepmom rang my uncle and they had a yarn on the phone for a half an hour. Four or five years ago it would have been a ten-minute yarn."

Like Van and his uncle, family members engage in conversations in which they share knowledge, feelings, and expectations, as well as news and insights about each other, with the consequence of increasing closeness and a family's sense of togetherness. In some cases, and perhaps all too frequently, kin may act in ways that discourage intimacy or are otherwise destructive, and as we have noted previously, alcoholism and substance abuse are common problems that intrude on family relationships. Lest we forget, for a minority, and especially adolescents, the counsel of elders regarding parents is expected but not particularly welcome. A conversation with Dirk, who was 18 at the time of our interview, illustrates how his uncle shared news about family members and encouraged him to be more considerate of his mother:

> My relationship with my mother [is] not really a good one. [My uncle] tries to give me advice on those sorts of things. He'd say, 'She's your mother, the only one you've got.'
>
> *RM: Is it good advice?*
> Yeah, I don't really listen to much of it.

Perhaps Dirk's comment is more recalcitrant bravado than disinterest because he went on to say that talking about his mom with his uncle does allow him to "vent my frustrations or whatever." The exchange illustrates an important circumstance in that the outcome of advice giving or attempts to influence another are not always successful, or successful in ways intended or anticipated.

On rare occasions, at least in these interviews, aunts may rely on third parties to communicate with or otherwise judge the well-being of their nieces. Aunt Barbara prides herself and her family on the idea of open communication. As she says, "we talk about just about everything," with one exception, the divorce of her niece's parents. "This was the one place I couldn't talk to [my niece]. She just didn't want to hear of it, so I had to back away a little bit." Barbara's niece was 13 at the time her parents split up, and while Aunt Barbara shared a close relationship with her niece and continues to do so, this was one area about which they did not communicate, at least not directly. Given her concern about her niece, Barbara asked her niece's friends how they thought she was doing. "She's fine," they said. Barbara valued the assessment of her niece's friends in part because many of them had divorced parents, and "knew the ropes." She understood as well that friends were an important resource for her niece as she worked through a personal understanding of her parents' separation. The case is interesting because Barbara knew her niece well enough to judge when it was inappropriate to press an issue, and well enough to know her niece's friends, to whom she then turned for insight. Here the business of family work, of caring for young people, is cast broadly to include the friends of a niece.

Of course not all friendships are considered desirable, although it is wise to recognize that some are, even if perhaps just as often they are not. Barbara shared how she and her niece's father were concerned about her niece's first boyfriend. They spoke of the developing relationship and jointly agreed that the last thing they should do is intervene directly. It would have "backfired completely," she said. And then, "we are not a family that will butt our noses into a developing situation if we can feel reasonably sure that she'll come out okay." Father and aunt decided an indirect approach was the best tactic, and a long trip to Australia provided the necessary distraction. Fortunately, separation of the young lovers did not make the hearts grow fonder and their relationship dwindled. "We just keep an eye out; hope for the best," said Barbara.

KIN WORK

In addition to talking about parents, aunts and uncles talked about other family members. This kin work took essentially two forms, with some conversation directed at maintaining particular relationships (e.g., an aunt advising her niece about getting along with a grandparent) and some at maintaining families (e.g., an uncle and nephew planning a family reunion). Relationship-centered kin work, or kin keeping as it is commonly referred to,[5] includes instances of problem solving – and often with regard to a

---

[5] Leach & Braithwaite, 1996; Rosenthal, 1985.

particular family relationship – attempts to better understand another's actions or motives for actions, attempts to be heard or have one's point of view understood, and sharing information on other family members with or without judgment.

Grandparents and siblings were frequent topics of conversation, with talk about other family members less frequent. Occasionally it is as straightforward as helping younger family members understand their elders and deal with them more effectively. Michele recounts how her grandmother "is a very interesting lady, a lovely person, but definitely has her way of doing things" and how her aunt has counseled her on communicating effectively with her grandmother. Learning how to manage relationships with people of a different generation and perhaps differing values can be an important role of aunts and uncles, and both commonly seem to mentor their nieces and nephews in this regard.

Occasionally kin keeping and mentoring of relationships with kin can be reciprocal, or reversed, as nieces or nephews advise their aunts and uncles in regard to other family members or take direct responsibility for enhancing kin relations. Hattie is fully aware that her mom and aunt have a contested relationship with her grandmother, who has "interesting" views she says, "like the Bible would be better if it were written by women." Hattie sees herself as often cast into the role of arbitrator in family conflicts, and given the insights she has regarding the eccentricities of her mother, father, aunt, and grandmother, she is a consummate kin keeper.

Occasionally an aunt or uncle can provide a welcome alternative perspective on family members or provide information that is not forthcoming from parents. Archie's grandfather recently died; his grandmother has Alzheimer's disease and is residing in an assisted living facility. Archie felt his mother was unwilling to share details of his grandparents' lives, especially regarding the current caregiving arrangements for his grandmother. For this, Archie turned to his uncle, who "told me what was going on and stuff." The "stuff" to which Archie refers includes some diversity of opinions among Archie's parents and their siblings regarding the provision of care for his grandmother, all of which Archie's mom was unwilling to share with him directly, but they were matters about which Archie was concerned. His uncle provided the background he desired and that his parents were unable to provide and, in so doing, enriched Archie's knowledge of his family, and perhaps his ties to all family members.

In some severely distressing circumstances, nieces and nephews sought out their aunts and uncles to share their experience of the death of a family member, often a grandparent, and more rarely the premature death of a parent or sibling. Aunts and uncles were especially important when parents seemed overwhelmed by their grief. On these occasions, aunts and uncles serve to help their nieces and nephews understand their own feelings, and possibly those of parents and other family members.

The siblings of nieces and nephews are a common topic of conversation, and perhaps in this area, aunts and uncles can offer an important element of support for families, including parents as well as their children. Aunt Denise speaks of her frequent visits with her 7-year-old niece, who in a typical conversation "chats about the day, or things that are bugging her, and her [twin] sister. She always has to complain about her sister." In these sorts of ordinary circumstance, aunts and uncles can offer direct advice in dealing with siblings or understanding another's perspective, or they may simply listen to the concerns of their nieces and nephews without judgment and thus provide emotional support. For instance, of his uncle, Heath says, "It is not necessary for him to give advice, just listen."

Yet another important and common element of kin work involves sharing information about third parties. Such conversations reestablish common interests and common knowledge and thereby solidify the interdependencies linking family members. Yvette and her aunt talk about Yvette's younger sister. "My mom's been having a hard time with my sister because she is 17 and all that. [My aunt and I] talk about [my sister] all the time actually."

Conversations about third parties, although common, are not necessarily positive in their tone or likely consequences. Yvette and her aunt also talk about the new wife of one of Yvette's uncles. Neither aunt nor niece approve of or especially like the new member of the family. "We just trash-talk her," Yvette says. She goes on to observe that having negative opinions about others and sharing them does not necessarily facilitate constructive conversation. On the other hand, such talk can function to distinguish a family's unique identity, membership, and meaning from images of outsiders and the new values, attitudes, and customs they represent. The challenge for families is to balance the innovations and new resources that new family members occasion with an interest in maintaining long-standing traditions that define family identities.

Sharing information about third parties is an important way that family members keep informed of one another's activities and well-being; it often includes an evaluative component, although subtly so. Zoey acts as a conduit of news about her brother for her aunt and mother, and both rely on her for such news, which they cannot obtain directly. Zoey notes that she is really close to her brother, although she readily admits he is not terribly communicative and does not return phone calls. "He's just in his own world, doing other things, [and] that's just how he's always been." Zoey manages to stay in contact with her brother and in a way ennobles his lack of sociability by casting it in the realm of consistent and acceptable behavior. She laughs as she recalls her parents' typical reaction to her brother: "[My parents] are always like, 'why do you even have a cell phone? You don't even answer it.'" By serving as a communication link between her brother, mother, and aunt and by casting her brother's lack of responsiveness as an acceptable component of an otherwise loveable person, Zoey ensures that mother and aunt are informed and any conflict over her brother's unresponsiveness is minimized.

Uncle Jessie relies on his 18-year-old nephew for advice regarding some members of the family, particularly his "wife's side," people whom he believes his nephew knows better. He regards his nephew as "a little more level headed [than his wife] when it comes to realizing there are flaws in his family as well as everyone's." "So I am able to talk things out with him. He's a very mature young man," Jessie says.

Perhaps one of the most expressive instances of family work, and one that demonstrates the permeability of family relationships, occurred in my interview with Cora. As she explained, "the things I tell my mom often get retold to everyone else," and by this Cora especially meant her aunts. She shared an example of asking her mom not to tell her sisters about a new boyfriend, and especially not to say anything about his nose ring or tattoos. Cora wanted her new friend to be judged on his own merits and felt certain he would make a good impression in person. "And sure enough [my mom] told them so they knew ahead of time," Cora says with some degree of consternation. My guess is that in small-town Maine, nose rings and tattoos are delectable topics of conversation.

Later in our interview Cora reflected back on her mother and her sisters. "Yeah, I'm pretty open. There isn't a lot that I hide from them." Family intimacies are born of such shared knowledge, family intimacies that transcend households.

Family-centered kin keeping commonly appears when aunts and uncles plan special events with their nieces and nephews. Aunt Ilse and her niece Lana, for instance, planned an elaborate dinner and menu in celebration of the anniversary of Lana's parents. The family gathering was a surprise for Lana's parents and orchestrated entirely by Lana and Aunt Ilse. The joint activity is now a remembrance for Lana and Ilse, a fond memory of something they did together. It is likely a remembrance for Lana's parents, and perhaps other family members as well.

Zoey and her aunt planned a surprise birthday party for Zoey's grandmother, who turned 80. The entire clan attended the event. Certainly Zoey and her aunt's planning was an important element in building their own relationship, their relationship with Zoey's grandmother, and the relationship between an aunt and her mother. Birthday parties, weddings, and anniversary celebrations can reach much further, however, and have implications for all family members and their understanding of their own unique imprint. These events may center on an individual or couple, but they are as well celebrations of entire families and instances of family-centered kin keeping. One hopes such events go well, that conflicts are minimal, that Uncle Ronnie does not become belligerent, that nobody takes their clothes off in the exuberance of a moment, that no one's feelings are hurt, and that all return home safely. Perfection is not possible, however. Sometimes people act badly. Not all kin work has positive intensions or outcomes. Fortunately it commonly does.

INTERGENERATIONAL BUFFERS

Aunts and uncles can act as buffers in the inevitable daily conflicts that ensue among family members, and they do so in a variety of ways with varying success. Uncles and aunts bring to bear their own personal experience and knowledge of parents and in this way act as *comparative mediators* in conflicts between nephews, nieces, and their parents, siblings, or other family members.

> When I decided not to take some standardized tests in high school, my parents were upset. My uncle told a story of when my father was young and in his last year of high school. He bought a motorcycle and took off from school. He went to Virginia for three months and that kind of put things in perspective. Nothing I would do was anywhere near as significant. The whole family laughed about that. (Gaston, age 21)

In this instance, an uncle acted as a mediator between Gaston and his parents in a comparative style by recalling a past bit of adolescent bravado on the part of Gaston's father at a young age. From the perspective of Gaston, his uncle's storytelling had the effect of ameliorating any concern his parent's had regarding his own more recent indiscretions.

Nieces and nephews spoke about how their aunts and uncles were able to "bridge the gap" between themselves and their parents. Aunts and uncles did so by reminding parents of their own experiences as children, adolescences, or young adults and by sharing their contemporary experiences as parents.

Archie's parents left him in charge of their home while they were off for a weekend holiday. We might ask: will Archie act responsibly in his newfound caretaking capacity, or will he stage an evening gathering of friends? When his parents returned home, they were surprised by a few broken furnishings, and what looked like the aftermath of a home invasion. Here again, an uncle intervened. Archie remembers his uncle spoke to his parents saying: "Don't worry about it. The same thing happened with me and my kids. I came home and there were people lying in the bathtub." Archie said this "sort of calmed" his parents. I asked him if it was a good party. He replied: "Yeah, Mom and Dad still talk about it every time they go away. 'Don't trash the house,' they say." The initial transgression has now become part of the family lore, with an uncle and his relationships to parents and nephew central to the drama. The incident also suggests that perfection is not of this world, and certainly not of adolescence. Aunts and uncles can help remind us when we most need the reminder.

In addition to this form of comparative mediation, aunts and uncles intervened directly by acting as either *partisan supporters or critics* of nieces and nephews in their disputes with parents.

RM: Does [your nephew] talk about having arguments with his dad?

Yes [but] it really depends on what the argument was. A lot of times he gets told to suck it up. [Or] sometimes I say I'll talk to your dad or I'll talk to your mom. I really am this buffer in between them. (Uncle John)

Aunts and uncles seem to side at times with nieces and nephews and at times with parents. They encourage children and parents to empathize with one another by reminding nieces and nephews of their parents' good intensions and love for them and by reminding parents of their own adolescent indiscretions.

Una has her share of disputes with her mother. Although mom likes Una's boyfriend, she doesn't quite approve of them living together, and then there is the issue of Una's plans to go south for spring break, which mom definitely doesn't like. Una's aunt supports her in many ways, including her vacation plans, but at the same time encourages her to try and understand her mother's perspective. I asked Una if her aunt was helpful. "I think I understand what she's trying to say, I just don't accept it." Not all interventions are successful, or successful in the ways intended.

Janice described how her parents divorced and her mom was "constantly bad mouthing" her father. "You can only take so much of that," she said.

Janice's aunt often stepped in, acting as an intermediary and encouraging her parents to refrain from casting their daughter in the midst of their personal disputes, consciously or not. Janice's aunt supported her by encouraging civil behavior between her parents.

Certainly not all nieces experienced long-standing conflict with their mothers or fathers, but it does seem common enough to warrant attention. Of the 28 aunts with nieces older than 12 and of the 21 nieces I interviewed, 13 reported relationships among mothers and daughters that were high in conflict.[6] Among fathers and sons, conflicted relationships are less likely, but then again fathers are more likely to be entirely inactive.[7]

Aunts often report intervening in such conflicts when they do occur. Susan, for instance, reported a good deal of conflict between her niece, Nika, and her niece's mother, Susan's sister. In fact, Susan is close to each of her three nieces and keeps in regular contact. I interviewed her at her rural home just before she packed up her young son and left for a business meeting. As we began talking about her nieces, she drew out photos of each and displayed them with obvious pride. Nika's parents divorced when she was young, and Susan often provided child care. She continues to be a confidant for her niece, and her niece continues to experience conflict with her mother. Susan says there has always been "kind of a thing" between mother and daughter. I asked if by "kind of a thing" she meant a competition. "I don't know if it would be a competition," she said. "They've always had kind of a rub between them, and they still do. I've always been a kind of balancing wheel because I'm very close to her mother, and I'm very close to [Nika]." Whether the relationship between mother and daughter could be characterized as competitive is not entirely clear, but it is suggested in some regards. For instance, when Nika planned her wedding for late September, her mother planned her own remarriage for earlier that very September, much to the chagrin of her daughter. Perhaps the more important issue is that relationships between parents and children can be complex; conflict can be routine. When conflicts do emerge as a constant, aunts can serve as singular mediators, as Susan did throughout her niece's childhood, adolescence, and young adulthood.

---

[6] Aunts were less likely to report high-conflict relationships between nieces and their mothers (5 of 28; 18%) than nieces (8 of 21; 38%). For a discussion of mother–daughter relationships across three generations including those high and relatively low in conflict, see Miller-Day (2004).
[7] Of those nephews who lived with or visited their fathers, approximately 4 of 43 had high-conflict relationships with fathers. Recall, however, that 8 nephews had little or no contact with their biological fathers.

No doubt issues of separation and identity development can be difficult for both parents and adolescents, and aunts and uncles can ease those transitions. Estella believes she is closer to her aunt than to her mother and often stays with her aunt when she returns home rather than with either of her divorced parents. When she first applied to a highly competitive university and planned to major in engineering, the move from her home in the southwestern United States to a major metropolitan center in the Midwest did not excite her mother. "I fought my mom a lot on letting me go there when I got the acceptance letter. Finally she bought a plane ticket so that I could go to school. I was really excited about that." Later in the interview, Estella added: "It was her final acceptance of letting me go I guess." Throughout this period, Estella's aunt, who happens to be single and an engineer herself, supported her niece but at the same time encouraged her to be more understanding of her mother.

As often as aunts and uncles supported their nieces and nephews, they just as commonly supported parents. Fiona is close to both her aunt and her mother and routinely seeks out the advice of both adult women, although she is more apt to go to her aunt when the issue is "embarrassing," which she explained as "things you would not talk with your mother about." Fiona then added that she turns to her aunt for "a second opinion when I don't agree with things my mom says. But she always says the same thing as my mom." The impression is one of close, supportive relationships among daughter, mother, and aunt and a good deal of communal parenting. Later in the interview Fiona shared that "[My aunt] is just very supportive and also very protective of her big sister [my mother] and tries to stick up for her." Fiona's comment suggests that there is more to the relationship of aunt and mother, that it is not simply a matter of an aunt acting in ways that are supportive of a parent. Their relationship has deeper, older sources that are rooted firmly in the lifelong intimacy of sisters, and because of this foundation, it is irreplaceable.

The context of lifelong relationships among siblings is important because it can influence relationships among aunts and uncles with their nieces and nephews, but that context is not always a positive influence. When I asked Mark if his uncle was ever critical, he replied: "No, if anything he is sort of an enabler of deviant behavior to the extent that he would cover up, say, if I was out late." Mark explained that his uncle believed his mother was too controlling, just as she was with Mark's uncle when he was a child. In this instance, the relational history of Mark's mother and uncle when they were young continues to influence their current relationship as well as that of Mark and his uncle.

Of course, support does not always imply agreement. At times aunts and uncles were clearly critical of their nieces and nephews and the actions they took, or choices made. Of her aunt, Elspeth said: "Yeah, she's definitely told me, you know, you're being an idiot here. Wake up and smell the coffee." At the same time, Elspeth's aunt shared her own experience as a teenager for whom conflicts with her own mom were common. In this way, Elspeth's aunt essentially normalized mother–teen daughter conflict, while expecting her niece to be more understanding of her parents and more civil in her actions.

Aunts and uncles alike often laced their partisan positions with calls for better understanding of family members. They were often quick to recall attempts to encourage their nieces and nephews to appreciate their parents' positions. Francesca explained how her niece has relatively few conflicts with her parents, but her nephew has a more turbulent relationship and moved in with his aunt for several months. Her nephew would complain that his mom is "always nagging on me," to which Francesca replied, "that's part of a parent's job to nag. What do you think my parents did? They nagged."

The interviews were replete with the promotion of empathy. In a typical conversation, nieces and nephews issue a complaint about parents. It can be, and often is, of a general nature such as, "My mother is driving me crazy," or a complaint may concern a specific instance of injustice, such as "my father won't let me buy a horse." Aunts and uncles encourage their nieces and nephews to understand their parents' position, their motivations, and their worries, and they recognized that sometimes nieces and nephews just need to complain.

In some instances, the low emotional tone of relationships with aunts and uncles allows nieces and nephews to hear another perspective and gain some insight into their parent's positions. Aunts and uncles can share the same essential message with nieces and nephews but get a very different response from that received by parents.

> If my mother and I were fighting about something I could talk to my aunt and hash it out and I didn't have the same aggravation talking to her about things as I did with my mom.

> My aunt helped me look at the problem through [my mother's] eyes . . . and [my aunt would say], "you really shouldn't be going out with boys until 2 in the morning."

> She would say "I don't blame your mother for being upset" but . . . she would sort of change it around so I could see it. And I would never be angry with her 'cause she was always so nice.

Janice seemed to have more than the usual amount of conflict with her mother, perhaps complicated by her parent's divorce when she was 18 and her estranged relationship with her father. Fortunately she has had a close relationship with her aunt, who is uniquely able to encourage some understanding of Janice's mother. Although Janice might not be able to voice agreement directly with her mother's position that as a young teenager she should not be "going out with boys until 2 in the morning," her comment suggests she is able to come to an understanding of her mother's sentiment, an understanding her aunt was able to promote if not entirely orchestrate.

In other cases, parents seem to be well aware of the limitations of their ability to give their children advice in contested areas, and parents actively encouraged relationships with aunts and uncles who acted as intermediaries. At other times, mothers and fathers actively sought out the advice of aunts or uncles regarding their children. In one instance, a father of an 18-year-old son relied on his brother as a mediator, an indirect line of additional communication with his son, as well as an intimate with whom the father discussed his experience of fathering with its occasional frustrations. Uncles can act as a buffer for both sons and fathers, and similarly aunts may act as intergenerational buffers. Denise's brother will often call her when his 7-year-old daughter is being particularly challenging. He'll say, "Lauren wants to talk with you. She just had a meltdown." Denise does her part by first hearing her brother's request and then listening to her niece's complaint and later encouraging her to be mindful of her own actions and their consequences. Dorthea has a similar relationship with her sister and her sister's adolescent daughter and often serves as an intermediary, one on whom her sister relies. "Sometimes [my sister] will call me when they [mother and daughter] had a big blow-out fight. She'll say, 'Here talk to her!'" Dorthea says that mother and daughter have "fights over make-up, clothing, weather." Dorthea seems well suited to the role of family ambassador.

Although many aunts and uncles successfully enact their roles as inter-generational buffers, there are instances when they clearly fail to do so. One uncle shared such an instance. I asked Sammy if he ever discussed family matters with his nephew.

Not really. Five or six years ago my sister [Carla] divorced from her [second] husband. [My nephew] was pretty attached to his [stepdad]. They had a lot of things in common. They were both carpenters. And when she divorced [my nephew] was pretty upset about that. He liked [his stepfather] and didn't really want them to split up. And to make matters worse, she then moved a couple hours away and he really felt like he was abandoned by her even though at this point he was in his mid-20s. Still he was pretty bitter about it. Everybody knew about it but I don't know that anybody really sat and had a heart-to-heart with him about it.

Here the relationship between uncle and nephew never seemed to develop, and one consequence is that there was little or no opportunity for the nephew to share his concerns or for the uncle to intervene on behalf of his nephew or mother. Later in the interview, Sammy shared that his nephew "keeps his distance" from the family and how his sister Carla complains that her son seldom visits. In fact, Sammy is fairly well informed about his nephew and Carla's concerns. The family relationships are complex and overlapping. Sammy speaks with his mother daily by e-mail, and she in turn speaks daily with Carla. Sammy also speaks directly with Carla several times per month, and his wife speaks with Carla more often. Although the family actively communicates, Sammy's relationship with his nephew has never flourished.

MEANING KEEPERS

Aunts and uncles participate in family work of a more general nature by encouraging a sense of family togetherness, and they do so through the practice of creating and participating in family traditions, rituals, and storytelling – activities that maintain a family's unique biography and each individual's sense of self. In fact the two overlap; individual and family biographies are cowritten, neither existing without the other, and each is threaded into generations past and future.

Family traditions commonly take the form of spending holidays together as well as enjoying more frequent visits. Aunts and uncles spoke of weekly get-togethers where family members freely visited one another, events that are variously organized around meals and evening or weekend get-togethers.[8] Some events are more ritualized than others, some more or less organized, but all share the common purpose of encouraging mutual interaction and celebration among family members. John routinely visits his niece and her single mother, John's sister. Once a year they take a vacation as a family. John is single and gay. He says of these outings: "[My niece's] mom is a student and they have no money. We travel as a family. So it's a really nice thing for everybody. It gives me a sense of actually having a family."

---

[8] At least 29% of the aunts and uncles in this study visit their siblings weekly.

And it gives my niece overseas trips, which is great when you are a kid." John is equally generous and committed to visiting his brother, sister-in-law, and teenage nephew, of whom he says, "nothing comes before him at all." For many uncles and aunts, social worlds are constructed around frequent visits with their parents, adult siblings, and their children. For John visits with his siblings and their children are especially significant because these occasions provide him with a sense of family membership and an opportunity to parent children.

For gay uncles and lesbian aunts who are childless, their roles as uncles and aunts respectively may be a particularly important route through which they gain access to parents and their children and the heightened sense of family membership these relationships provide. In a study of gays and lesbians and their relationships with straight friends, Anna Muraco examines how gay males develop close relationships with their straight female friends, who provide them with opportunities to mentor children. For instance, "Scott explained that through his 25-year friendship with Ruth and her now-teenage daughter, he has been able to experience childrearing."[9] In this instance, Ruth and her daughter became de facto members of Scott's chosen family with likely consequences for his lifelong friendship with Ruth and her daughter, and perhaps for his own development as well. Curiously, previous inquiries report that gay men engage in more kin work than their lesbian counterparts, which would appear entirely inconsistent with the typical gendered practices in which women are more active.[10]

Aunt Connie spoke of monthly parties in which all birthdays occurring in a given month are celebrated. Connie and her sisters recently orchestrated this as a solution to overcrowded social calendars when as many as seven family birthdays occur in a given month. Otherwise, as Connie says, "if you work full time you're always going to someone's house every night, and even though I enjoy it, it cuts into your time." Alexandra spoke of *Friday fudge nights* where all of her sisters, brothers, and their spouses and children would gather at her mother's home. "That's where everything was decided," she recalled. "How people would vote [and] how they felt about certain issues." Personal biographies are public constructions, at least in part.

Maya, her sisters, and their daughters gather on Sunday afternoons at her mother's home. Maya attends the gatherings but "only if I have a chance," suggesting the somewhat informal nature of the gatherings. A fete they are not. I asked her where the men were. Although her husband works on

[9] Muraco, 2006, p. 1319.
[10] Blumstein & Schwartz, 1983; Carrington, 1999.

weekends, the husbands of her sisters – she has three – stay at home. I then asked if she, her mother, and her sisters ever talk about the absence of the men. "No," she said, "we never really talk about that."

Fiona spoke about her family's social gatherings, which often involve outdoor bonfires with gender segregation, where "the men talk about sports, and the women talk about life." As an element of family gatherings, bonfires are not an uncommon tradition among rural Maine families, although I cannot speak about the gendered separation of sports and life, having participated only in the one.

In each of these families, and many more about which aunts, uncles, nieces, and nephews spoke, routine family gatherings were important and highly valued. Routine gatherings probably have an element of demand or common expectation that family members will attend, but there is also an element of personal discretion. Connie parenthetically notes how too many gatherings can "cut into your time," and Maya attends weekly gatherings of her mother and sisters but "only if I get a chance." For some families, routine gatherings are relatively ungendered; both men and women attend as do their children. Alexandra describes Friday fudge nights that are socially integrated, although the labor involved in producing them may not be. We might ask who made the fudge. Likely it was women, which is yet another ingredient of kin keeping.

For others, gatherings are gendered. For instance adult sisters gather, often including their daughters, at the home of their mother or a sister, and occasionally their gatherings are organized around public events such as shopping, concerts, and dining out. Connie and her sisters plan occasional trips together to urban areas. Their most recent involved a trip to New York City in which the sisters "got two hours of sleep every night," and not insignificantly Connie's favored niece was invited to come. "She's one of us now," Connie says.

For some, family gatherings occur only rarely and on major holidays such as Thanksgiving or Christmas. Geographic distance can separate families and limit their visiting, as may long-standing feuds. In these cases, although contact across households was limited, I did not get the impression it was not valued, at least in principle.

Beatrice recalled an unpleasant episode that occurred in her childhood involving a dispute among her parents and their siblings after which visiting ceased. As children, Beatrice and her sisters made a pact that such a falling out would never happen to them. Having missed the opportunity to develop relationships with her own aunts, uncles, and cousins, she and her siblings are now committed to providing such opportunities for their own children.

It is an unusual story in that Beatrice links visiting with her siblings and their children back to her own childhood experience and a decision on the part of her and her siblings to value family togetherness in their own adult lives, which they now enact in a truly generative fashion.

Holidays are especially valued and often laden with rituals, some distinctly in the service of kin keeping and a concern for future generations. Cora's family is especially inventive. Every Christmas her aunt prepares calendars for each of her siblings' families on which birthdays, anniversaries, and dates significant to the wider family are noted. On Christmas, each family member brings a gift for the future, gifts that are encased in a time capsule to be opened in the distant future. Of course there are immediate needs that are well recognized. Cora's mom places whoopee pies in each person's Christmas stocking. Whoopee pies are a traditional Maine treat available throughout the year in nearly every country store and consisting of some sort of white, creamy, disgustingly sweet confection sandwiched between two portions of chocolate cake. I have never tried one, but I hope to someday when fortitude is at a premium, and indiscretion is unbounded.

Building a sense of family commonly occurred as aunts and uncles shared stories about family members, particularly about the parents of nieces and nephews, and in doing so acknowledged the family's unique history.[11] Storytelling serves a number of purposes. Stories recount significant events, relational histories, or personal anecdotes. They can underscore a common shared biography, a unique lesson, or simply serve as dramatic entertainment. The purpose and effects of storytelling are often far reaching because they promote a common sense of a family's origin, an enriched understanding of others, and a comparative understanding of the self.[12]

Stella and her husband create scrapbooks of family vacations, holidays, and significant family events. For Stella, the books are an important way to reckon her family's history.

> It's not just a matter of putting that picture there, but you write about what's going on, what it means to you.... It's about family history, putting down memories, telling about things that have happened [and] what we want to remember, because even though we say we're always going to remember, your mind has ways that you don't. By putting these down on paper, you can be artistic with it if you want, you can be as creative or as uncreative as you want to, but the important thing is to tell that story . . . so

[11] Slightly more than half of uncles (57%, or 12 cases) and nephews (55%, or 17 cases) reported instances of family storytelling, as did most aunts (72%, or 22 cases) and nieces (95%, or 20 cases).
[12] Langellier & Peterson, 2004.

that when someone's not around you can look at that picture and know who, what, where, and when.... [The contents of the scrapbooks] are things I want to remember and years from now I want other people to see.

Stella is surprisingly insightful, committed, and organized in her recording of family history, articulate in her understanding of its importance, and certainly generative in her compiling of memories for future generations. She shares her passion with her niece, and they occupy a day constructing a scrapbook as a gift for a friend. "It's wonderful," she says. "You sit and talk while you are doing it and its one of those things where all of the sudden the day is gone." In Stella's family, scrapbooks are often the focus of visits, encouraging family members to reminisce, to recount stories and thus co-construct the joint enterprise of family, framing what each member brings to that enterprise and what each takes away. Family identities, and to a certain extent personal identities, are defined and embossed for future generations. I wonder, too, if they are not continuously being re-created as the scrapbooks are discussed among brothers, sisters, parents, and children and details are added along with personal reflections unique to each person. Through their conversations, memories become a negotiated co-construction in much the same way that couples, when recalling events of the past – perhaps a vacation or holiday – each add unique details that prompt one another's recall and add to the detail and significance of the story being told.[13] Michele recalls how her mother and aunt tell stories together "because what one can't remember the other one does." Memories are transactive affairs, socially constructed and re-created over time.

Most aunts and uncles I interviewed were not quite as organized as Stella or as structured in their treatment of family storytelling, although some were equally deliberate, or nearly so. Evin provides his version of the family's history in answering a query from his nephew. "He's very interested in the extended family, understanding who is out there. I organized a family reunion and gave him a family history." By learning about his relations, Evin's nephew may gain a better understanding of himself and his extended family and perhaps a renewed sense of belonging. Barbara remarks how family history and genealogy "keeps you connected, rooted in a way." Barbara's mother started the local historical society and also served as her family's personal historian, a role that has now been passed on to Barbara. "We enjoy talking to each other," she says of her siblings and their families, and

---

[13] For a discussion of jointly constructed memories among couples, or *transactive memory*, see Wegner, Erber, and Raymond (1991).

then with a smile adds, "We're a great crowd of people that don't solve any problems." For Barbara's family, and many families like theirs, storytelling is a valued and routine part of their interactions.

Storytelling can also have a measure of entertainment value. Janice, Cora, and Zoey all mentioned laughter – stories told and retold because they are fun, for both the actors and audience, as well as instrumental in emphasizing common experiences unique to each family. "She's a good storyteller," Janice says of her aunt. "I like her stories because she gets so incredibly worked up that she will cry; she will get laughing so hard. It's fun to see."

In the sharing of personal experiences – and especially stories about parents as young children, adolescents, and young adults – aunts and uncles help their nieces and nephews gain a better perspective on family members. The consequence of doing so is to help nieces and nephews understand themselves and their origins as well as that of their parents. Al does not consider himself the family storyteller per se – "I think my sister is probably the bigger storyteller than I am" – but nonetheless he does provide his nephew with a perspective. "Yeah there are some stories about his father in high school, I mean because I went to high school with him and stuff. I can sort of talk about the crazy things we did." Family storytelling provides nieces and nephews with information about their parents or family history that is otherwise unavailable. Rog speaks of his uncle: "You get the old family stories. What Dad used to be like sort of thing. It is quite helpful, because Dad, being the sort of person he is, isn't likely to pass the information on his own in a lot of cases."

Nieces and nephew rely on aunts and uncles to help them understand relational histories (e.g., why a parent might not get along with a grand-parent) or personal idiosyncrasies (e.g., why a parent might seem overly concerned with finances). Mark uses the information about his mother's early experience provided by his uncle to better understand her current actions.

> I wouldn't say I really ask for advice – like how I should deal with my mother – but I definitely like to inquire about their relationship when they were younger. . . . Kind of like from a historic vantage point, where is my mother coming from. So it allows a little deeper understanding of the present without asking him "I'm having a problem with my mom, how should I deal with it right now?"

At times nieces and nephews actively sought out such information in an attempt to understand themselves, their parents, and occasionally their grandparents, aunts, and uncles. This form of storytelling is especially important when family histories are complex and nieces or nephews are estranged from a parent, typically fathers. In one case, an uncle, Greco, described a reunion with his nephew whom he hadn't seen in many years. In fact, Greco had been estranged from his stepsister and her children, as well as his own children, with whom he is just beginning to reestablish contact.

> It really started when I had to go into the hospital. My nephew, who is 26... wanted to come and see me in the hospital. I hadn't seen him since he was 7 or 8. He felt that there was a large void in his family, in his awareness of this family, awareness of himself, or whatever. I had gone through some years where I had some trouble. I had trouble with booze, trouble with drugs.
>
> [My nephew] really asked a lot of questions. He wanted to know about stuff I had done in the past. What it was like growing up with my sister. And he wanted to share what he knew about his mother. Hearing about her as a sister and sharing his feeling about her as a mother and how those two stories sort of match.... He also wanted to know about things that could make it easier to understand his brothers because they all had been involved with different fathers.
>
> *RM: Were you able to help [your nephew] understand his mother better?*
>
> Well I have to imagine that it did. He didn't understand how many changes she had gone through.

In this case, Greco was able to provide a perspective that was important to his nephew in his attempt to understand his own family. The reunion provided the nephew with details about a number of family members, including his mother, father, and stepfathers. Greco's nephew gained insight into why his parents divorced, the challenges that faced his mother as a single parent, and some qualities in his family that were not very flattering, including his uncle's substance abuse. The contact, which began when Greco was gravely ill in a hospital, was also important to Greco's own development. Later in the interview, Greco said: "I mean it was like from the mouths of babes comes all this wisdom about how you just have to keep trying to keep the communication going in families." Audience and actor are mutually influenced, each reconnected to one another and their respective families. Greco's story illustrates how storytelling contributes to the development of personal identities, providing an enriched understandings of others and ultimately oneself.

At times aunts and uncles provide information about parents indirectly and perhaps unwittingly, especially when parents and their siblings engage one another as playmates and social companions. In these circumstances, nieces and nephews gain insights into their parents as individuals. Buddy's comments about his uncle and mother are illustrative:

> When [my uncle] and my mother get together my mother tends to become a completely different person. He has got quite a calming effect on her. Often around home she'll let the smallest thing worry her. She doesn't worry a lot when she is with my uncle. They are often just there to have fun. It is quite good to see her like that.

For Buddy, interactions between his uncle and mother *transform his attention* by allowing him to cast his mother in a broader role, rather than as simply a parent who, in his words, "annoyed him." Transformations of attention can be an important and unique opportunity for nephews and nieces to view their parents in roles they may not otherwise reveal. When parents interact with siblings and friends, they are not necessarily parents, but spirited playmates. Janice recalls how her mother, when in the company of her mother's friends and sisters, becomes a different person who is "silly [and] talks about inappropriate things [like] guys, dating." Janice draws the line however in refusing to go dancing with her mom and her "50-year-old friends at the local dance hall." She says, "I love you mom, but it's really not my bag."

Angela sees her mom transform when she interacts with her sisters. In this circumstance, her mom laughs more and is more fun, whereas at home mom "gets upset about little things, like [if] the house is not clean." In this instance and it seems in many others as well, both mother's and daughter's attention are transformed; each is able to see the other in a new light.

Aunts and uncles were often entirely aware of such transformations. Pat believed his nephew benefited from observing him, his sister, and their other brother interact. "Watching us interact was kind of like watching people who knew each other from a different world. . . . I think [my nephew] learned a lot because my sister acts a bit different when I am there."

In other instances, aunts and uncles, through their direct storytelling with nieces and nephews, can help them transform the way they view their parents or how they understand their parents as unique individuals. Raymond's uncle has shared stories with him about his father as a young man. Raymond says, "Things that my father would never admit to me. Through [my uncle] I saw my father as a person just like me." With great insight on his own part, Raymond understands that his uncle sees in him his father as a young man; in a sense, their relationship is a way for his uncle to reconnect with his past and perhaps with his relationship with his brother (Raymond's father). For Raymond, his uncle's reminiscing has the effect of allowing him to understand his father and his own similarities to a man he does not know very well. Of his relationship with his father, Raymond says: "It's like two adults sitting in a bar talking about the weather. We don't really have a father–son relationship."

CONCLUSION

Generative communities require intergenerational buffers and meaning keepers, both of which are central components of kin keeping and the enterprise of sustaining families. Kin keeping can be simply defined as "efforts expended on behalf of keeping family members in touch with one another."[14] Among these efforts are expressions of kin keeping that are demonstrative, direct, and visible (e.g., an uncle encourages his nephew to communicate more regularly with his parents) and expressions that are less visible and direct (e.g., an aunt worries about her niece's adjustment to a parental divorce and queries a third party about the niece's well-being). This basic framework can usefully be expanded to include a variety of activities, including facilitating communication among family members and thus sharing knowledge and coming to understand one another's past experiences, current activities, and future aspirations. Kin keeping also commonly includes the provision of services and exchanges of support, sanctioning behavior considered inappropriate, the organization of celebrations and gatherings, the creation of rituals (e.g., family fudge nights), administrative labor directed at maintaining ties and family record keeping, and the making of decisions regarding intensifying or neglecting ties.[15] Although one individual family member is often regarded as primarily responsible for kin keeping, usually a grandmother or elder sister,[16] our inquiry demonstrates that the expression of kin keeping and the work associated with developing and maintaining ties with kin involves a variety of family members including aunts and uncles, their siblings, and partners of siblings, in addition to nieces and nephews. Virtually all of the forms of kin keeping appear in our inquiry, and many of our respondents, including young adults, reported engaging in kin-keeping activities. It is perhaps an oversimplification to regard kin keeping as the providence of a single family member.

Kin keeping is the work family members engage to develop and sustain their relationships and maintain their view of a common family culture. As

---

[14] Rosenthal, 1985, p. 965.
[15] Regarding the construction of kin groups and the deliberate inclusion or exclusion of members, see Carrington, 1999; di Leonardo, 1987; Leach & Braithwaite, 1996.
[16] Rosenthal, 1985; Leach & Braithwaite, 1996.

this chapter has demonstrated, family work can serve to promote understanding and knowledge of another. Uncle Greco shared stories with his nephew about his mother and her life in the hope of increasing his nephew's understanding of his mother. On the other hand, family work can also serve to promote disengagement. An aunt encouraged her niece to distance herself from her father's destructive behaviors.

We examined four forms of family work or social locations in which individuals participate in kin keeping. These included talk about relationships with parents; talk about other family members including the siblings of aunts and uncles, the siblings of nieces and nephews, and grandparents; intergenerational buffering and in particular occasions when one family member acts as a comparative mediator, partisan supporter, or critic of another family member; and finally instances of family storytelling, an activity that directly services the co-construction of personal and family biographies.

A concern for future generations advances when older community members advocate for younger members as well as each other. Aunts and uncles at times advocate for nieces and nephews and just as commonly they advocate for parents. In this mix, it is difficult to separate an aunt's concern for her niece from her concern for her niece's parents, one of whom is often a sibling. Generative action is relational in origin and expression and often crosses multiple generations.

Similarly, generativity appears when older members share their experiences and knowledge of family members. Meaning keeping and storytelling are generative actions firmly rooted in multiple overlapping relationships. Multiple family members often participate in the construction, assembly, and interpretation of stories. We see instances of this joint construction when families, like Stella's, gather around family photo albums, each sharing in the storytelling, each contributing their unique memories and interpretations. In this way, family storytelling is often a transactive affair with each member contributing his or her own recounting of events and contributing details that may not be available to others. Generative actions occur routinely among the aunts and uncles, nieces and nephews in this study, but the generative culture of families is broader, more textured, and diverse and occurs in a social configuration of overlapping relationships and households.

Of course not all stories are told. Not all aunts and uncles are equally supportive of their nieces and nephews or their parents. Not all family relationships are generative, and we should be mindful of such limitations. Aunts and uncles, perhaps quite commonly, fail to develop significant relationships with their nieces and nephews. From this study, we cannot say with any certainty just how often meaningful relationships emerge, or just how often they fail to do so. We can infer that relationships vary in closeness; some are highly valued, and some are complex intersections of multiple generations.

We have seen here how kin keeping emerges as an important way to view the relationships of aunts and uncles with their nieces and nephews as well as other family members – most notably, parents and grandparents. Kin keeping is largely generative action; although often seen as the providence of women, this, too, differs across families. In some, like those of Connie and Maya, gatherings of kin largely revolve around mothers and sisters who occasionally include their adult or near adult nieces in their social events. However, some families seemed to be less segregated by gender, as in Aunt Alexandra's family, where sisters, brothers, spouses, and children gather for Friday fudge nights, "where everything is decided." Some parents routinely relied on their siblings to support their parenting, and this appeared in relationships with uncles as well as aunts. Kin keeping is clearly a central feature of many families, an activity that is at times rewarding and highly valued and a critical element of generativity. Concerns for future generations are largely expressed through relations with kin.

When families work well and when members are able to maintain frequent contact, kin keeping is often reciprocal; generativity is often a mix of reciprocal caregiving. Although aunts and uncles support their nieces and nephews by complementing the work that parents do or by acting as surrogate parents, they are just as often nurtured by the very children for whom they are responsible, at least in part. "From the mouth of babes came all this wisdom," said one uncle. Aunts and uncles often rely on their younger relatives to better understand and negotiate family matters. Nieces and nephews enact their concerns for people who are important to them, such as aunts, uncles, and grandparents. Generativity is lived within a context of multiple generations and represents a concern for future generations shared by both young and old.

7

Friendship

In the mix of generative roles, whether aunts and uncles are acting as mentors or family historians, engaging in partisan support or intergenerational mediation, there are many instances in which their relationships with nieces and nephews take on the character of a friendship.[1] Aunts and nieces, uncles and nephews share common interests and spend time together engaged in those interests. They offer each other advice, often about family members, and at other times plainly enjoy one another's company. A similarity of interests and reciprocal provisions of support are common themes in friendship, but the longevity of their shared family relationships is perhaps not as common. It is the distinguishing feature that casts friendships among kin apart from those with nonkin, and it is one central feature from which generativity emerges. Aunts and uncles are unique among family members in that they share a long history with the parents of nieces and nephews as siblings, a history and role relationship that sets them apart from grandparents and frames their relationships with nieces and nephews, at times accelerating such relationships and at times discouraging them from developing.

INTIMACY AND COMMITMENT

Aunts and uncles may develop relationships with nieces and nephews that begin at birth and may include nearly all significant developmental milestones in infancy, childhood, adolescence, and early adulthood. This shared co-biography represents a depth and longevity of acquaintance that appears only rarely among nonkin. When I asked Beatrice how or even if her friendship with her niece differed from a friendship with an adult peer, she replied:

---

[1] Thirty-four of 52 aunts and nieces reported being friends, as did 16 of 52 uncles and nephews.

"I know the stories of her when she was a baby and I can talk about her first birthday party." Janice shared a similar sentiment about her aunt. "We have a shared history that goes back to my birth." The foundations of their relationships run deep. This common knowledge, a sharing of nearly all significant life experience pooled within common array of shared relationships, is irreplaceable. Intimacy is growing old together and sharing significant moments, as well as insignificant moments, that few others would know or even care to know. In contrast, friendships among nonkin are typically rather short-lived and based on shared interests as well as circumstance, much of which is ephemeral and subject to change. Alterations in occupations, living arrangements, and primary partnerships can lead to substantial changes in people's network of intimates. Even intimate ties are relatively unstable over time.

In a rare longitudinal panel study, sociologist Barry Wellman and his colleagues mapped the social ties of a small sample of Torontonians over 10 years.[2] Only 27% of the personal relationships with kin and friends that were considered intimate remained so over a decade. The ties individuals maintain with immediate kin are the most stable (i.e., parents, parents-in-law, siblings, and adult children), followed by extended kin and friends. In addition, the termination of primary partnerships, such as marriage, can significantly change the composition of one's personal ties. Approximately half of all predivorce contacts are lost following divorce, including relationships with in-laws and mutual friends once shared by spouses, and these net declines in the core networks of former partners seem to be persistent over subsequent years.[3] Resilient ties that span decades are relatively uncommon.

The friendships that develop between aunts and nieces and uncles and nephews seem to have at their core a number of additional features, and chief among them is a perceived commonality of interests and sensibilities. Those who regard their favored kin as close friends often emphasize qualities such as empathy or feeling understood, mutual support emotionally and instrumentally, resiliency or feeling like the friend will always be there for you, familiarity or feeling comfortable in the other's presence, mutuality and a balance of personal disclosures with each partner sharing personal intimacies with the other, trust and an interpersonal climate of unconditional acceptance, and an array of common interests including recreational pastimes. These are features that define the deep structure of close friendships among peers,[4] and as with unrelated peers, the

[2] Wellman, Wong, Tindall, & Nazer, 1997.   [3] Terhell, van Groenou, & van Tilburg, 2004.
[4] Hartup & Stevens, 1997; VanLear, Koerner, & Allen, 2006.

friendships that develop among kin are largely discretionary.[5] Partners have a certain degree of freedom in electing to develop a close relationship. Aunts and uncles may acknowledge a responsibility to mentor or at least take an interest in their nieces and nephews, but whether they develop a close friendship is a matter of personal choice on the part of both generations. In short, the qualities of friendship present among aunts and uncles with nieces and nephews parallels the prototypical qualities that comprise friendships among peers,[6] as well as the friendships of older adults.[7]

Certainly not all aunts develop close friendships with a niece and not all of their nieces become their friends. As noted earlier, cross-generational relationships are enhanced when personal conditions such as career commitments are not perceived as all consuming, when parents and their siblings enjoy positive relationships, and when family traditions and lore encourage relationships with kin both within and across generations. Geographic separation affects the development and maintenance of close relationships, but such limitations can be and often are overcome.

Although distance often separated Maya, who was 53 at the time of our interview, and her 41-year-old niece Vicky, their friendship continued to endure as they earned college degrees, developed careers, married, and had children. Maya says of her friendship with Vicky, "I would trust her more with my feelings than I would with anybody else. She knows me so well and she is a lot like me." Similarly Fiona speaks of her aunt as her best friend. "I'm closer to her than any friend," she says. Compatibility, common interests, and life experience combine to encourage their relationships. In both of these cases, aunt and niece were relatively similar in age, with 12 years separating them, a distance that likely became increasingly unimportant as the nieces aged. Fiona, who was 18 when interviewed, says of her aunt, "She is only 12 years older than me so she's more like a friend than an aunt." For some pairs, relative similarity of age may yield a greater sense of commonality,[8] although among children this is not likely to be a contributing factor. To a 9-year-old niece, the world of a 21-year-old aunt might seem distant, mysterious, inaccessible. Similarity of age is relative. The same age differences that separate a child and aunt (in these examples, 12 years) may seem rather trivial to an older niece. Nevertheless, we might usefully question how relationships with young children become enduring friendships as nieces transition into young adulthood.

[5] Allan, 1998; Finch & Mason, 1993; Spencer & Pahl, 2006.
[6] Allan, 2008; Davis & Todd, 1985; Spencer & Pahl, 2006; VanLear et al., 2006.
[7] Blieszner, 2006; Blieszner & Adams, 1992.   [8] Ellingson & Sotirin, 2006.

Two features seem to be important factors for both aunts and uncles: personal commitment and moral commitment. Here we borrow from the work of Michael Johnson and his colleagues, who distinguish between *personal commitment*, a commitment to follow a line of action based on individual discretion, and *moral commitment*, a belief that a particular line of action is the right thing to do based on a sense of morality, obligation, or duty.[9] Aunts and uncles who maintained close relationships with their nieces and nephews were similar in their abiding commitment to the longevity of their relationships. A personal commitment to seeing such relationships continue into the future and, to a certain extent, a moral commitment or belief that such relationships are the responsible course of action for family members combine to fuel the development of friendships. When I asked Beatrice what she expected of her relationship with her niece in the future, she replied: "It is my hope and expectation that it will remain close." She then added with determination, "I think she has a sense that I am committed to her for her whole life." John shares a similar sentiment when he says of his nephew that "he knows with me nothing comes before him at all."

Personal and moral commitments define essential qualities of personal relationships, or what we might refer to as *deep structures*, the core or essential underpinnings of relationships.[10] Deep structures such as commitment are thought to be more stable than surface structures, such as the typical activities in which partners engage. Developmental changes commonly trigger changes in surface structures in the sense of what partners do together and how often they do it. For instance, as nieces and nephews move through childhood, their needs change, idiosyncratic interests emerge, and the activities they engage in with their aunts and uncles likely change. Deep structures, like commitment, are apt to be more stable over time, and perhaps less apt to be influenced by developmental change. Consequently relationships that are based on blends of personal and moral commitment, as well as core attributes that typify adult friendships, like mutual compatibilities and mutual supportiveness, are apt to be more stable.

FORECASTING FRIENDSHIP

Eight of the aunts of young nieces explicitly spoke of their interest and keen anticipation in seeing their relationships develop into close friendships as

---

[9] M. P. Johnson, Caughlin, & Huston, 1999; for a comprehensive discussion of commitment, see Rusbult, Coolsen, Kirchner, & Clarke, 2006.
[10] Hartup & Stevens, 1997.

their nieces transition into adulthood. Not insignificantly, all of these aunts were themselves childless. Perhaps their status as childless adults provides aunts with the time and opportunity to invest in their relationships with favored nieces, and perhaps just as important, or more important, their nieces represented the children they did not have and the prospect of a highly valued lifelong intimate relationship. Here again the origin and expectations surrounding relationships among aunts and nieces, when they are close, are unique and differ from close associations among unrelated peers. I can hardly imagine an adult waiting for a neighbor's child to reach adulthood in anticipation of an enduring friendship emerging from their occasional, or even frequent, play sessions. The social fact of kinship is profoundly important and amplified for women and perhaps more so for childless women.

Sandy was planning a special birthday celebration for her niece, Mimi, who was soon to turn 16. The plan was to visit New York City, go to the theater, and visit the studio production of a television show. Sandy is herself married and childless and works as a playwright and producer. Her niece often discusses with her a future career in television production. Of this interest, Sandy said, "She's very interested, and she's very good at it. She'll watch a show and her analysis of it is really extremely good, I think, from a writer's point of view.... She doesn't just see the show, she sees what goes on to make it happen." Sandy takes obvious pride in Mimi's creative interests and abilities, and, like many aunts and uncles, enjoys providing enrichment opportunities and mentoring Mimi; in so doing, she is supplementing the work of her parents. However, one important feature of their relationship deserves special attention. Elements of a mutual friendship based on similarities of interests, temperament, and experiences underscore their relationship. Sandy is quick to point out their common creative interests as well as their common experience of family life as middle children. "I see a lot of what she goes through in her life is similar to what I went through in my childhood, so I can relate to that and maybe give her a little insight." By sharing her own similar experiences and understandings, Sandy is able to mentor Mimi in the fine art of managing relationships with family members. From Sandy's perspective, and possibly her niece's as well, they share important similarities not only in their personal interests and creative pursuits but also in their experiences of family life. Later in the interview, Sandy reflects on how her relationship with Mimi is developing into a mutual and reciprocal friendship in which Sandy is "more likely to share her concerns and ask [Mimi's] opinion." She adds, "The older Mimi gets, the more I have that [element of friendship] and the more I'm looking forward to it when she becomes an adult."

When asked if she expects her relationships with her 7-year-old twin nieces to develop into friendships in the future, Denise replies, "I really have a hard time picturing it any other way." Although Denise is quick to point out that she loves the twins equally, she also observes how her relationships with them are distinct. "One of them," she says, "and I love them exactly the same, but one of them more so than the other is more of a buddy and we talk about her day and my day." Denise shares how one of her nieces is more independent, rarely calls, and doesn't appear to need frequent contact. The other, Lauren, is more communicative. "Lauren really needs to talk to me on the phone. She'll check in on me, or if I haven't seen them for four or five days she'll wonder why I'm not coming down. She calls on Wednesdays, her auntie day, usually Wednesday evenings."

Denise is single and childless, an active aunt, clearly devoted to both her nieces, but even at an early age, she recognizes a somewhat closer bond with one of her nieces that is based on a pattern of routine contact and sharing of personal experiences that may well form the basis of an adult friendship.

Of course not all expectations regarding the future course of a relationship will be met. Aunts and uncles as well are quick to recognize the many competing demands on children as they move into adolescence and early adulthood. They recognize how relationships with peers become increasingly central as children mature and may compete with their relationships with extended kin. I asked Ilse, who is childless, if she expected to be friends with her niece in the future. "I hope so," she immediately replied. But her reply was tinged with a degree of ambivalence and uncertainty. Ilse says, "My good friend, who has a good relationship with her niece, has said to me, 'Enjoy these years, once she's off on her own you'll never see her again.'" Ilse and her niece Lana, who is now 16, have a tradition of taking a camping holiday each summer, and they have talked about a longer trip to the western United States, where they both have an interest in visiting. "I've brought it up from time to time. Is this the year for us to do it? [My niece] looks at the various other things she's doing, and for one reason or another, we've decided not to." Later she says, "I have a feeling that that trip may not happen." Ilse's experience points out two important features of friendship: it is voluntary and based on mutual interest. Although an aunt or uncle may prefer a close friendship, a niece or nephew may be less enthusiastic or find that relationships with peers overwhelm relationships with nonpeers, including endearing relationships with extended kin.

Uncles did not seem as likely to voice a keen expectation that a close tie with a young nephew would one day develop into a peerlike friendship. Uncles with young nephews spoke of their responsibilities as mentors and role models, as adjuncts to parents or substitute parents, but unlike some aunts, they did not routinely disclose an expectation that their relationships would develop into friendships as their nephews became adults. To be sure, some uncles were highly involved in the lives of their young adult nephews, and there were clearly instances of mutual friendships. Uncles and nephews share common recreational interests, their future plans, and their common family experiences. They talk and sometimes give one another advice about personal matters, work and career, expensive purchases like a new truck, and a wide array of routine daily concerns. They talk about their relationships with other family members and advise each other on future courses of action or simply commiserate and acknowledge one another's concerns. "We consider each other not just nephew and uncle, but we also consider ourselves friends," says Uncle Jessie. "He is as close as any of my adult friends."

Nonetheless, the friendships of uncles and nephews were often paired with a mentoring function. Raymond says of his uncle, "We are just like two old bar buddies having a good time," but in the same conversation he adds another element: "Nothing gets [my uncle] down and he's taught me not to let life beat you down. [He says,] 'Don't worry about things you don't have control over.'" From Raymond's perspective, their friendship is rewarding and steeped in a wide variety of common interests, but unlike peer-based friendships, it is tinged with elements of mentoring as an older man shares his essential observations on life's lessons with a younger man. In the same way, Uncle Robert discusses how he enjoys "hanging out" with his nephew and spending recreational time with one another, while at the same time, Robert acts the part of an elder by recognizing the importance of "just being another person who can help him find his way," particularly because his father died recently. For some uncles, friendship themes were easily merged with mentoring, and for others, mentoring seemed to take precedence over developing a friendship.

For some aunts and uncles, their relationships, although close, were not regarded as peer-based friendships, at least not entirely. Michele is married with two of her own children. She regards her aunt as a "good friend" but at the same time views her with a degree of respect more consistent with an esteemed elder. Of her aunt, she says, "I still revere her as my aunt and I call her Aunt Lauren; it's not just Lauren." Aunts and uncles occasionally pointed out how their relationships are characterized by friendship themes, as well as responsibilities for mentoring and role modeling. Relationships that become like friendships are not necessarily one-dimensional. They are sometimes complex arrangements of both peerlike friendships based on a certain degree of mutuality in which each party is responsive and responsible for the conduct of the relationship and its maintenance, as well as *mentorships,* or asymmetrical relationships in which an elder is responsible for a younger person in a truly generative fashion.

GAY AND LESBIAN STATUS

In some cases, an aunt or uncle's sexual orientation seemed to have little effect on relationships with a niece, nephew, or other family members; in other cases, it was central, although not always in anticipated ways. For Uncle Ricky, being gay was relatively inconsequential in regard to his relationships with his nephew, brother, and elderly uncle who lived next door. "Both my uncle and nephew know I'm gay and they are both accepting. It's a nonissue with them. Actually with the whole family it's a nonissue." I asked Ricky if his gayness was ever discussed. He replied:

> Sure in that if I happen to have someone over for a holiday I guess it's discussed. Or who I'm dating, or how things are going if I am in a relationship. They are very comfortable discussing "How are you and your boyfriend doing?"

Jonnie maintains a modest relationship with his uncle, not necessarily close but neither is it distant. He is quick to recall special memories of times spent with his uncle throughout his childhood and adolescence. More recently their paths have diverged. Whereas Jonnie has completed advanced degrees, his uncle never attended college, and from his perspective this divergence is symptomatic of how little they have in common as adults. Jonnie's family is somewhat accepting of his gay status, although not terribly communicative on the issue. "I think [being gay] has impacted my relationship with everyone. Like there used to be the conversation about who is hot and who's not for women. And obviously that doesn't occur now." And yet he still admires his uncle's integrity and family values. "One thing that comes to mind when I think of my uncle, is his commitment. If you needed something, he would be someone you could call. You just know he would drop what he was doing to help you out. He is a very family-centered person." We might suspect that Jonnie's sexual orientation adds to the divergent life experience that separates him and his uncle. Apart from some fondly recalled childhood memories of joint recreational activities, like hunting, they now have little common experience or interests on which to base a friendship.

Families vary in how well they accept the sexual orientation of their members. Most families, but not all, seem to accept the choices of their members. Raye spoke of her own aunt who was a very successful professional and local politician, much admired in her community. Nonetheless, for Raye her aunt's lesbian lifestyle negated all of her many achievements. "It just cancels out anything that she might achieve in her life." Raye's sentiment is unusually strong among the family members I spoke with but likely not uncommon.

In contrast, Addie thought her aunt's coming out "was kind of cool." Addie clearly admired her aunt for her "toughness" and her ability to adopt her own standards, solve her own problems, regardless of what others might have thought. Addie reflects on her aunt and the source of her admiration: "so I think part of why it was cool was not so much that she was a lesbian, but that she found her life [and] what made her happy." Later in our conversation, Addie recalls her aunt telling her, "it doesn't matter what other people think about you, it only matters what you think about you." For Addie this was and continues to be sage advice.

For still others, gay or lesbian status is relatively inconsequential. I asked Roslyn if being a lesbian was in any way consequential in her relationship with her niece Nina. She thought not, because Nina's mom is also a lesbian.

Rebecca recalls how her niece has developed a strong relationship with Marty, her partner, and talks with her about all manner of issues, including sensitive topics regarding other family members. Rebecca suggests that Marty is more objective and more skilled given her training as a social worker. In this instance, the sexual orientation of aunt and her partner are perhaps of less consequence than their personal commitment to their niece and the individual skills they bring to that relationship.

Chris is a 60-year-old gay uncle who lives with his elderly partner in a well-kept and spacious home. I met Chris at his home as he was just emerging from his verdant gardens. Chris maintains a close relationship with his 43-year-old nephew, Sumner, who is gay and HIV-positive. Chris recalls babysitting for Sumner when he was an infant. Now they visit at least monthly, although they live far from each other (a one hour flight), and talk weekly on the phone. I asked Chris if the fact that both he and his nephew were gay influenced their relationship.

No, the fact is I was struggling [in my earlier years] with my sexual orientation and that decreased the bond I think if anything. And so it took from when Sumner was in his teens, well into his twenties [that we became closer] . . . and that's when he was having a hard time with his parents. [We vacationed in Australia with my partner and talked] about a whole row of issues, him growing up, his parents and when he was young, and that's when he told us he was HIV-positive. So the contact has grown from there.

Later in the interview, Chris talks about the friendship he now has with his nephew.

Well it is very special that Sumner can understand me better than any of my other nephews and nieces, and I can understand him. So that is a very special bond. And if he comes and stays we can go out and enjoy the same environments together [like gay clubs], which we do.

A similarity of family history, values, and interests that is at least partly rooted in their shared sexual orientation has deepened their friendship. Still the relationship does take on some additional tones that are atypical of friendships. Uncle Chris provides advice to his nephew about understanding his parents, as well as occasional financial help.

So he came back to New Zealand and stayed here to build bridges with his parents. Unfortunately they told him how they loved him, but that love was on their terms. He wasn't to talk about his relationships, he wasn't to talk about how he caught a virus . . . all he really wanted was for them to accept him for who he was. I told [my nephew] why I felt his father is like that. . . . Whereas I am very fond of my sister, in some areas there is a limit. . . . When they [the sister and family] found out [my nephew] was HIV-positive they all very nicely sat down and signed a get-well card and sent it to him, which shows very little comprehension about the virus.

The friendship of Chris and Sumner is unique in some regards. Their shared sexual orientation adds to their commonality of experience within the context of their family. For Sumner, his sexual orientation added some degree of conflict to his relationship with his parents, which continues to be strained. Chris and Sumner's friendship exists in a heterosexual family culture, a fact that sets them apart from other family members and provides them with an array of similar experiences, some of which are rooted in the misunderstandings, conflicts, and lack of acceptance that occur in their separate family relationships. At the same time, they share a common gay culture, knowledge of which is unavailable to other family members, and this, too, sets their relationship apart. The heterosexual context forming the backdrop for their relationship seems to have the effect of magnifying the significance of their commonality.

Like many aunts, uncles, nieces, and nephews, Chris and Sumner have a deep understanding of each other's perspectives and experiences in dealing with family members. They know the players and, like good friends, can commiserate in their frustrations. Like other uncles and nephews, their relationship has developed and endured over decades and with it brought a convoy of shared experiences, relational and family milestones, personal achievements, and individual challenges.

Fundamental to their friendship is their gay lifestyle and shared understanding of gay culture. Chris remarks how they enjoy the same social venues that cater to gay and lesbian audiences. Like good friends of virtually any persuasion, Chris relishes that his nephew can understand him, and conversely he can understand his nephew, an understanding cast in essential acceptance and tolerance.

Complementing their friendship is Chris's concern about his nephew's health. Chris encourages his nephew to be mindful of his well-being, and offers to finance health care as well as their monthly social visits. Here again friendship is paired with mentoring and caregiving, all of which speaks of Chris's deep commitment to his nephew and his generative concern over his nephew's continued well-being.

It is a bit of a paradox that their shared status as gay men frames their friendship, and yet the processes and events that underlay their relationship are not at all unique but typify close friendships among men or women regardless of their sexual orientation, and the depth and longevity of their relationship places them among the closest of uncles and nephews.

ANOTHER SIDE OF FRIENDSHIP AND GENERATIVITY

When I was about 16 or 17 [my uncle and I] were on the job and he lit up a joint, and he passed it to me. I took it. I smoked pot. And ever since we always smoke weed once in a while with each other and stuff. This was straight out of the blue. I had no idea he did and I don't know if he had any idea I did. Actually I think he did because my parents caught me and they might have told him.

RM: How did your parents feel about this?

I eventually told them. They know I do and they are just like, "Well, whatever." They have never had too many bad things to say about it.

To understand further the basis of their relationship, I asked this nephew, Nat, how he referred to his uncle.

> I called him Uncle Mike for a while and then it became a bit of a joke. Like I'd call him Uncle Mike, and he'd call me Nephew Nat. After a while I kind a got the hint he probably doesn't want me to call him that anymore. After a while it was just Mike. . . . He is a super nice guy.

Like any good friendship, Nat's relationship with his uncle has a reciprocal element. Occasionally Uncle Mike shares his personal concerns, as Nat related: "Yeah, he tells me things I don't know, things that happen, things that bother him. Stuff like that."

In our discussions, we have cast friendship into the mix of central ingredients for a generative culture. Typically we think of friendship as a rather positive affiliation. Friends have fun. They support one another. They are dependable. We might not expect friends to experience conflict, but of course they do. Aunts sometimes criticize the choices of their younger nieces. Nephews sometimes question the wisdom of an uncle's overindulgence in alcohol. Further, when a friendship involves an uncle or aunt, with a niece or nephew, we can expect that friendship to include a measure of mentoring. Usually we think of mentoring as a rather positive contribution by an older person to the life of a younger person, or, as we have learned, not infrequently younger people mentor older people by providing them with advice and support, again with some positive benefit or at least good intension. Nat's story about his uncle raises some questions about these core assumptions and, more important, how we understand generativity and how we represent that understanding.

In some instances, generativity lies in the eyes of the beholder and is consequently subject to individual judgment. One clear example of the ambiguity inherent in any a priori judgment of generative action is evidenced in Uncle Mike's decision to share a marijuana cigarette with Nat during a break in their work-related activity. On the one hand, Nat reported a close relationship with his uncle. They visited often throughout Nat's childhood, adolescence, and young adulthood. There were frequent occasions of mentoring where Uncle Mike provided advice regarding family, schooling, work, and relationships. But on this one occasion, we might view the sharing of a marijuana cigarette as a turning point in their relationship from avuncular elder to that of a peer friendship. The question is whether the incident was generative. At the time, possession of marijuana was illegal, and quite apart from its legality, some would question the wisdom of this activity, particularly because it occurred on a work site.

The incident points out the relative nature of the concept of generativity and especially how decisions regarding what constitutes "a concern for others" is largely dependent on morality rooted in individual beliefs, community norms, and institutions, all of which are subject to change. For instance, drinking alcohol was once prohibited universally in the United States and elsewhere. Laws and expectations governing individual conduct change. They vary by culture. Alcohol consumption is permitted among adolescents in some cultures but not others. At some point in time, in one particular cultural context, sharing a marijuana cigarette would be considered at most an indication of an adult welcoming an older adolescent into the world of adulthood. At another point in time, in another cultural context, using marijuana would be considered a certain infraction of law, custom, or both. What we consider generative is both historically and culturally relative, as well as a matter of individual taste. Uncle Mike likely considered his actions appropriate, and Nat's parents, at least from Nat's perspective, had little concern. The action was given in the spirit of friendship. Possibly the local minister and sheriff would have felt differently.

On the other hand, perhaps the only relevant issue is the actor's intention – a demonstrated concern for others – and in this way any action intended to benefit another's welfare is generative regardless of the current or future evaluation of observers. We cannot know whether future generations will consider those actions generative. Futures are capricious. In locating the relationships of uncles and nephews, aunts and nieces, we have found instances of frequent, diverse, and intimate experience dwelling in shared family biographies. From this location, generativity appears throughout the relationships of aunts, uncles, nieces, and nephews – not universally but frequently enough that we should take notice.

THE SUFFUSION OF FRIENDSHIP AND KINSHIP

Kinships and friendships are often viewed as distinct types of relationships, and in some ways, as we have seen, they are distinct. Relationships with kinfolk are often based on a sense of obligation; relationships with friends are based on a large measure of personal discretion. The distinctions are crude; they apply to Western enactments of personal relationships, but only sparingly. There are two key findings derivative of our developing understanding of the relationships of aunts and uncles that bear on the distinctions between kinship and friendship and deserve emphasis. Kinship is not a uniform social category, and friendship and kinship are not always separate social categories. Kin vary in regard to normative expectations that accompany their position in a family.[11] We expect parents to act differently than grandparents, siblings differently than cousins. If nothing else, kin relations vary in the obligations attributed to each position. Parents are expected to enact a greater sense of obligation for their children than grandparents or aunts and uncles. The roles of kinfolk also vary across generations with consequences for their relationships. The lifelong relationships between parents and children are distinct from the lifelong relationships likely to develop among siblings.[12] Parents, for instance, are more apt to provide financial aid to an adult child than siblings are to one another. On the other hand, relationships among siblings are more egalitarian and amongst the most enduring and pervasive of personal relationships.[13] The ways in which obligations are understood, interpreted, and enacted vary as a function of social placement in a family.

Aunts and uncles are unique because they are often of the same generation as parents. Siblings typically share an entire biography and come to know each other as peers, when relatively similar in age, or at least as near peers, when age discrepancies are large. Even those related by marriage may experience extensive relationships existing over long periods of time. Several aunts and uncles, for instance, mentioned they knew their future sister or brother-in-law (i.e., a niece's or nephew's parent) during the early years of their siblings' courtship, and sometimes even earlier as childhood friends. For instance, Al has an exceptionally long relationship with both of his nephew's parents, one of whom is Al's sister, and the other a childhood friend with whom Al attended high school. The experiences of siblings are distinct from those of parents (or grandparents) and ground the relationships they may later form with nieces and nephews.

At this point, we might question the distinction commonly made between family and friends. Among aunts and uncles and their nieces and nephews, the two forms of relationships – kinship and friendship – are occasionally suffused or blended.[14] To be sure, some kin are but distant acquaintances, yet others maintain among the closest of relationships. Such ties often suffuse qualities expected among close kin, such as a sense of obligation and an expectation that the relationship will continue in the distant future, with qualities more typical of intimates who are unrelated, including

---

[11] Rossi & Rossi, 1990; Schnieder & Cottrell, 1975.
[12] Wellman & Wortley, 1989.
[13] Eriksen & Gerstel, 2002; Matthews, 2005; White, 2001.
[14] I am indebted here to British sociologists Liz Spencer and Ray Pahl (2006) and their excellent book on friendship and family relations. Graham Allan (1998, 2008) also offers insights into the distinction between friendship and kinship bonds.

the sharing of similar interests and pastimes, having fun together, feeling uniquely understood, and disclosing intimacies.

The distinguishing element of personal discretion so important in underlying friendship is present as well. Aunts and uncles note special bonds or connections they feel to some nieces and nephews and not others, usually based on shared interests and sensibilities, and they suffuse elements of friendship into their relationships because of this perceived similarity and connection. More broadly, close ties with kin are based on biological and relational connectedness as well as personal discretions derivative of mutual liking, affection, common interests, and values.[15] In the friendships that develop among aunts and nieces, uncles and nephews, *given ties*, forged by shared genealogies or marriage, become blended with *chosen ties*, forged by personal choice.

Aunts and uncles may differ in some regards in how frequently their relationships with nieces and nephews become suffused. In this relatively small and decidedly nonrepresentative sample, aunts were more likely to report being friends with their nieces, about 65%, than uncles were with their nephews, about 31%. Aunts seemed more apt to anticipate eagerly that their relationship with a young niece would develop into a mutual friendship in the future and spoke openly of their desire, particularly aunts who were themselves childless. Perhaps aunts are more likely to develop blended relationships with strong elements of friendship. Generally speaking, women report a wider array of confidants and close associates than men.[16] As a group, we might expect aunts to witness more friendships developing with nieces. Although it is too soon to say with any certainty, possibly uncles are less likely to supplant their responsibilities as mentors and parental figures with peer-based friendship themes.

CONCLUSION

Aunts and uncles at times merge their generative roles and responsibilities as mentors, supplemental or surrogate parents, intergenerational buffers, and family historians with friendship themes, and they do so effectively, enriching themselves and strengthening their family ties. Core ingredients

[15] Allan, 2008; Finch & Mason, 1993; Pahl & Prevalin, 2005.

[16] In a study of spouses and their confidants, 6% of wives and 25% of husbands reported having no close friends (Helms et al., 2003). In a recent nationally representative study in the United States, fully 24.6% of adults reported having no confidants – that is, a person with whom they discussed important matters (McPherson, Smith-Lovin, & Brashers, 2006).

of friendship, or what we have referred to as their deep structure, include sharing common interests and sensibilities, as well as fostering a climate of mutual acceptance, personal disclosure, trust, and commitment. Although kinship ties with their basis in obligation, and friendship ties with their basis in personal choice, are typically viewed as distinct, this inquiry demonstrates how the two are suffused or blended. In their friendships with nieces and nephews, aunts and uncles share common interests, recreational pastimes, personal concerns, advice, and occasional criticism, but at the same time aunts and uncles maintain their sense of responsibility for their younger family members. In this way, the friendships of aunts and uncles with nieces and nephews are unique because of their generative components. Although generativity is simply defined as a concern for future generations, in fact the application of this definition to lived experiences is not quite so straightforward. The most graphic example was the case in which Uncle Mike shared an illegal substance with his nephew. Mike's intentions may have been admirable, but it is unlikely all would agree that the activity was appropriate. The instance demonstrates how decisions regarding generative actions are relative and apt to vary across families, communities, and cultures, as well as over historical time.

A variety of questions remain, including the issue of cross-sex friendships among aunts and nephews, as well as uncles and nieces. To be sure, the aunts and uncles in this study mentioned such relationships, but we would be hard-pressed to offer insights into how such relationships might differ or even how often they occur. We can also question whether friendship themes characterize other family relationships and especially relationships among grandparents and grandchildren. In large part, the available literature on grandparenting centers on issues of supplemental caregiving and parenting[17] without much regard for older grandchildren with whom grandparents might develop strong friendship ties. The suffusion of kinship and friendship themes need not be unique to aunts and uncles and their relationships with nieces and nephews.

We might additionally question whether aunts and uncles are aware of the uniqueness of their position in their families. Do aunts and uncles share a common understanding of their obligations; do they share a common culture of aunting and uncling? I explore these issues in depth in the next chapter.

---

[17] Robertson, 1995; Silverstein & Marenco, 2001.

8

The Social Reproduction of Aunts and Uncles

The roles of aunts and uncles are likely flexible in their expression and in the accompanying expectations held by family members. As we have learned throughout the earlier chapters, aunts and uncles vary in their enactment of relationships with siblings and their children. As with many social positions, there is a certain amount of personal discretion involved; to a certain extent, individuals freely elect to develop and maintain personal relationships, or they elect not to do so. Further, like many social positions, there is a certain degree of flexibility in the expectations family members have of each other, expectations that define patterns of obligation and rules of engagement. And then, too, relationships and the social positions that comprise them are negotiated enterprises. Personal preferences must be negotiated with relational partners, and there are many. Developing and sustaining a relationship with a niece depends in part on the niece's preferences, her parents, grandparents, and quite possibly other family members. The expression of aunting and uncling and the expectations that pair with those expressions are continually being created and recreated in the ordinary discourse of family life.[1] Earlier we referred to elements of this discourse as marriage or relationship work in which spouses talk with friends and relatives about their primary relationships, sometimes seeking advice and just as often seeking a sympathetic listener. We discussed family work and "doing family" as ordinary discourse about family members, their circumstance, activities, and relationships in which the roles of members are continually being created, rehearsed, and given meaning. In this chapter, I further explore these issues by considering two simple questions. Do aunts and uncles talk about their roles, their understandings of what it means to be an aunt or uncle, and in doing this brand of family work, do they essentially define aunting and

---

[1] For a discussion of obligation in kin relations, see Rossi & Rossi, 1990; Stein, 1993.

uncling in broader terms? Second, is there a common culture of aunting and uncling, a system of shared beliefs regarding how relationships with nieces and nephews, as well as relationships with their parents, should develop? I explore the question of whether there are common beliefs that are held by the actors themselves – the aunts and uncles – as well as corresponding beliefs or expectations held by other family members, particularly parents. As we found throughout this study, aunts and uncles are occasionally central figures in families, and although it is impossible given the limitations of this sample to know how often or commonly they are central, for some "doing family" transcends the boundaries of nuclear family households. Adult siblings talk to each other about their lives, their partners, and their children, and they extend this talk, this doing family with others in their social worlds, including friends, coworkers, and other personal associates.

In using the phrase *doing family*, we are calling on a distinctly relational, interactive, and creative view of families. Rather than view families as naturally occurring sets of personal relationships with clear memberships and boundaries and clear assignments of roles and responsibilities, a perspective widely criticized,[2] we can usefully draw on an alternative view. This transactive perspective emphasizes the active social construction of families in the routine interaction of members who through their talk and activities define memberships (who's in and who's out), individual roles and responsibilities, acceptable and unacceptable behaviors, and who performs the work needed to continually define family members and their relationships.[3] Aunts and uncles construct their roles through negotiated family work and the ordinary discourse surrounding daily experience.

To explore further the social reproduction of aunts and uncles, I asked each to describe their experience as children and their relationships to their own aunts and uncles, as well as the current status of such relationships. In this way, we gain further insight into how contemporary aunts and uncles create and re-create their roles and responsibilities to children vis-à-vis their own experience. Do, for instance, aunts and uncles model their early childhood experience in developing relationships with nieces and nephews? Exploring the relationships of an earlier generation also permits us to search for continuities in how such relationships are played out in later generations and in this way further detail a culture of aunting and uncling.

Finally we examine how the expression of aunting and uncling influences the personal development of aunts and uncles, how they are personally

___

[2] K. R. Allen, Fine, & Demo, 2000; Hansen, 2005; Smith, 1993; Sprey, 2009.
[3] Carrington, 1999; Nelson, 2006; Sarkisian, 2006.

influenced by their family relationships and especially their relationships with children.

AUNTING AND UNCLING TALK

Aunts and uncles talk about their roles and their relationships with nieces and nephews as a matter of routine family work with spouses, partners, siblings, and parents, as a matter of ordinary disclosure about current events with social companions such as coworkers and friends; more rarely, they directly reflect on their responsibilities as aunts and uncles.

Aunting and uncling talk occurs in the wider context of family responsibilities, or indirectly as aunts and uncles share information about their nieces and nephews. For instance, one uncle, Robert, who is a Catholic priest, talked about his family and some of the family conversations they have had. He said, "We have never talked much about being an uncle or aunt but we've talked heaps about being a family and there is a lot of implication about being an uncle." In this way, uncling is discussed indirectly in the context of family values and the responsibilities of all family members to one another. Robert explained further:

> I remember when on holiday from the seminary I was going to stay with [some friends], and this particular time instead of going [home where my family lives, I thought] I'll stay a couple of days with these people in the south island. [My sister] sort of scowled at me. I had forgotten that it was [my nephew's] twenty-first birthday. So of course I declined the invitation with [my friends] and came up to [my nephew's birthday party]. And that was kind of my first experience of the sort of unwritten code of responsibility for my nephews.

Robert's experience suggests that the expectations of a parent and an uncle's responsibilities to a nephew are not necessarily explicit but are nonetheless understood, however obliquely communicated.

Another uncle, Evan, shared a similar sentiment in that uncling talk occurs in the context of directed family work. "I talk a lot with my wife about family relationships. Like what does my nephew need, or what does my brother need? Given what we know about their situation, is there anything we should be doing to help out?" The implication here is that uncling is seen in the context of a family responsibility tinged with a sense of obligation, and in this case toward a brother and his children.

Al raises a related theme in that his avuncular role is partly derivative of his relationships with his siblings. He stated, "At least for me it is an outgrowth of the relationship between siblings. So that the ones you're closest to, the siblings you're closest to, you in a sense have more interest in their kids because there are things that you are already sharing." In this case, Al does not talk directly about his role, but he does think about it and take an interest in his nephew in part because of his positive relationship with his siblings.

Talk about aunting or uncling is often embedded in a form of family work in which adult siblings talk about each other, their children, and their respective families. Freddie, when asked if he had ever talked about uncling with other family members, replied:

> Yes I have and yes I do, because I enjoy it so much. Numerous times in my own family we've talked about uncling and aunting. Four of us do not have kids and two do. The four of us really enjoy and have spoken about our enjoyment of uncling and aunting.

Discussions among siblings about aunting and uncling seem to occur relatively often and appear to be one forum in which mutual expectations are forged and the roles of aunts and uncles are defined. Alexandra talks with her younger sisters about their eldest sister, who is going through a divorce. The younger sisters are concerned about their elder sister's children, their nieces. Alexandra recalls how she and her sisters discuss "being involved" with their nieces and supporting them as their parents experience a separation and divorce. The sisters reached an agreement regarding the importance of their aunting and in doing so decided on a course of action with regard to their nieces. They are socially constructing their roles and their expectations of one another as sisters and aunts. In this case, the discussion is prompted by one sister's divorce; talk about aunting is cast within a discussion of a deteriorating marriage and the particular needs of the distressed spouses – and perhaps more important, their children. I can't say with any certainly if this issue was discussed on more than one occasion, but I suspect a divorce is important enough that the discussions prompted by it were many and ongoing.

Doing family is likely a rather ordinary, routine, and ongoing activity, perhaps more typical among sisters, or mixed groups of sisters and brothers. From Alexandra's story, and those of the many aunts and uncles like her who are involved in the lives of their nieces and nephews, we can surmise that talk about aunting and uncling is a common component of doing family, or, in other words, sharing information about family members, negotiating understandings or interpretations of current circumstance, and deciding on possible courses of action and generating expectations of one another.

The roles of aunts and uncles are continually being negotiated, defined, and enacted through multiple personal relationships.

Aunts and uncles talk about their activities with friends, among whom they share information about their nieces' and nephews' achievements, their routine visits, or their common interests. As Chris described, "I've often spoken about my nephew to people.... The fact that I am an uncle and have a gay nephew." Similarly, Francesca says of her relationship with her niece: "I think people who know me well, my friends, know that this is a very important relationship. [My niece] comes up in conversation a lot with me and my friends. I think I sort of naturally talk about it." In this way, aunts and uncles share details of their personal lives, interests, and activities with their close associates, and an important component of their lives are their relationships with nieces and nephews.

In describing routine visits, recent activities, and the personal accomplishments of their nieces and nephews, aunts and uncles are essentially doing family, defining what their roles mean to them as well as to other family members. Lena demonstrates these themes in her conversations with friends who are also aunts. In sharing their experiences, Lena said, "I think by describing what [my friends and I] are doing, we're saying 'this is what I think, this is what an aunt should be.'" The implicit roles of aunts and uncles are socially constructed as people engage in relationship work with friends and family members.

When people share ordinary details of their aunting and uncling, they are forging deeper friendships. For Aunt Denise, discussions of aunting occur in the context of her friendship with another aunt. Like good friends, they share details of their daily lives, including the current circumstance of their respective families. They are simultaneously discussing personal anecdotes and thus forging an intimate friendship, as well as engaging in family work. As Denise related about her typical conversations with her best friend, "We talk about the role we play, what we did over the weekend [with our nieces], or [about how our nieces'] parents weren't getting along well."

When aunts and uncles share with other aunts and uncles what they do with their nieces and nephews, they in a sense define their roles through a socially comparative process. Aunts Theriza and Ilse are both childless, and both talk about their nieces with good friends who are also aunts. With their friends they compare notes, make suggestions for activities, problem solve, offer advice in dealing with particularly thorny family matters, and generally support each other. Their talk about aunting is a means by which they can compare experiences in a mutually supportive context. For some, the support can take the form of an older aunt mentoring a younger one.

Francesca and Denise talked about sharing their experiences as aunts with friends and coworkers who have only recently become aunts, encouraging them to develop close relationships with their infant nieces. Said Denise to her friend, "wait and see how it's going to change your life." Denise and Francesca emphasized how learning of their friends' new relationships with infant nieces reminded them of their own early experiences, and they freely encourage their friends to engage fully in their new role as aunts while offering advice based on their own experiences.

Of course not all aunts and uncles have close relationships with siblings or their siblings' children; not all commonly engage in family work regarding their siblings, nieces, or nephews. Approximately 22% (7 of 31) of the aunts and 24% (5 of 21) of the uncles interviewed indicated they did not talk explicitly about their roles or their activities with nieces and nephews either to other family members or to friends.[4] Sylvia, when asked if she ever talked with anyone about what it means to be an aunt, replied in her own way: "No I don't think I have. There aren't too many people like you who come around asking me 50 questions [about aunting]." Of course Sylvia was quite correct and people do not generally wax over the meaning of aunting or uncling in abstract terms. Rather they talk about aunting and uncling in specific and personal terms, in relation to current events and current relational conditions. Talk about aunting and uncling occurs often enough to suggest it is rather routine and involves talking about family members and sharing details of one's ordinary activity.

THE FAMILY RELATIONSHIPS OF AUNTS AND UNCLES

In this section, I examine how aunts and uncles are socialized into their roles, how they understand their roles, and whether they themselves had a close relationship with an aunt or uncle. Uncles may model their own early experience of being uncled in developing their relationships with nephews, perhaps compensating for any shortcomings they may have experienced in their own relationships, much as parents do,[5] or, like fathers, they may emulate a number of male role models, including fathers, uncles, other kin, and peers.[6] Similarly, aunts may model the relationships they experienced

---

[4] We might expect that those people who report little aunting or uncling talk simply have less to talk about because they interact less with their nieces and nephews. This does not appear to be the case. Those who report talking about aunting and uncling interact no more or less with their nieces and nephews than their less talkative counterparts. Talkers and nontalkers alike interact about monthly, on average, with their nieces and nephews.
[5] See Marsiglio, 2004; Pleck, 1997.   [6] See Daly, 1993.

with their own aunts as children and adults, or they may draw on relational experiences with others, including mothers and grandmothers.[7]

Unlike aunts who seemed to experience relatively close relationships with their own aunts during their formative years – and some continue to maintain such relationships – uncles were less apt to recount significant relationships with their own uncles. Approximately 45% (10 of 22) of uncles reported no particular relationship with an uncle during their childhood, whereas only 16% (5 of 31) of aunts reported limited relationships with their own aunts during their childhood. Nonetheless, for some uncles, such relationships were influential, and for a select few, they continue to be.

Tom has close relationships with his 7-year-old twin nephews, whom he sees weekly or more often, and models his uncling on his own experience as a child. He said: "I always assumed that I would use [my uncles] as role models." He went on to state: "Yeah, well I'm really carrying on a tradition my mother's brothers taught me." Among uncles, this was the only direct mention of a tradition of uncling, although it is implied in uncles' descriptions of their own contemporary or past experience with great uncles.[8]

Another uncle, Michael, modeled his relationship with his nephew on his own family experience, experiences that often included strong educational components, as does his current relationship with his nephew.

> In my family we place value on things we believe in and one of them is education and we want to make sure that gets passed on. We don't specifically talk about these things; it happens by virtue of the things we do. My mother used to have a history day in which she would organize some activity or event on a summer weekend and we would all get together. One example was to go see an automobile museum that had a history in Maine. So she organized a day for the museum director to show [us] around and talk about the [autos] and so forth. Another day we organized it around visiting a nearby very very large tree. The whole family went and hung about this tree and had a picnic. I as an uncle do that sort of thing too.

Other uncles spoke about especially memorable childhood experiences with their own uncles (e.g., family outings or sporting trips), qualities they admired in their uncles (e.g., their sense of humor or constant encouragement and support), as well as qualities they did not particularly admire or wish to emulate. Said Pat, "In some ways, I learned what I didn't want to

---

[7] See Arendell, 2000; Miller, 2005; Miller-Day, 2004.

[8] For the purpose of clarity, I sometimes refer to this older generation of uncles and aunts as *great uncles* or *great aunts*.

be from [my] uncle." In contrast, Ricky's uncle served as a "father figure" throughout his childhood and continues to be an important influence in his life – "the one male role model that I always had," he said. Ricky is now 39, gay, and unpartnered. His uncle is 63 and lives next door. "I see him every day, sometimes three or four times a day. Every morning we chat and then usually visit each other after work." The relationship is uncommon for its longevity and closeness and likely influences Ricky's relationship to his own nephew.

Aunts generally reported more involvement with their own aunts during their childhood, although they did not always continue these relationships in adulthood. Sixteen aunts reported close relationships with an aunt when they were children, and nine of those relationships continued to be close into adulthood. Aunts, even those who reported modest relationships, had much to say about their experiences with their own aunts. They described relationships that are in many ways similar to their own relationships with nieces. They emphasized valuing their aunts for their humor, acceptance, caring, confirmation, and unconditional support. Of her great aunt, Alexandra said, "I could have told her that I was going to make a living sitting in trees and she would have been supportive."

Often the gifts bestowed by great aunts were given in the context of strong and positive relationships with parents, but for others they were viewed as unique. Stella contrasted her strained relationship with her mother – "we butted heads all our lives" – with her relationship with her aunt who was "somebody that accepted me for me." Stella's aunt was a significant source of support throughout her childhood and then later when Stella became a single parent. "She believed in me," Stella recounts, "and that's a role that I think an aunt can do." Stella is now 52, and her relationship with her aunt continues, sometimes in poignant ways. Stella views her elderly uncle as verbally abusive and overly critical of her aunt, and she encourages her aunt to have "confidence in herself." It is yet another instance of reverse mentoring in which a younger generation mentors an older generation.

Ilse found an important source of support in her lesbian aunt as she struggled with her own sexual identity and eventually self-identified as a lesbian. "I saw her the other day and she asked how my partner is, and that really meant a lot to me," she said. The gift of unconditional support is often startling in its consistency across generations. Addie said of her aunt, "if nothing else I always knew that [my aunt] cared about me, that she loved me, and that I always had a place to go."

Experiences with great aunts mimicked the contemporary relationships of aunts and nieces in additional ways. Aunts valued their experiences with their own aunts as models of alternative lifestyles, often expressing an admiration for their aunts' sense of independence, personal achievements, and strength of character, or as models of alternative career paths. Harriett recalled how her aunt was dean of a small liberal arts college and a woman who had traveled widely, including an extended working visit to China in 1916. "She gave me the idea of having strength," Harriett said. In some ways, Harriett followed in her aunt's footsteps; she traveled to China with her husband and children and spent a year there.

Olympia recalled her aunt, who was a single woman and legislative assistant on Capitol Hill. "I was attracted to her because she was kind of magical and also because she was so independent. Who knew a single woman?" she said. Addie expressed an admiration for her aunt as a "very forward and direct person. She didn't sugarcoat anything and was always honest with me about things." Francesca spoke of her aunt, who was a schoolteacher. She recalled a visit to her aunt's classroom as a young child and the distinct impression this professional woman made on her. Francesca is now a school principal, having followed in the professional footsteps of her aunt.

Great aunts clearly left distinct impressions on their nieces and often served as role models for their nieces' lives, marriages and partnerships, choices of careers, and emerging relationships with their own nieces. Some of the relationships with great aunts were close, but often it is not necessarily the closeness of a relationship that determines influence. Some of those who had relatively distant relationships with their aunts were nonetheless profoundly influenced. Kathryn spoke of her own aunt, whose name she shares, as an important influence in her life, although they have never lived near one another and saw each other infrequently. Throughout her childhood, her aunt was an important source of self-validation, and later a model for her adult life.

> My parents have a really very traditional marriage, my dad is pretty dominating in a lot of ways and didn't want his wife to work and that kind of thing, although I think my mother probably would have liked it. So here's my aunt and her husband who had a very different relationship. My uncle was a professional photographer, was a press spokesman for a governor in Nebraska at one time, and then he bought some small-town newspapers, and they lived in this really small town, and ran the newspaper, and Aunt Kathryn worked with him on that, the whole family worked on it, but she was an integral part of that whole business, so she and my Uncle Woodrow had a working relationship, and I hadn't thought about this before, but maybe that is a part of the model of what [my husband] and I do. I certainly didn't get it from my parents, and maybe

I saw enough of what [my aunt and uncle] were doing [to illustrate] that was something that sometimes people did. That had an influence on me. They had a very loving relationship and cared about each other very deeply, really cherished each other.

Kathryn's family moved often during her childhood, including several years living abroad, and yet throughout her childhood, her aunt remained an important figure in her life. She and her husband are highly successful professionals in similar fields, often sharing adjacent offices. Visits with her aunt are less than annual but nonetheless highly valued and influential. In a family with a strong, opinionated, and domineering father who engendered contentious relationships with his children, an aunt served and continues to serve as a voice of reason. Of her aunt, Kathryn said, "She puts me in the context of being a reasonable person."

Like the contemporary relationships of aunts and nieces, aunts were in many ways mentored by their great aunts, and aunts of this middle generation occasionally reversed roles and mentored their great aunts or became caretakers by assisting their elder aunts in their daily living. Isabella recalled in rich detail a close and lifelong relationship with her aunt, one that "shaped how I wanted my relationships to my nieces to be." She recalled their last visit when her aunt was dying of cancer.

I realized that [my aunt] didn't think my mother loved her. I almost fell off the chair and just spontaneously I said, "My mother loved you and you know she always spoke of you with such affection." And [my aunt] just sat there with this pained look on her face, and I thought this is the reason I came. I came to tell her that my mother loved her. And then later her husband said, "I want to tell you that it was so important because she laid to rest her pain related to her sister." She died five days later. [The visit] was crucial for her, and maybe it was crucial for me.

For Isabella and her aunt, their last visit represented a kind of generative redemption sequence in which the fears of an older woman are accepted and laid to rest by the care of a younger woman.

Aunts were quick to acknowledge the roles their great aunts played in their lives and how they served as role models for their own relationships with nieces. Of her great aunt, Connie said, "I just hope I can be half the [aunt] she was." And to a certain extent, this was true of uncles as well. The experiences of aunts and uncles were at times rooted in relatively close relationships with great aunts and uncles and, at other times, framed within relatively modest relationships with infrequent opportunities for direct interaction that were nonetheless influential. The impact of these relationships is perhaps best illustrated in the similarities of themes that appear. Aunts and uncles valued the support of their great aunts and uncles, their encouragement, mentoring, and modeling of alternative lifestyles, just as younger nieces and nephews described similar features they value in their contemporary relationships. Like their younger nieces and nephews, aunts and uncles sometimes identified qualities of their great aunts and uncles that they sought to avoid in their own relationships, such as overbearing personalities, unstable relationships, and substance abuse. Some themes are especially unique in the relationships of aunts and nieces, relative to uncles and nephews, as discussed in Chapter 5 on mentoring. Aunts valued the qualities of independence and visions of nontraditional lifestyles that their great aunts offered, much as nieces valued these same qualities in their contemporary relationships with aunts. These themes did not appear in the depictions of relationships of uncles and nephews of either generation; they are themes unique to women. Perhaps this issue was best acknowledged in my conversations with Kathryn, who, on reflecting on the significant women in her family's ancestry, said: "You know, the women get lost in family history, even their names get lost, and I do feel a special need to try to encourage the girls."

GENERATIVITY AND PERSONAL DEVELOPMENT

> There is something that I understand about my niece that reflects back on how I need to understand myself. I feel that as I nurture her, I am maybe also nurturing myself. . . . If you see something in someone else that maybe they're having some difficulties with, and it's something also that you're dealing with yourself, if you're showing kindness and acceptance to this other person, then it also helps you be a little kinder and more accepting [of yourself]. (Aunt Harriett)

The very fact of aunting and uncling, of mentoring, advising, and befriending nieces and nephews, of taking an interest in their lives and that of their parents, can have important and far-reaching consequences for aunts and uncles and their own personal development. Then too, in much the same way that children influence the development of their parents,[9] nieces and nephews may influence the personal development of their aunts and uncles. Harriett, in her astonishingly insightful comment, suggested that by coming to understand her niece and her struggles, she is given the opportunity to better understand herself. "As I nurture her, I am maybe

---

[9] Crouter & Booth, 2003.

also nurturing myself." The act of being generative influences the personal development of both generations.

Aunts and uncles were quick to point out how they felt "lucky" or "blessed" in having positive relationships with nieces and nephews. Susan said of her nieces, "I don't know how I would live without them. They have given me more than I will ever give as an aunt." Aunting and uncling, when it works well, provides gratification and introduces meaning to a life, connects one to an ensemble of family relationships, provides companionship and a sense of place in time with a past and future, and services a need to parent – to be generative.

In some cases, aunts and uncles were very clear that their experiences with nieces and nephews had brought on unanticipated and life-changing consequences – and in one case, a profound change in an uncle's connections to his family and his own health and well-being. This particular uncle, Greco, was hospitalized for complications arising from a life of substance abuse, a life that estranged him from his family and children for 14 years. Of his years with booze and drugs, Greco said, "the underlying problem [is that] there [was] a lot of emotional void." His nephew, who was 26 and who Greco hadn't seen since his nephew was 7 or 8 years old, came to visit him in the hospital. Much to Greco's surprise, his nephew was interested and believed "I was filling an empty space for him.... He felt that there was a large void in his awareness of his family, awareness of himself, or whatever." Through the first few months of their visiting, Greco answered his nephew's questions. Although surprised by the intensity of his nephew's interest, he answered questions about his nephew's stepfather, about the fathers of his nephew's brothers, about his mother (Greco's sister), and their early family life, which was marked by an abusive and volatile father. Of this time, he said, "The kids [his nephews and nieces] were instrumental in helping me to take a look at things a little more differently . . . and [gave me] reasons to appreciate things. . . . I have to say I have been getting tutelage by being around my sister's kids again." Greco's reconnection brought about by his nephew's visits has had the effect of renewing his connection with his sister, her children, and, in the end, his own children.

> I wouldn't have had the wherewithal to reconnect with them as much as they have with me. They're stronger in their awareness and their thirst for family than I was. And their clarity in being able to communicate was stronger than mine. The result is something to build on, to look forward to. I see a real sense of permanence in this kind of affection and caring. I see this as real positive in its promise.

Greco's story is unusual in many respects. His estrangement from his family, including his own children, spouse, and siblings, was complete and spanned over a decade. His nephew's visit during a prolonged hospitalization was prophetic and brought about a change of lifestyle. Where there had been no contact with his sister and her children, there is now routine involvement. After recovering from his illness, Greco elected to remain in Maine and live near his sister rather than move back to Philadelphia, where he had spent much of his adult life. The events Greco describes represent a *generative redemption sequence* in which the downward spiral of a misguided life of substance abuse and isolation is abruptly transformed by a nephew's simple questions about himself and his family. Developmental psychologists Dan McAdams and Regina Logan define redemption sequences as "extremely bad events [that] are followed by good outcomes (e.g., growth, enlightenment)."[10] In this instance, a simple query about community and a young man's place in it calls on an uncle to act in an agentic fashion and reopen his connection to that community, to reformulate his self-understanding and personal commitments to others.

More typically, relationships with nieces and nephews brought about important, but perhaps less profound, changes in an aunt's or an uncle's personal development. Two single and childless uncles reflected on their experience when I asked if being an uncle changed the way they viewed themselves. Michael said, "Well to a certain extent it has. This is the closest thing I have to kids and so I recognize that [it] is the next generation and so forth. So they are the future." In a similar way, another childless uncle, Robert, who happens to be a Catholic priest, reflected:

> Having really good relationships with my nephews and nieces I think satisfied a lot of my need for generativity and seems to [resolve] my own need for children and it made my decision for celibacy, and therefore not having children, [a less] painful decision in that respect. It was painful in the partner respect. I get enormous satisfaction through my nephews and nieces.

In other cases, the personal development of uncles changed the way they viewed their nephews. An example of the latter is Benny, who is married and now in his 40s; he described his recent experience of a critical illness: "It just changed the way I was prepared to help [my nephews]. [I became] much more willing [and] less selfish." Another uncle, Mark, describes his

[10] McAdams & Logan, 2004, p. 25.

own introspective process as one that led to a desire to reconnect with his brother and nephew.

> I started into personal therapy trying to look at relationships and a whole range of issues and the issue of being an uncle came up as one of the dimensions of that. It was just trying to look at the family constellation, my involvement with my brother, with his family, how to improve in a sense my own life. And I saw that [i. e., my relationship with my nephew] as one of the things that was sort of an undone piece that I wanted to begin to work on. So I have been more intentional over the last 10 years in trying to be involved, than I was in the earlier time.

For both aunts and uncles, relationships with nieces and nephews, as well as with their parents, can have a variety of positive consequences providing a source of personal satisfaction, a sense of place and connection to community, and purposeful life embedded in a configuration of family relationships. For a rare few, such relationships are profoundly meaningful, occasioning a generative redemption from a field of self-destructive behaviors. Personal experiences like that of Greco, and to a certain extent Benny and Mark, are unique and perhaps represent instances of generative redemption more typically experienced by men. None of the aunts discussed such profound estrangements from their families, although some reported periods of distraught relationships with family members and occasions of substance abuse. As noted earlier, 14 nieces and nephews reported little or no relationship with their biological fathers or were reported by their aunt or uncle as having no such paternal relationships. In contrast, only one nephew, and none of the nieces, reported having no contact with his mother (who suffered from substance abuse) (see Table 4.2). Perhaps women are less likely to experience the extremes of family estrangements reported by men, and for these men, developing relationships with nephews can profoundly affect their relationships with siblings and their own children. For many aunts and uncles, relationships with nieces and nephews have decidedly positive consequences; for a select few, they are redemptive.

CONCLUSION

Aunts and uncles are socialized and actively participate in the creation and re-creation of their roles and responsibilities to family members through their experience of great aunts and uncles, through their direct experience of aunting and uncling, and through their talk about such activities with family members and other close associates. Across generations there is remarkable consistency in the expression of aunting and uncling and in the expectations of parents. Great aunts and uncles are valued because of their unconditional support, appreciated for their personal qualities, and, among women, admired for their sense of independence. This is an array of qualities not unlike what nieces and nephews report admiring in their own aunts and uncles. For nieces and nephews of either generation, aunts and uncles often complement parents, particularly by offering contrasting lifestyles, career choices, or individual interests. At the same time, they are often active participants in family life, supplementing what parents do as well as acting as intergenerational buffers – sometimes supporting parents, sometimes supporting children. Then, too, among nieces and nephews of either generation, aunts and uncles occasionally model life choices that are not especially admirable, including a personal history of distressed relationships or unhealthy choices such as a history of substance abuse.

The roles of aunts and uncles are similar in many ways, perhaps sharing more similarities than differences. Nonetheless, there are some important differences. Aunts seem more likely to establish or continue relationships with their great aunts and to assume caretaking responsibilities for their elderly great aunts. Uncles did not seem to maintain relationships with great uncles with the regularity that women did, although there were clear exceptions.

Unlike uncles, aunts of either generation are valued for their sense of independence – an issue that often emerges in terms of an unusual choice of careers, relative to parents; a sense of professionalism that is viewed as unique relative to other women in the family; a perceived balance of family life and parenting with personal interests; or a unique choice of lifestyle. This is a common theme across both generations; nieces often value aunts whom they view as independent women who established a balance of family life with personal interests. It is a common theme throughout my interviews – and a common theme in parallel studies of mothering. Tina Miller, in her insightful work with young mothers, recounts the difficultly women face in balancing childrearing with personal needs. Shelia, a participant in Miller's study, said: "I'm quite happy at home, I'm my own person now since I've got these twins ... but I still want ... my independence."[11] Nieces are attuned to such issues, recognizing the value of caregiving and mothering while asserting the need to be autonomous and independent, to be understood as unique individuals and not essentialized by their biologies. The issue was germane for aunts in their own childhood impressions of their great aunts,

[11] Miller, 2005, p. 117.

and it continues to be germane for nieces of a younger generation. It is not a theme that appears in my interviews with uncles or nephews. For men, establishing independence in terms of career choices or personal interests is a privilege hardly recognized as such.[12]

Aunting and uncling can have a profound affect on children, as well as their parents, and serve to bind families in a web of interdependent relationships, but it also can have a profound affect on aunts and uncles and their own personal development. The relationships aunts and uncles establish can provide personal satisfaction, opportunities for the development of lifelong friendships, a connection to family and community, a sense of place located in a convoy of generations, and opportunities to enact generative themes. For some, such relationships provide unique opportunities for personal growth and development. For Harriett, coming to understand her niece and her niece's difficulties forecasted a better understanding of her own life. In the generative act of caring for her niece, Harriett comes to understand and accept herself. In a life largely lived in isolation from his family, Greco was suddenly drawn into a web of family ties that gave new meaning to his life, occasioned by a spontaneous visit by his nephew. In her last visit with an ailing aunt, Isabella appears to intervene in mending a torn relationship between sisters, her aunt and her mother. In each instance, contact with a niece or nephew yields a generative redemption sequence. The experiences of Harriett, Greco, and Isabella speak to the potential power of intergenerational family ties to heal and to the long reach of a culture of aunting and uncling.

[12] For a discussion of male privilege, see Marks, 2001.

9

Balancing the Composition

Families are often defined in rather prosaic terms, with more than a hint of ideology. A family comprising parents and children in one nuclear household becomes the standard-bearer, and of course many families are organized in this way; but many are not. In defining families simply in terms of the physical location of parents and young children, we properly underscore the importance of parent–child relationships, but at the same time overlook other ways in which families evolve, including households headed by single parents, blended families, and adults who reside together without children (e.g., because their children are living independently or because they are childless). We neglect asking the all-important question of where the grandparents and adult siblings are living and how often they communicate and become active in supporting each other, including sharing in child care. Standard definitions of families as singular households are in part a simple description of how people live and organize some of their relationships, however inaccurate, and in part implicit prescriptions for how lives should be lived. In one insightful view, feminist scholar Dorothy Smith defines the Standard North American Family (SNAF) as an ideological code representing a legally married heterosexual couple sharing a household with children. As an ideology, it is pernicious:

> SNAF infected texts are all around us. They give discursive body and substance to a version of the family that masks the actualities of people's lives or at best inserts an implicit evaluation into accounts of ways of living together in households or forming economically and emotionally supportive relationships outside that do not accord with SNAF.[1]

[1] Smith, 1993, p. 63.

It is tempting to invoke ideology as an explanation for why families are so misrepresented in public discourse and the enterprise of social science, for despite continuing evidence to the contrary, standardized views of what family means ignore how we actually live in relationships with brothers and sisters, with children of our own parentage or not, with aging parents, with long-standing friends whom we regard like kin. The labors of aunts, uncles, nieces, and nephews require that we take exception to a restrictive view of the SNAF and entertain a more integrated view of families living in highly interdependent relationships distributed across multiple households.

SITUATING FAMILIES IN A RELATIONAL CONTEXT

Scholars have long focused on the health of families, and often this concern surfaces as a cautionary tale about deteriorating conditions, and particularly the loss in the utility, importance, and presence of kin in everyday life. Where once kin were seen as a prime source of support in a wide array of arenas, contemporary families are dispersed, highly mobile, flexible in their expectations of one another, and not especially stable.[2] More recently social critics have continued in this vein, arguing that individuals are becoming increasingly isolated,[3] and in some regards, limited empirical research seems to support this view. Large surveys intended to be representative of noninstitutionalized adults in the United States find declining core networks of intimates, the people with whom individuals discuss important matters. Nearly one quarter of adults report having no regular confidants in their core networks, and this figure represents a substantial rise from similar figures collected two decades earlier, or so it seems.[4] It is tempting to conclude that families are isolated, that networks of intimates are declining in importance, and that close relations with kin are relatively unimportant, even if they happen quaintly to persist.

What is not immediately apparent is that arguments over the isolation of families and the demise of the importance of kinship have a long and curious academic history. Writing in the mid-1950s, Elizabeth Bott commented: "It is a commonplace of sociology and anthropology that kinship does not play a very important part in industrialized societies. The elementary family of father, mother, and dependent children is said to stand alone."[5] Bott

[2] Adams, 1999; Amato, Booth, Johnson, & Rogers, 2007; Popenoe, 1993.
[3] Bauman, 2000; Olds & Schwartz 2009; Putnam, 2000.
[4] McPherson, Smith-Lovin, & Brashears, 2006, 2008.
[5] Bott, 1971, p. 115.

was sharply critical of this view largely because it did not characterize the diversity of families and their experience as it was reported in the literature of the time or the experience of the London families she studied. Although some families were relatively uninvolved with kin, others were clearly heavily involved, particularly working-class families, who reported a good deal of contact with kin. The assumption of an invariant configuration of families organized in separate households with little contact was for Bott too simplistic. She went on to argue: "The elementary family does not stand alone; its members keep up frequent and intimate relationships with parents and with at least some of the siblings, uncles and aunts, and cousins of the husband and wife."[6] Similar observations appear in a mid-twentieth-century study of kinship ties among older adults living on this side of the Atlantic in the urban midwestern United States. In their study of kinship, Elaine Cumming and David Schneider concluded: "the ideal American family is a nuclear family, but the real American family is often an extended one."[7] Similarly Carol Stack, in her now classic study of Black Americans, found that families were thickly organized around kinship and neighborhood ties.[8]

In the decades following the work of Elizabeth Bott and many others, the theme of displaced families and minimal contact with kin continues, but not without its occasional detractors, who, like Bott, find their own study of families to be far more nuanced. Family sociologists Diane Holmberg, Terri Orbuch, and Joe Veroff, in their study of couples in the early years of marriage, emphasized the importance of kin and friends, intimates who constitute the supporting characters of a family. "Marriage is not a duet," they concluded, "but rather a complex orchestral arrangement, one in which many different people's needs and preferences must be considered and negotiated."[9] Parents, siblings, grandparents, friends, and coworkers enter into the narrative descriptions of couples as they recount their weddings, honeymoons, the birth and rearing of children, the challenges of balancing work and family, and more generally the ordinary business of family life. The preferences of family members and other close associates of both spouses are apparent in the planning of weddings and continue throughout marriage. Similarly sociologist Karen Hansen in her in-depth study of parenting practices challenges the view of self-contained nuclear families raising children independently and without connection to community. She concluded: "parents consciously and creatively construct networks of interdependence.

---

[6] Bott, 1971, p. 116.
[8] Stack, 1974.

[7] Cumming & Schneider, 1961, p. 499.
[9] Holmberg, Orbuch, & Veroff, 2004, p. 154.

They regularly and intentionally tap people beyond their immediate family for aid in the care of their children."[10] Not surprisingly, parents regularly tap their siblings for help in child care; their siblings respond and in part regard their service to parents and their children as enjoyable, rewarding, and fun. They live in what Hansen practically denoted as *not-so-nuclear families*, and in this way her study emphasizes the juxtaposition of independent SNAFs with the lived experience of interdependent households.

Similar themes of interdependence are evident in studies of grandparents, parents, and children. In a longitudinal study of multiple generations of families that spans 30 years, social gerontologist Vern Bengtson and his colleagues consistently find high levels of intergenerational solidarity that reflect close emotional ties among grandparents, parents, and grandchildren, and this pattern of emotional closeness is stable over the course of the study. Just as important, their work finds that not all intergenerational ties are positive or without discord. One in five relationships is characterized by significant conflict or detachment. Nonetheless, Bengtson concluded: "For many Americans, multigenerational bonds are becoming more important than nuclear family ties for well-being and support over the course of their lives."[11]

A number of parallel lines of research offer additional evidence for the importance and regularity of ties with kin. The recent mass survey of adults we visited earlier, although finding what now appear to be, at the very most, modest declines over the previous two decades in the size of core discussion networks, still found that kin represent a substantial proportion of core network members (40%) for those adults who identify at least one confidant with whom they discuss important matters.[12] Because this survey centers on a very narrow band of friendship in the form of personal confidants, we can expect that it underestimates involvement with the diversity of kin and friends that typically constitute personal networks. Detailed inquiries into the nature of friendship find that friends vary widely in the complexity and depth of their relationships. Confidants, or the people with whom we discuss important matters, are but one form of close tie, and they may or may not overlap with close ties we rely on for practical help or those we rely on for emotional support.[13] Individuals vary as well in the composition and size of their personal communities of associates whom they consider

[10] Hansen, 2005, p. 3.   [11] Bengtson, 2001, p. 5.

[12] The decline in the size of core networks reported by McPherson and her coauthors (2006; 2008) is hotly contested, and for good reason. For a discussion of key issues in this research see Fischer, 2009.

[13] Spencer & Pahl, 2006.

important. Some personal communities or personal networks are relatively large and comprise kin, some are dominated by friends unrelated by blood or marriage, and others contain a mix of kin and nonkin.[14] These basic patterns seem to vary little across a number of cultures; diversity in family ties is common.[15] The consistent theme is simply that people vary in the number, composition, and organization of personal ties, but they are hardly isolated.

More germane for our purposes are investigations of relationships among adult siblings, and here we find strong evidence of persistent close connections: adult siblings commonly exchange practical support including child care,[16] siblings are commonly among the closest friends of adults, approximately 50% of adults report monthly contacts with siblings, and approximately one third would rely on a sibling in an emergency.[17] Further, as noted earlier in this text, the mobility and convenience of cell phones and a rapidly developing array of computer-mediated forms of communication appear to strengthen ties among family members by increasing communication among intimates, near-intimates, and distant kin.[18]

Taken together, the picture that emerges from a variety of work on marriage, parenting, intergenerational relations, adult siblings, and the contemporary use of new mediums such as e-mail and the Internet is generally consistent – for many, kin continue to be important in the lives of adults. Families are far from isolated nuclear units living in discrete households. It seems likely that some aunts and uncles are deeply involved with their siblings and with their nieces and nephews, and for some, these relationships become among the longest and most intimate in a lifetime. Then, too, families are flexible arrangements. Just as Elizabeth Bott concluded from her study of urban families in the mid-twentieth-century, more contemporary work on families concludes that families are diverse in their social arrangements. Some are remarkably close and maintain this affective solidarity over long periods of time; others experience change as relationships once close become distant or vice versa, and still others are marked by persistent conflict and distant relationships. We cannot say with any certainty that the participants in this study are representative of any known population, but then neither can we say they are unique. We can say that much like

---

[14] Spencer & Pahl, 2006; Widmer, 1999; Widmer & Sapin, 2008.
[15] Murphy, 2008.
[16] Eriksen & Gerstel, 2002; Voorpostel & Blieszner, 2008; Voorpostel & Van Der Lippe, 2007.
[17] White, 2001; White & Riedman, 1992.
[18] Boase et al., 2006; Igarashi et al., 2005; Katz & Rice, 2002; Rainie et al., 2000.

Mark Twain's response to a press report of his early demise, the isolation of contemporary families is greatly exaggerated.[19]

THE EXPRESSION AND MEANING OF GENERATIVITY

Generative inclinations and activities appear routinely among the aunts, uncles, nieces, and nephews of this study. Mentoring, intergenerational buffering, meaning keeping, and friendship describe the essentials of generativity, and each of these dimensions saturates the culture of some families and appears weakly, if at all, in others. To appreciate fully the meaning and construction of generativity in the lives of individuals, we need to apply a sociological imagination,[20] one that emphasizes the intersections of personality and individual biography with personal relationships and social configurations of overlapping families and households. The framework of this study was well suited to the task because the essentials of generativity are all in large part relational features that take their meaning and expression within a configuration of family relationships. Our sociological imagination is limited in some respects because the study has generated few insights into variations of generativity across key social locations such as ethnicity, race, class, or culture, and such diversity may add insight into the dimensionality of generativity.[21] Nonetheless our micro-sociological focus sharply illustrates a highly textured view of generativity, emphasizing features commonly experienced although uncommonly recognized, as well as a broader view of families, emphasizing solidarities within and across generations. Here we expand on these themes and in particular on how this inquiry alters our initial representation of generativity.

Developmental psychologist Eric Erikson described middle age as a unique period of the adult life course in which generativity is a central concern. Having earlier developed a sense of self, of personal identity, and a connection with a select few persons preferred as intimates, the developmental task in midlife becomes one of turning attentions to the needs of others and the care of future generations. Although still acknowledging that generative inclinations can appear among younger or older adults, Erikson believed generativity typically dominates in middle adulthood, struggling with the competing demand of self-absorption. Current students of life-span development emphasize a more flexible view because personal choice,

---

[19] In response to an Associated Press report of his death in 1897, Mr. Twain is said to have cabled from Europe, "The reports of my death are greatly exaggerated."
[20] Mills, 1959; Shanahan & Macmillan, 2008.
[21] W. Allen & Connor, 1997.

relational and parental statuses, health and poverty, economic and political climates peculiar to a particular historical period, and cultural beliefs all influence the development and timing or appearance of psychosocial concerns like generativity.[22] Among adults, age has less to do with an emerging concern for future generations than becoming a parent, or perhaps an aunt, uncle, or grandparent, and all of these statuses can occur over a broad spectrum of the life span. In short, individuals do not suddenly become concerned with generativity because they turned 35, or any other age, any more than they suddenly become parents, aunts, or uncles because they have reached a particular age. Human development is far more flexible and adaptive to personal, social, historical, and environmental conditions.

Contemporary developmental psychologists view generative inclinations and behaviors as more salient among middle-aged adults in part because of cultural expectations – expectations that may vary across cultures.[23] "One of the reasons that generativity emerges as a psychosocial issue in the *adult* years is that society comes to demand that adults take responsibility for the next generation."[24] Undoubtedly there is some appeal to this argument. We expect younger adults to redirect some of their attentions to future generations as they become older and settled into work habits and family lives. To a certain extent, research supports this view, at least in part. Generative actions and concerns appear more commonly among American adults in the midlife years relative to young adulthood or old age, but such group differences are often minimal and exceptions relatively common.[25]

Our visits with the aunts and uncles of this study are illustrative of how age-graded concerns are moderated by other factors, especially the personal and relational conditions of actors. Such moderating factors are illustrated in the experiences of a number of uncles and aunts, including Aunt Olympia, with whom we visited earlier. When Aunt Olympia was still in her mid-20s, single and childless, she became deeply involved with her sister's young daughter. Aunt Olympia's sister was recently divorced, and her need for help in child care was significant. The sisters had a close relationship, and Olympia had the time and interest in developing a relationship with her niece. In this instance, and in many similar instances, generative relationships with nieces and nephews emerge from personal circumstance, and central among such circumstances is childlessness. Additional features that encourage generative relationships include the quality of relationships

[22] Kotre, 1984; McAdams & Logan, 2004; Shanahan & Macmillan, 2008.
[23] McAdams et al., 1998; McAdams & Logan, 2004.
[24] McAdams et al., 1998, p. 10.
[25] McAdams & de St. Aubin, 1992; McAdams et al., 1998.

among adult siblings, family circumstances such as the needs of adult siblings for help in child care, and family traditions such as the belief that nurturing relationships among collateral kin are valuable. As they mature, the personal preferences of nieces and nephews also become important, and they may elect to pursue relationships with aunts and uncles or to forgo such relationships. Perhaps the age of aunts and uncles plays some part in the emergence of generativity, but its influence seems to be overwhelmed by the distinct elements of family culture, the personal attributes of family members, and the primacy and character of their relationships. Generativity, rather than being driven by age, personal condition, or developmental task, is largely derivative of intersections – the interplay of conditions describing the lives of kin, parents, and children and their relationships. If and when age matters, it matters least.

When relationships among aunts and uncles with nieces and nephews are relatively close – and they are not always close – they are often reciprocal. We saw many examples of this reciprocity as older generations mentor younger generations and in turn are themselves mentored, which we often referred to as reverse mentoring. Nieces and nephews advised their aunts and uncles on matters of relationships with their own children as well as relationships with other family members. Nieces and nephews provided personal advice regarding careers and advanced education, managing relationships with coworkers and employers, and the ordinary mix of daily life. Intimate relationships among adults and children create fertile conditions for generativity. When generativity emerges in the relationships of intimates, it is often reciprocal, although this is not to say it is necessarily balanced. Nieces and nephews were often deeply concerned about their favored aunts and uncles – and in this sense generative in their inclinations and actions. Age seems to matter less than we might expect in both the onset of generative inclinations as well as the object of generative actions. Younger persons quite freely act in generative ways toward older persons. In the realm of families, generativity emerges out of layered personal relationships – an aunt's or uncle's relationships with adult siblings, their children, and perhaps grandparents and other close associates. Generativity as it emerges in families is often a mix of reciprocal caregiving, a concern for future generations as well as future relationships, and it is not uncommonly a constellation of concerns shared by nieces and nephews regarding their parents, siblings, grandparents, aunts, and uncles.

Given the significance of family relationships in the emergence and expression of generativity, it is surprising that common instances of kin keeping are largely absent from the traditional paper-and-pencil measures of generativity. Such measures like the Loyola Generativity Scale (LGS) and the Generative Behavior Checklist (GBC)[26] omit sampling instances of what appear to be rather common ways in which family members enact generative actions. For example, of the 20 items that comprise the LGS, there is no mention of core family members or other close associates or the all-important relational contexts wherein generativity often resides.[27] From the perspective of our emerging understanding of generativity, this is an oversight.

Typical items in the LGS may well tap generative inclinations, but they are too abstract to capture the nuances of how generative inclinations are lived, and the result is a somewhat distorted conceptualization and an incomplete assessment. Nonetheless, the LGS does tap generative inclinations that may emerge outside of the realm of intimate relationships. For instance, selected items inquire about creative contributions ("I try to be creative in most things that I do"), community activism ("I do volunteer work for a charity"), or creating a long-lasting legacy of personal contributions that may or may not include family relationships ("I feel as though my contributions will exist after I die"). The question is whether an aunt or uncle who maintains a close relationship with a niece or nephew would score high on these items. In a very general sense, the measure captures some of what we mean by generativity, but it is a rather shallow description without context. Aunt Olympia may feel she is creative, and she may volunteer for charities; this would lead us to regard her as generative. Yet the thick description of her core generative inclinations and actions that are rooted in her relationships with her niece and niece's mother would go undetected. Aunt Olympia's responses to a brief questionnaire would fail to reveal the core of her generativity, the relational context in which it occurs, and properties derivative of that context. We would fail to appreciate how Olympia's generativity is directed at a constellation of family relationships that include a contemporary (Olympia's older sister) and a child who has now matured into an adult, parent, and intimate of Olympia. In this way, Olympia's generativity is directed at multiple generations. We would fail to realize the significance of personal exigency (the sister's divorce, or Olympia's initial status as a young adult both single and childless), and the relative insignificance of age (Olympia was in her 20s when she became an active aunt). We would also fail to realize the importance of family development and changes in personal

---

[26] McAdams & de St. Aubin, 1992.

[27] The GBC is slightly better in this regard because it includes at least four items, among the 49 items that constitute this measure, that specifically center on providing care to children.

relationships. When interviewed, Olympia was 52 and her niece 35. Over the course of better than three decades, Olympia and her niece became close friends as both were mothers with professional careers. Olympia continued to mentor her adult niece, but she also valued her niece's counsel. As their relationship added a distinct element of friendship, it became increasingly characterized by a mutual interdependence and generativity, with each generation caring for the other, each centered on caring for the future of the family ensemble.

In short, for family members, queries about their relationships, whether strong or weak, reveal much about the very nature or core of generative expression. Generativity is apt to be largely rooted in family relationships with important implications for how and when generative inclinations develop and where and by whom generative actions are expressed. Quite possibly close relationships in which generative inclinations develop and are expressed are common among aunts and uncles in their relationships with their siblings, nieces, and nephews.

In locating the relationships of aunts and uncles with their siblings and children, we uncover instances of frequent, diverse, and intimate experience dwelling in shared family biographies. From this location, generativity unfolds in expressions of mentoring, meaning keeping, and intergenerational buffering. The elements of generativity are cast within a relationship that shares similarities with parenting – and sometimes quite explicitly, as in cases where a nephew views an uncle as like a "father" or a niece views an aunt as a "second mom." When acting as surrogate parents or supplementing the work of actively involved parents, the contributions of aunts and uncles are unique, in part because of their social locations as contemporaries of parents who bring to bear their sometimes quite intimate knowledge of multiple generations of family members. At other times, generativity is cast within a relationship that suffuses themes common to peer-based friendship with themes more common to kinship. The mix of parenting and friendship themes demonstrates that the expression of generative inclinations is dynamic because of its placement in the developing and co-occurring biographies of family members. Among families with young children, the generative inclinations of aunts and uncles are apt to take a form different from the generative inclinations that emerge in the same family constellation with much older children. In this way, generativity emerges in a developmental and relational context that happens to be entirely missing from existing conceptualizations and measures. Relationships framed by generative inclinations substantially and uniquely benefit parents, their children, and the aunts and uncles themselves. In this social landscape, a new understanding of generativity emerges, one deeply rooted in a convoy of personal relationships.

BALANCING THE COMPOSITION

In a wonderfully interesting essay, family sociologist Kerry Daly[28] begins with a simple observation that families as we represent them in the logic of theory or the empiricism of research, and families as they are lived, are quite different. To detail his observation, Daly uses a metaphor of *negative spaces.* In the world of art, negative spaces are the areas around or between objects. The area around a cup or the area between the body of a cup and its handle is negative space. Artists understand the importance of negative spaces – what a social scientist might call context – because negative spaces help define a subject and add balance to a composition. To take the metaphor a step further, artists freely acknowledge that focusing on the area around a cup in order to represent the cup yields a more accurate painting. Without context, still-life painting (a subject matter that has occupied artists for centuries and, judging by the artistic activity in my own household, will continue to do so well into the future) would be just another bowl of fruit. Negative spaces help to define context and thereby the subjects of interest. This study in many ways is a representation of negative spaces or the personal and relational background of parents and children – what we social scientists ordinarily don't see but which families themselves experience quite routinely in their relationships with kith and kin.

The study of aunts and uncles adds context and expands how we come to understand and represent families as dynamic social entities. This study illustrates how families are configurations of interdependent relationships arranged across households. I learned, for instance, of my nephew's new relationship with a young New York architect and social activist by speaking with my niece, who in turn has recently spoken to her mother, where she garnered the relational news about her brother, which she so readily shared with her uncle. To portray a family as a single household – that is to say, as a still life without context – would be rather tidy and nuclear, but not nearly as interesting, nuanced, or factual. The social spaces of families are replete with relationships that cross household boundaries, including those of immediate kin such as grandparents, parents, and children, as well

[28] Daly, 2003.

as collateral kin including aunts, uncles, nieces, and nephews. Of course, a balanced composition must recognize the cast members as well as the diversity of their associations. The relationships of adult siblings with each other and their children are routinely intimate, and perhaps just as routinely distant, a diversity that Elizabeth Bott easily recorded in the mid-twentieth-century and one that continues to be reported more recently.[29] The relationships of siblings include habits of mutual support as well as habits of tension, conflict, ambivalence, and distance. Relationships among adult siblings and their children change in response to major events such as marriage, parenthood, divorce, illness, and death, and they co-occur in a developmental context that influences the subjective and behavioral manifestation of their relationships.

An understanding of families organized across multiple households or as convoys of intersecting relationships that change over the life course of cast members is distinct from a rather simplistic view of families comprising one or two biological parents and their children. The aunts, uncles, nieces, and nephews in this study describe relationships that vary in the intensity and breadth of their interdependencies. Their relationships emerge as distinctly less normatively bound and certainly more active than is often assumed. Aunts are at times closer to their sisters than the aunts are to their husbands. Uncles, however close they are to their own children, find uniquely intimate relationships with a favored nephew who is regarded as like a son and like an honored friend. The ties among aunts and uncles with their nieces and nephews are commonly founded in shared ancestry or marriage, but such foundations belie a critical relational architecture that is socially constructed. In our postmodern portrait, the domestic life of adult partners and parents with children is recentered. Parenting is no longer simply a matter of the engagement of a custodial parent and child. Parenting is a far richer enterprise, frequently involving kin and close associates who are regarded as kin, as well as more distant acquaintances who are nonetheless consequential.[30] Parents seek out the counsel of their adult siblings, or direct help in child care; aunts offer their perspectives, which are sometimes quite different from the perspectives of parents; uncles intervene in disputes between parents and children; nieces and nephews find their understandings of their parents transformed through the storytelling of their aunts and uncles; people of all ages sometimes mentor one another.

Our foray into aunting and uncling encourages a broader understanding of families and how they are actually lived, and a certain drift away

[29] Bott, 1971; Widmer, 1999.   [30] Blau & Fingerman, 2009.

from the rather rigid and sometime distinctly misguided normative views of families and their relationships. One of the more interesting elements of aunting and uncling is how these positions retain some common expectations that are widely held by parents and their siblings but at the same time allow for some deviation from what we normally consider appropriate maternal or paternal activities. Aunts and uncles are in part freelance parent/friends and, as a result, inventive. Aunts often violate traditional feminine directives, seemingly unencumbered by "maternal instincts" or codes that define appropriate maternal behavior, and they are valued for their inventiveness, a position communication scholars Patricia Sotirin and Laura Ellingson also distill from their study of nieces.[31] In their role as aunts, women are free to model alternate lifestyles and deviate from heteronormative conventions that prescribe the expressions of domesticity, maternity, and femininity – conventions that are largely restrictive. To a lesser extent, uncles who describe close relationships with their nephews breach masculine conventions that limit the emergence of their family intimacies and kin keeping, a position consistent with Karen Hansen's reports of the contributions of uncles in caregiving networks.[32] Nieces and nephews approved of the breach. Aunts and uncles often modeled alternative lifestyles and values, and were highly valued for doing so. I did not get the impression, however, that the breach from traditional conventions is entirely derivative of atypical statuses. For instance, those aunts and uncles who were single, childless, gay, or lesbian were not necessarily valued more than their counterparts who were traditionally married parents. Parents and nonparents, homosexuals, and heterosexuals are valued as aunts and uncles in part because the social conventions that define aunting and uncling simply permit, and sometimes even encourage, nonconventionality. Oddly enough, the expectation of eccentric and nonconventional behaviors among aunts and uncles is somewhat codified judging from the number of children's books that immortalize such characters,[33] as well as their appearance in popular treatments of aunts and uncles.[34] Aunts and uncles in some ways undo conventional depictions of gender. They are family contrarians.

In the end, knowing about the negative spaces or social contexts, here represented by aunts and uncles, informs our knowledge about the ordinary lives of families, about parenting and raising children, about friendships. From this perspective, families are often not terribly nuclear in practice,

---

[31] Sotirin & Ellingson, 2006.   [32] Hansen, 2005.

[33] For examples, see Lima & Lima, 2001; Warhola, 2003.

[34] Sturgis, 2004; Wild, 2000.

but then neither are they particularly unusual. The understanding of families that emerges from this study suggests how very odd and surprisingly persistent the ideology of the SNAF is because it fails to acknowledge expressly the ordinary relationships among family members like adult brothers or sisters.

I began this inquiry with a distinctly personal interest and some lingering personal memories of my own family, my own aunts and uncles, a curiosity born of experience and profession. The inquiry most certainly led to places I could never have imagined. I initiated the project thinking it would take no more than a year, occupy a leave from my home institution, and perhaps yield a fine article or two. In the end, the project expanded annually and occupied the better part of my professional life for 7 years.

Although this has been the first in-depth study of aunts and uncles, I hope it will not be the last. Perhaps we have built a foundation for expanding an understanding of the organization and interdependence of family ensembles that figure so prominently in the lives of adults and children. Speaking with the 104 participants was immensely rewarding; it ultimately enriched our understanding of how families operate, how aunts and uncles become significant for parents and children as well as our understanding of generativity and its relational and developmental genesis. We have come to better understand how visions of isolation from kin – and intimate friends for that matter – seem to persist without much critical analysis, and in the face of over a half century of evidence to the contrary. Such is the power of residual ideology. But perhaps most important, this study permits a richer appreciation for how to go about understanding a collection of kin relations who are not typically or clearly recognized for their contributions. Some of us – and I include both the participants and myself in this category – can hardly imagine life without them. And being a child of the culture of rock and roll, I hope you don't mind if I end with a line that might have been penned by Robert Hunter, one of the principal lyricists for the Grateful Dead: *what a long and curious trip it's been.*[35]

---

[35] The line from the Grateful Dead song *Truckin'* typically is voiced as "what a long, strange trip it's been," and I've always understood that strange, for Hippies, implies curiosity in the best sense. For instance, one might say, "Groovy man, this is one strange book," which would mean very good and you should most certainly buy a copy. Many thanks to Alan Trist and the folks at Ice Nine for permission to quote from Robert Hunter's lyrics for the song *Truckin'*, Copyright © 1971, Ice Nine Publishing Company.

APPENDIX

All interviews were digitally recorded and transcribed verbatim into text. The transcripts were then parsed into meaning units, typically a sentence or paragraph on a common subject, and coded into one of the themes detailed here. A meaning unit was usually assigned exclusively to one code, but on occasion the comments of participants included multiple meanings and were assigned multiple codes as appropriate. For example, in speaking of her 23-year-old niece, Aunt Rebecca shared the following: "[My niece] is bright and she seems to have great aptitude with math, and she wanted to be a math teacher for a long time. . . . I've tried to really encourage her . . . and I think it's nice for women to be in math and science fields, because there's not many of them, and her mom sort of discourages her." In this example, Aunt Rebecca is clearly being supportive of her niece (Code 3.1: General support), but at the same time she is mentoring a nontraditional gender identity on the part of her niece (Code 3.5: Mentoring gender) and supplementing the likely position of her niece's mother, as Rebecca implies in the last sentence (Code 2.2: Supplemental parenting).

The coding scheme allows us to describe the *dramatis personae* and identify common themes that appear in their relationships. Most of the themes were anticipated, and specific interview questions were purposefully designed to explore particular issues (e.g., mentoring and family work). Some themes were entirely unanticipated and developed in the course of the study. The mentoring of aunts and uncles by nieces and nephews is one example (Code 3.7: Reverse mentoring). In all, the coding protocol consists of eight primary codes and a number of secondary codes:

1. Individual and relational descriptors – individual characteristics and activity patterns. Basic descriptors of the aunts, uncles, nieces, and nephews, what they do together and how often they do it.
   1.1. Personal attributes of aunts, uncles, nieces and nephews – age, race or ethnicity, education, occupation, income, sexual orientation, marital status, number of children, lineage, and absence of niece's or nephew's parents.
   1.2. Frequency of interaction – how often partners visit, call, or e-mail.
   1.3. Closeness/intimacy – references to the closeness or intimacy of the relationship. This code includes comments about limited intimacy and closeness.
   1.4. Family influence – references to how parents or grandparents encourage or discourage the relationships of aunts and uncles with nieces and nephews.
   1.5. Activities – what partners do together (e.g., visit with or without parents present, engage in recreational pursuits, play, provide child care, or visit with other family members).
   1.6. Talk – learning about each others activities, life, catching up.
   1.7. Understanding – interviewee's understanding of target as a unique individual.
   1.8. Third-party talk – learning about another indirectly through a third-party, such as a sibling (e.g., nieces' and nephews' parents) or another family member. For example, an aunt talks to her sister and learns about the activities of her niece.
   1.9. Role modeling – a reference to aunts or uncles as role models, either positive or negative.
   1.10. Admirable personal qualities – qualities nieces and nephews admire, or do not admire, in aunts and uncles.
2. The culture of aunting and uncling: how aunts and uncles understand their roles including family members' beliefs and expectations regarding aunts and uncles and their relationships with nieces and nephews.
   2.1. Role enactments of aunts and uncles – aunts' and uncles' understanding of their role and responsibilities to nieces and nephews. This code includes ideas about the unique contributions of aunts or uncles, as well as how aunts and uncles differ from parents.
   2.2. Aunts and uncles as supplemental parents – direct references to parenting or supplementing what parents do, for example, providing child care, short- or long-term housing or alternate life choices (e.g., with regard to schooling, careers, or relationships).

2.3. Third-party perspectives – an aunt's or uncle's reference to an outsider's perspective regarding nieces and nephews and their relationships to their parents and siblings.

2.4. Father or mother substitute – reference to an aunt or uncle acting as a father or mother figure, especially in cases where fathers or mothers are absent through desertion, divorce, or death.

2.5. Boundary issues – recognizing parents' priority, or not doing so. This code includes conflicts with parents about the degree or type of involvement of aunts and uncles with nieces and nephews.

2.6. Eccentric behaviors – direct comments by nieces or nephews about eccentric or unusual behaviors or habits of aunts or uncles (e.g., dancing nude). This can mean acting in ways that are considered contrary to traditional views of femininity or masculinity.

2.7. Ethnicity or race – the influence of ethnicity or race on the relationship.

2.8. Sexual orientation – the influence of the sexual orientation of aunts, uncles, nieces, or nephews on their relationship.

2.9. Childlessness – of an aunt or uncle and influence on relationships with nieces or nephews.

2.10. Niece and nephew differences – discussion of differences between nieces and nephews, and differences between nieces and nephews and an aunt's or uncle's own children.

2.11. Naming – references to how nieces and nephews refer to aunts or uncles (e.g., with or without the salutation of aunt or auntie).

2.12. Interview effect – any reference to the effect of the interview on the respondents' thoughts about their relationship with an aunt, uncle, niece, or nephew.

3. Mentoring – direct exchanges of support and advice.

  3.1. General support or advice giving – sharing information or wisdom regarding school, career, family members, and intimate relationships with peers and friends.

    3.1.1. Instrumental support – exchanges of material aid such as money or lending a car.

    3.1.2. Emotional support – exchanges of positive regard and emotional support.

    3.1.3. Mixed support – exchanges that include elements of instrumental and emotional support.

  3.2. Criticism – direct exchanges of criticism of a niece's or nephew's choices or actions (e.g., quitting school, staying out late).

  3.3. Supportive listening without judgment or evaluation.

3.4. Spiritual advice – discussions of spiritual or religious issues.

3.5. Mentoring gender – lessons or talk about gender-appropriate behavior. This code includes talk about gender (in)appropriate behavior and may include traditional or nontraditional elements.

3.6. Nefarious activity – engaging in any activity with the potential for negative outcomes such as the use of drugs or alcohol.

3.7. Reverse mentoring – instances in which nieces and nephews provide support, criticism, or advice to an aunt or uncle.

3.8. Parental support – instances in which aunts or uncles provide support for parents or instances in which parents directly seek out the advice or support of an aunt or uncle.

4. Meaning keeping and family work – communications that influence a family's solidarity and knowledge about family history, as well as communications about particular individuals or in regard to particular relationships with family members.

　　4.1. Family storytelling/transformations of attention – sharing stories and historical information about family members with nieces and nephews, especially stories about parents when they were young. May include instances in which nieces and nephews learn about parents' early history as children, adolescents, and siblings from an aunt or uncle directly through conversation or indirectly through observing aunts or uncles interacting with parents.

　　4.2. Creating or managing family traditions – including holidays, family events, and gatherings that encourage a unique sense of family solidarity.

　　4.3. General family work/talk – sharing information and feelings about the current circumstances of family members or their relationships (e.g., parent's impending divorce, an aunt's spouse or partner, or any other family member).

　　4.4. Child-minding talk – parents, aunts, and uncles talk about children.

　　4.5. Absent parents – talk about the long-term absence of a father (typical) or mother (atypical) due to desertion, divorce, or death.

5. Intergenerational buffers – acting as an intermediary in relationships between family members.

　　5.1. Mediators – mediating disputes between family members, especially nieces and nephews with parents or siblings as a neutral party, partisan supporter, or critic.

　　5.2. Empathy – providing a way to understand a family member's point of view, as in that of a parent (typically) or grandparent (occasionally), or encouraging parents to understand nieces and nephews, often by providing comparisons to the parent's childhood or adolescence.

6. Friendship (fellow travelers) – basic friendship themes in the relationships of uncles and aunts with nieces and nephews. All of these themes suggest a peer or near-peer based relationship characterized by a mutuality or mutual benefit and admiration.

   6.1. Companionship themes – comments about liking to be with the other, spending time together, or enjoying one another's company as peers or near-peers.

   6.2. Shared interests – sharing in a common activity such as recreational pursuits, common interests, or simply spending time together in unstructured activity.

   6.3. Mutual support – sharing or expressing mutual support.

7. Aunting and uncling as it affects personal development – the influence of nieces and nephews on aunts and uncles, or changes in the way aunts and uncles view themselves as a result of aunting or uncling.

8. Socialization of aunts and uncles – an aunt's or uncle's formal and informal preparation for the role.

   8.1. Personal memories – an aunt's or uncle's personal experience with his or her own aunts and uncles (including ongoing relationships, should they exist).

   8.2. Aunting and uncling talk – conversations of aunts and uncles with friends or family members about the responsibilities or importance of aunting or uncling for nieces and nephews, or sharing day-to-day accounts with friends or family members about relationships with nieces and nephews.

Table A1. *Descriptive statistics for uncles (n = 21) and nephews (n = 31) by country*

	Uncles		Nephews	
Variables	US	NZ	US	NZ
Age, Mean (SD)	49.2 (8.9)	41.8 (11.6)	23.1 (2.8)	19.2 (1.5)
White, non-Hispanic	100	90	75	90
Education				
High school	9	0	8	0
Some college	27	22	75	100
College degree(s)	64	78	17	0
Occupation				
Professional	73	60	8	0
Blue collar	18	0	17	0
Student	9	20	75	100
Retired/disabled	0	20	0	0
Annual income (in thousand USD), Mean (SD)[a]	55.0 (22.6)	N/A	11.8 (4.0)	N/A
Heterosexual	91	80	92	100
Marital status				
Single	18	30	92	95
Married/cohabiting	73	60	8	5
Divorced	9	10	0	0
Childless	27.3	70.0	100	100
Uncle's nephew's age, Mean (SD)	21.9 (6.7)	17.8 (9.7)	N/A	N/A
Nephew's uncle's age, Mean (SD)	N/A	N/A	47.7 (7.0)	45.1 (10.5)
Uncle's nephew's sexual orientation – Heterosexual	100	90	N/A	N/A
Nephew's uncle's sexual orientation – Heterosexual	N/A	N/A	100	100
Frequency of interaction				
Annually or less	18.2	10	0	15.8
Biannual	9.1	10	8.3	15.8
Bimonthly	27.3	20	41.7	31.6
Monthly	9.1	10	25	10.5
Biweekly	18.2	10	8.3	10.5
Weekly or greater	18.2	40	16.7	15.8
Length of interview (in minutes) Mean (SD)	52.5 (18.7)	36.0 (6.3)	26.8 (21.2)	20.1 (6.2)
Uncle's relationship to nephew's parents				
Mother's brother	54.5	50.0	58.3	47.4
Father's brother	27.3	30.0	33.3	31.6
Brother-in-law	18.2	20	8.3	21.1

Note: All figures are in percentages unless otherwise noted. NZ = New Zealand; US = United States.
[a] Incomes not available for the NZ sample.

REFERENCES

Adams, B. N. (1999). Cross-cultural and U. S. Kinship. In M. Sussman, S. K. Steinmetz, & G. W. Peterson (Eds.), *Handbook of marriage and the family* (2nd ed., pp. 77–91). New York: Plenum Press.

Allan, G. (1998). Friendship and the private sphere. In R. G. Adams & G. Allan (Eds.), *Placing friendship in context* (pp. 71–91). New York: Cambridge University Press.

Allan, G. (2008). Flexibility, friendship and family. *Personal Relationships, 15*, 1–16.

Allen, K. R., Fine, M. A., & Demo, D. H. (2000). An overview of family diversity: Controversies, questions and values. In D. H. Demo, K. R. Allen, & M. A. Fine (Eds.), *Handbook of family diversity* (pp. 1–14). New York: Oxford University Press.

Allen, W., & Connor, W. (1997). An African American perspective on generative fathering. In A. Hawkins & D. Dollahite (Eds.), *Generative fathering: Beyond deficit perspectives* (pp. 52–70). Thousand Oaks, CA: Sage.

Amato, P. R., Booth, A., Johnson, D. R., & Rogers, S. J. (2007). *Alone together: How marriage in America is changing.* Cambridge, MA: Harvard University Press.

Ambert, A. M., Adler, P. A., Adler, P., & Detzner, D. (1995). Understanding qualitative research. *Journal of Marriage and the Family, 57*, 879–893.

America Online. (2000). *American Online/Roper Starch Cyberstudy 2000.* Roper #CNT375.

Arendell, T. (2000). Conceiving and investigating motherhood: The decade's scholarship. *Journal of Marriage and the Family, 62*, 1192–1207.

Bauman, Z. (2000). *Liquid modernity.* Cambridge, UK: Polity Press.

Bengtson, V. L. (2001). Beyond the nuclear family: The increasing importance of multigenerational bonds. *Journal of Marriage and Family, 63*, 1–16.

Bianchi, S. M. (2006). Mothers and daughters "do," fathers "don't do" family: Gender and generational bonds. *Journal of Marriage and Family, 68*, 812–816.

Blau, M., & Fingerman, K. L. (2009). *Consequential strangers: The power of people who don't seem to matter.* New York: W. W. Norton.

Blieszner, R. (2006). Close relationships in middle and late adulthood. In A. L. Vangelisti & D. Perlman (Eds.), *The Cambridge handbook of personal relationships* (pp. 211–227). New York: Cambridge University Press.

Blieszner, R., & Adams, R. G. (1992). *Adult friendship.* Newbury Park, CA: Sage.

211

Blume, L. B., & Blume, T. W. (2003). Towards a dialectical model of family gender discourse: Body, identity and sexuality. *Journal of Marriage and Family, 65,* 785–794.

Blumstein, P., & Schwartz, P. (1983). *American couples.* New York: Morrow.

Boase, J., Horrigan, J. B., Wellman, B., & Rainie, L. (2006). *The strength of Internet ties.* Washington, DC: Pew Internet & American Life Project.

Boase, J., & Wellman, B. (2006). Personal relationships: On and off the internet. In A. L. Vangelisti & D. Perlman (Eds.), *The Cambridge handbook of personal relationships* (pp. 709–723). New York: Cambridge University Press.

Bott, E. (1971). *Family and social network* (2nd ed.). New York: Free Press.

Burger, E., & Milardo, R. M. (1995). Marital interdependence and social networks. *Journal of Social and Personal Relationships, 12,* 403–415.

Caputo, R. K. (2001). Grandparents and coresident grandchildren in a youth cohort. *Journal of Family Issues, 22,* 541–556.

Carrington, C. (1999). *No place like home: Relationships and family life among lesbians and gay men.* Chicago: University of Chicago Press.

Chebra, J. M. (1991). *Aunts' and uncles' relationship with their nieces and nephews: An exploratory study.* Unpublished master's thesis. Kent State University, Ohio.

Cherlin, A. J., & Furstenberg, F. F. (1986). *The new American grandparent.* New York: Basic Books.

Chiroro, P., Viki, T. G., Frodi, A., Muromo, T., & Tsigah, A. (2006). Nature and prevalence of childhood sexual abuse among high school girls and college students in Zimbabwe. *Journal of Psychology in Africa, 16,* 17–26.

Cogan, J. (2002). *The uncle book: Everything you need to know to be a kid's favorite relative.* New York: Marlowe.

Cohler, B. J., Hostetler, A. J., & Boxer, A. M. (1998). Generativity, social context, and lived experience: Narratives of gay men in middle adulthood. In D. P. McAdams & E. de St. Albin (Eds.), *Generativity and adult development* (pp. 265–309). Washington, DC: American Psychological Association.

Coltrane, S. (2000). Research on household labor: Modeling and measuring the social embeddedness of routine family work. *Journal of Marriage and the Family, 62,* 1208–1233.

Connidis, I. A. (1992). Life transitions and the adult sibling tie: A qualitative study. *Journal of Marriage and the Family, 54,* 972–982.

Connidis, I. A. (2001). *Family ties and aging.* Thousand Oaks, CA: Sage.

Cooney, T. M., & Smith, L. A. (1996). Young adults' relations with grandparents following recent divorce. *The Journal of Gerontology, 51,* 91–95.

Copen, C., & Silverstein, M. (2007). Transmission of religious beliefs across generations: Do grandparents matter? *Journal of Comparative Family Studies, 38,* 497–510.

Cox, D. (2003). Private transfers within the family: Mothers, fathers, sons, and daughters. In A. H. Munnell & A. Sunden (Eds.), *Deaths and dollars: The role of gifts and bequests in America* (pp. 168–197). Washington, DC: Brookings Institute Press.

Crouter, A. C., & Booth, A. (Eds.). (2003). *Children's influence on family dynamics: The neglected side of family relationships.* Mahwah, NJ: Erlbaum.

Cumming, E., & Schneider, D. M. (1961). Sibling solidarity: A property of American kinship. *American Anthropologist, 63*, 498–507.

Daly, K. (1993). Reshaping fatherhood: Finding the models. *Journal of Family Issues, 14*, 510–530.

Daly, K. (2003). Family theory versus the theories families live by. *Journal of Marriage and Family, 65*, 771–784.

Davidson, B. (1997). Service needs of relative caregivers: A qualitative analysis. *Families in Society, 78*(5), 502–510.

Davis, K. E., & Todd, M. J. (1985). Assessing friendship: Prototypes, paradigm cases and relationship description. In S. Duck & D. Perlman (Eds.), *Understanding personal relationships: An interdisciplinary approach* (pp. 17–38). Beverly Hills, CA: Sage.

de St. Aubin, E., McAdams, D. P., & Kim, T. (Eds.) (2004). *The generative society: Caring for future generations.* Washington, DC: American Psychological Association.

Deutsch, F. M. (2007). Undoing gender. *Gender and Society, 21*, 106–127.

di Leonardo, M. (1984). *The varieties of ethnic experience: Kinship, class, and gender among California Italian-Americans.* Ithaca, NY: Cornell University Press.

di Leonardo, M. (1987). The female world of cards and holidays: Women, families, and the work of kinship. *Signs, 12*, 440–452.

DiPerna, P. (1998). Becoming Aunt Paula. *Parents, 73*(8), 152–154.

Downs, B. (2003). Fertility of American women: June 2002. *Current Population Reports,* P20-548. Washington, DC: U.S. Bureau of the Census.

Doyle, C. (2001.) Surviving and coping with emotional abuse in childhood. *Child Clinical Psychology and Psychiatry, 6*, 387–402.

Dubas, J. S. (2001). How gender moderates the grandparent-grandchild relationship: A comparison of kin-keeper and kin-selector theories. *Journal of Family Issues, 22*, 478–492.

Dunifon, R., & Kowaleski-Jones, L. (2007). The influence of grandparents in single-mother families. *Journal of Marriage and Family, 69*, 465–481.

Ellingson, L. L., & Sotirin, P. J. (2006). Exploring young adults' perspectives on communication with aunts. *Journal of Social and Personal Relationships, 23*, 483–501.

Eriksen, S., & Gerstel, N. (2002). A labor of love or labor itself: Care work among adult brothers and sisters. *Journal of Family Issues, 23*, 836–856.

Falicov, C. J. (1999). The Latino family lifecycle. In B. Carter & M. McGoldrick (Eds.), *The expanded family life cycle: Individual, family, and social perspectives* (3rd ed., pp. 141–152). Boston: Allyn & Bacon.

Faubion, J. D. (2001). *The ethics of kinship.* Oxford: Rowman & Littlefield.

Finch, J., & Mason, J. (1993). *Negotiating family responsibilities.* London: Routledge.

Fingerman, K. L. (2004). The role of offspring and in-laws in grandparents' ties to their grandchildren. *Journal of Family Issues, 25*, 1026–1049.

Fingerman, K. L., & Hay, E. L. (2002). Searching under the streetlight?: Age biases in the personal and family relationships literature. *Personal Relationships, 9*, 415–433.

Fingerman, K. L., Hay, E. L., & Birditt, K. S. (2004). The best of ties, the worst of ties: Close, problematic, and ambivalent social relationships. *Journal of Marriage and Family, 66*, 792–808.

Fischer, C. S. (1982). *To dwell among friends.* Chicago: University of Chicago Press.

Fischer, C. S. (2009). The 2004 GSS finding of shrunken social networks: An artifact? *American Sociologial Review, 74*, 657–669.

Gerstel, N., & Gallagher, S. K. (1996). Kinkeeping and distress: Gender, recipients of care, and work-family conflict. *Journal of Marriage and the Family, 55*, 598–608.

Gerstel, N., & Sarkisian, N. (2006). Marriage: The good, the bad, and the greedy. *Context, 5*, 16–21.

Gibbs, N. (2008, February 18). A day to forget: The best gift for Valentine's Day is to ignore it altogether. *Time, 171*, 64.

Glaser, B., & Strauss, A. L. (1997). *The discovery of grounded theory: Strategies for qualitative research.* New York: Aldine.

Goodman, C. C. (2007). Family dynamics in three-generational grandfamilies. *Journal of Family Issues, 28*, 355–379.

Hanks, R. S. (2001). "Grandma, what big teeth you have!": The social construction of grandparenting in American business and academe. *Journal of Family Issues, 22*, 652–676.

Hansen, K. V. (2005). *Not-so-nuclear families: Class, gender, and networks of care.* New Brunswick, NJ: Rutgers University Press.

Hartup, W. W., & Stevens, N. (1997). Friendships and adaptation in the life course. *Psychological Bulletin, 121*, 355–370.

Harvey, J. H., & Wenzel, A. (2006). Theoretical perspectives in the study of close relationships. In A. L. Vangelisti & D. Perlman (Eds.), *The Cambridge handbook of personal relationships* (pp. 35–49). New York: Cambridge University Press.

Hawkins, A. J., & Dollahite, D. C. (Eds.). (1997). *Generative fathering: Beyond deficit perspectives.* Thousand Oaks, CA: Sage.

Helms, H. M., Crouter, A. C., & McHale, S. M. (2003). Marital quality and spouses' marriage work with close friends and each other. *Journal of Marriage and Family, 65*, 963–977.

Hochschild, A. R. (1979). Emotion work, feeling rules and social structure. *American Journal of Sociology, 85*, 551–575.

Holmberg, D., Orbuch, T. L., & Veroff, J. (2004). *Thrice told tales: Married couples tell their stories.* Mahwah, NJ: Erlbaum.

Hosley, C. A., & Montemayor, R. (1997). Fathers and adolescents. In M. E. Lamb (Ed.), *The role of the father in child development* (3rd ed., pp. 162–178). New York: Wiley.

Igarashi, T., Takai, J., & Yoshida, T. (2005). Gender differences in social network development via mobile phone text messages: A longitudinal study. *Journal of Social and Personal Relationships, 22*, 691–713.

Johnson, C. L. (1988). Active and latent functions of grandparenting during the divorce process. *Gerontologist, 28*, 330–335.

Johnson, C. L. (2000). Kinship and gender. In D. Demo, K. Allen, & M. A. Fine (Eds.), *Handbook of family diversity* (pp. 128–148). New York: Oxford University Press.

Johnson, M. P., Caughlin, J. P., & Huston, T. L. (1999). The tripartite nature of marital commitment: Personal, moral, and structural reasons to stay married. *Journal of Marriage and the Family, 61*, 160–177.

Johnson-Garner, M. Y., & Meyers, S. A. (2003). What factors contribute to the resilience of African-American children within kinship care? *Child & Youth Care Forum, 32,* 255–269.

Katz, J. E., & Rice, R. E. (2002). *The social consequences of Internet use: Access, involvement, and interaction.* Cambridge, MA: The MIT Press.

Katz, R., Lowenstein, A. Phillips, J., & Daatland, S. O. (2005). Theorizing intergenerational family relations: Solidarity, conflict, and ambivalence in cross-national contexts. In V. Bengtson, A. C. Acock, K. R. Allen, P. Dilworth-Anderson, & D. M. Klein (Eds.), *Sourcebook of family theory & research* (pp. 393–420). Thousand Oaks, CA: Sage.

Kenrick, D. T., & Trost, M. R. (1997). Evolutionary approaches to relationships. In S. Duck, K. Dindia, B. Ickes, R. Milardo, R. Mills, & B. Sarason (Eds.), *Handbook of personal relationships* (2nd ed., pp. 151–177). New York: Wiley.

Keyes, C. L. M., & Ryff, C. D. (1998). Generativity in adult lives: Social structural contours and quality of life consequences. In D. P. McAdams, & E. de St. Albin (Eds.), *Generativity and adult development* (pp. 227–263). Washington, DC: American Psychological Association.

Klein, R. C. A., & Milardo, R. M. (2000). The social context of couple conflict: Support and criticism from informal third parties. *Journal of Social and Personal Relationships, 17,* 618–637.

Kotre, J. (1984). *Outliving the self: Generativity and the interpretation of lives.* Baltimore, MD: Johns Hopkins University Press.

Kotre, J. (2004). Generativity and culture: What meaning can do. In E. de St. Aubin, D. P. McAdams, & T. Kim (Eds.), *The generative society: Caring for future generations* (pp. 35–49). Washington, DC: American Psychological Association.

Kotre, J., & Kotre, K. B. (1998). Intergenerational buffers: "The damage stops here." In D. P. McAdams & E. de St. Albin (Eds.), *Generativity and adult development* (pp. 367–390). Washington, DC: American Psychological Association.

Kruk, E., & Hall, B. L. (1995). The disengagement of parental grandparents subsequent to divorce. *Journal of Divorce and Remarriage, 23,* 131–147.

Langellier, K. M., & Peterson, E. E. (2004). *Storytelling in daily life.* Philadelphia: Temple University Press.

LaRossa, R. (2005). Grounded theory methods and qualitative family research. *Journal of Marriage and Family, 67,* 837–857.

Leach, M. S., & Braithwaite, D. O. (1996). A binding tie: Supportive communication of family kinkeepers. *Journal of Applied Communication Research, 24,* 200–216.

Lima, C., & Lima, J. (2001). *A to zoo: Subject access to children's picture books.* Westport, CT: Bowker and Greenwood.

Litwak, E., & Kulin, S. (1987). Technology, proximity, and measures of kin support. *Journal of Marriage and the Family, 49,* 649–662.

Margolin, L. (1994). Child sexual abuse by uncles: A risk assessment. *Child Abuse and Neglect, 18,* 215–224.

Marks, S. R. (2001). Teasing out the lessons of the 1960's: Family diversity and family privilege. In R. M. Milardo (Ed.), *Understanding families into the new millennium: A decade in review* (pp. 66–79). Minneapolis, MN: National Council on Family Relations.

Marsiglio, W. (2004). Studying fathering trajectories: In-depth interviewing and sensitizing concepts. In R. D. Day & M. E. Lamb (Eds.), *Conceptualizing and measuring father involvement* (pp. 61–82). Mahwah, NJ: Erlbaum.

Marsiglio, W., Amato, P., Day, R. D., & Lamb, M. (2000). Scholarship on fatherhood in the 1990's and beyond. *Journal of Marriage and the Family, 62*, 392–410.

Matthews, S. H. (2005). Reaching beyond the dyad: Research on adult siblings. In V. Bengtson, A. C. Acock, K. R. Allen, P. Dilworth-Anderson, & D. M. Klein (Eds.), *Sourcebook of family theory and research* (pp. 181–184). Thousand Oaks, CA: Sage.

Mauthner, M. L. (2002). *Sistering: Power and change in female relationships.* New York: Palgrave Macmillan.

McAdams, D. P., & de St. Aubin, E. (1992). A theory of generativity and its assessment through self-report, behavioral acts, and narrative themes in autobiography. *Journal of Personality and Social Psychology, 62*, 1003–1015.

McAdams, D. P., Hart, H. M., & Maruna, S. (1998). The anatomy of generativity. In D. P. McAdams & E. de St. Albin (Eds.), *Generativity and adult development* (pp. 7–43). Washington, DC: American Psychological Association.

McAdams, D. P., & Logan, R. L. (2004). What is generativity? In E. de St. Aubin, D. P. McAdams, & T. Kim (Eds.), *The generative society: Caring for future generations* (pp. 15–31). Washington, DC: American Psychological Association.

McDermid, S. M., Franz, C. E., & De Reus, L. A. (1998). Generativity: At the cross-roads of social roles and personality. In D. P. McAdams & E. de St. Albin (Eds.), *Generativity and adult development* (pp. 181–226). Washington, DC: American Psychological Association.

McPherson, M., Smith-Lovin, L., & Brashers, M. E. (2006). Social isolation in America: Changes in core discussion networks over two decades. *American Sociological Review, 71*, 353–375.

McPherson, M., Smith-Lovin, L., & Brashers, M. E. (2006). ERATTA: Social isolation in America: Changes in core discussion networks over two decades. *American Sociological Review, 61*, 528–537.

Mikkelson, A. C. (2006). Communication among peers: Adult sibling relationships. In K. Floyd & M. T. Morman (Eds.), *Widening the family circle: New research on family communication* (pp. 21–35). Thousand Oaks, CA: Sage.

Milardo, R. M. (Ed.). (2000). *Understanding families into the new millennium: A decade in review.* Minneapolis, MN: National Council on Family Relations.

Milardo, R. M. (2005). Generative uncle and nephew relationships. *Journal of Marriage and Family, 67*, 1226–1236.

Milardo, R. M., & Helms-Erikson, H. (2000). Network overlap and third-party influence in close relationships. In C. Hendrick & S. Hendrick (Eds.), *Close relationships: A sourcebook.* Thousand Oaks: Sage.

Miller, T. (2005). *Making sense of motherhood: A narrative approach.* Cambridge University Press.

Miller-Day, M. A. (2004). *Communication among grandmothers, mothers, and adult daughters: A qualitative study of maternal relationships.* Mahwah, NJ: Erlbaum.

Mills, C. W. (1959). *The sociological imagination.* New York: Oxford University Press.

Monserud, M. A. (2008). Intergenerational relationships and affectual solidarity between grandparents and young adults. *Journal of Marriage and Family, 70,* 182–195.

Muraco, A. (2006). Intentional families: Fictive kin ties between cross-gender, different sexual orientation friends. *Journal of Marriage and Family, 68,* 1313–1325.

Murphy, M. (2008). Variations in kinship across geographic and social space. *Population and Development Review, 34,* 19–49.

Nahemow, N. (1985). The changing nature of grandparenthood. *Medical Aspects of Human Sexuality, 19,* 185–190.

Nelson, M. (2006). Single mothers "do" family. *Journal of Marriage and Family, 68,* 781–795.

Olds, J., & Schwartz, R. S. (2009). *The lonely Americans: Drifting apart in the twenty-first century.* Boston: Beacon Press.

Oliker, S. J. (1989). *Best friends and marriage.* Berkeley: University of California Press.

Oswald, R. F. (2002). Resilience within the family networks of lesbians and gay men: Intentionality and redefinition. *Journal of Marriage and Family, 64,* 374–383.

Pahl, R., & Pevalin, D. J. (2005). Between family and friends: A longitudinal study of friendship choice. *The British Journal of Sociology, 56,* 433–450.

Parkin, R., & Stone, L. (2004). *Kinship and family: An anthropological reader.* Malden, MA: Blackwell.

Perry-Jenkins, M., & Salamon, S. (2002). Blue-collar kin and community in the small-town Midwest. *Journal of Family Issues, 23,* 927–949.

Pleck, J. H. (1997). Paternal involvement: Levels, sources, and consequences. In M. E. Lamb (Ed.), *The role of the father in child development* (3rd ed., pp. 66–103). New York: Wiley.

Popenoe, D. (1993). American family decline, 1960–1990: A review and appraisal. *Journal of Marriage and the Family, 55,* 527–555.

Pratt, M. W., & Fiese, B. H. (2004). *Family stories and the life course: Across time and generations.* Malwah, NJ: Erlbaum.

Pratt, M. W., Norris, J. E., Hebblethwaite, S., & Arnold, M. L. (2008). Intergenerational transmission of values: Family generativity and adolescents' narratives of parent and grandparent value teaching. *Journal of Personality, 76,* 171–198.

Proulx, C. M., Helms, H. M., & Payne, C. C. (2004). Wives' "marriage work" with spouse and friend: Links to marital quality. *Family Relations, 53,* 393–404.

Putnam, R. D. (2000). *Bowling alone.* New York: Simon & Schuster.

Rainie, L., Fox, S., Harrigan, J., Lenhart, A., & Spooner, T. (2000). *Tracking online life: How women use the Internet to cultivate relationships with family and friends.* Washington, DC: Pew Internet & American Life Project.

Roberto, K. A., Allen, K. R., & Blieszner, R. (2001). Grandfathers' perceptions and expectations of relationships with their adult grandchildren. *Journal of Family Issues, 22,* 407–426.

Robertson, J. F. (1977). Grandmotherhood: A study of role conceptions. *Journal of Marriage and the Family, 39,* 165–174.

Robertson, J. F. (1995). Grandparenting in an era of rapid change. In R. Blieszner & V. H. Bedford (Eds.), *Handbook of aging and the family* (pp. 243–260). Westport, CT: Greenwood Press.

Rosenthal, C. S. (1985). Kinkeeping in the familial division of labor. *Journal of Marriage and the Family, 47*, 965–974.

Rossi, A. S., & Rossi, P. H. (1990). *Of human bonding: Parent–child relations across the life course.* New York: Aldine de Gruyter.

Ruiz, S. A., & Silverstein, M. (2007). Relationships with grandparents and the emotional well-being of late adolescent and young adult grandchildren. *Journal of Social Issues, 63*, 793–808.

Rusbult, C. E., Coolsen, M. K., Kirchner, J. L., & Clarke, J. A. (2006). Commitment. In A. L. Vangelisti & D. Perlman (Eds.), *The Cambridge handbook of personal relationships* (pp. 615–635). New York: Cambridge University Press.

Russell, D. E. H. (1986). *The secret trauma: Incest in the lives of girls and women.* New York: Basic Books.

Salmon, C. A. (1999). On the impact of sex and birth order on contact with kin. *Human Nature, 10*, 183–197.

Salmon, C. A., & Daly, M. (1996). On the importance of kin relations to Canadian women and men. *Ethology and Sociobiology, 17*, 289–297.

Sarkisian, N. (2006). "Doing family ambivalence": Nuclear and extended families in single mothers' lives. *Journal of Marriage and Family, 68*, 804–811.

Sarkisian, N., & Gerstel, N. (2008). Till marriage do us part: Adult children's relationships with their parents. *Journal of Marriage and Family, 70*, 360–376.

Sault, N. L. (2001). Godparenthood ties among Zapotec women and the effects of Protestant conversion. In J. W. Dow & A. R. Sandstrom (Eds.), *Holy saints and fiery preachers: The anthropology of Protestantism in Mexico and Central America* (pp. 117–146). Westport, CT: Praeger.

Schnieder, D. M., & Cottrell, C. B. (1975). *The American kin universe: A genealogical study* (The University of Chicago Studies in Anthropology Series, No. 3). Chicago: University of Chicago, Department of Anthropology.

Segura, D. A., & Pierce, J. L. (1998). Chicana/o family structure and gender personality: Chodorow, familism, and phychoanaytic sociology revisited. In K. V. Hansen & A. I. Garey (Eds.), *Families in the U.S.: Kinship and domestic politics* (pp. 295–314). Philadelphia: Temple University Press.

Shanahan, M. J., & Macmillan, R. (2008). *Biography and the sociological imagination: Contexts and contingencies.* New York: W. W. Norton.

Shklovski, I., Kiesler, S., & Kraut, R. (2006). The Internet and social interaction: A meta-analysis and critique of studies, 1995–2003. In R. Kraut, M. Brynin, & S. Kiesler (Eds.), *Computers, phones, and the Internet: Domesticating information technology* (pp. 251–264). New York: Oxford University Press.

Silverstein, M., Giarrusso, R., & Bengtson, V. L. (1998). Intergenerational solidarity and the grandparent role. In M. Szinovacz (Ed.), *Handbook on grandparenthood* (pp. 144–158). Westport, CT: Greenwood Press.

Silverstein, M., & Marenco, A. (2001). How Americans enact the grandparent role across the family life course. *Journal of Family Issues, 22*, 493–522.

Smith, D. E. (1993). The standard North American family: SNAF as an ideological code. *Journal of Family Issues, 14*, 50–65.

Snarey, J. (1993). *How fathers care for the next generation: A four-decade study.* Cambridge, MA: Harvard University Press.

Snow, D. A. (2004). Thoughts on alternative pathways to theoretical development: Theory generation, extension, and refinement. In C. C. Ragin, J. Nagel, & P. White (Eds.), *Workshop on scientific foundations of qualitative research* (pp. 132–136). Washington, DC: National Science Foundation.

Sotirin, P. J., & Ellingson, L. L. (2006). The "Other" women in family life: Aunt/niece/nephew communication. In K. Floyd & M. T. Morman (Eds.), *Widening the family circle: New research on family communication* (pp. 81–99). Thousand Oaks, CA: Sage.

Spencer, L., & Pahl, R. (2006). *Rethinking friendship: Hidden solidarities today.* Princeton, NJ: Princeton University Press.

Sprey, J. (2009). Institutionalization of the family and marriage: Questioning their cognitive and relational realities. *Journal of Family Theory and Review, 1,* 4–19.

Stack, C. (1974). *All our kin: Strategies for survival in a black community.* New York: Harper & Row.

Stafford, L. (2005). *Maintaining long-distant and cross-residential relationships.* Mahwah, NJ: Erlbaum.

Stein, C. H. (1993). Felt obligation in adult family relationships. In S. W. Duck (Ed.), *Understanding relationship processes 3: Social context of relationships* (pp. 78–99). Thousand Oaks, CA: Sage.

Stone, L. (2000). *Kinship and gender: An introduction.* Boulder, CO: Westview Press.

Strauss, A., & Corbin, J. (1990). *Basics of qualitative research: Grounded theory procedures and techniques.* Thousand Oaks, CA: Sage.

Sturgis, I. (Ed.). (2004). *Aunties: Thirty-five writers celebrate their other mothers.* New York: Ballantine.

Terhell, E. L., van Groenou, M. I. B., & van Tilburg, T. (2004). Network dynamics in the long-term period after divorce. *Journal of Social and Personal Relationships, 21,* 719–738.

Thiele, D. M., & Whelan, T. A. (2008). The relationships between grandparent satisfaction, meaning, and generativity. *International Journal of Aging and Human Development, 66,* 21–48.

Thomas, J. L. (1986). Age and sex differences in perceptions of grandparenting. *Journal of Gerontology, 41,* 417–423.

Thorne, B., & Yalom, M. (Eds.). (1992). *Rethinking the family: Some feminist questions.* Boston: Northeastern University Press.

Traeder, T., & Bennett, J. (1998). *Aunties: Our older, cooler, wiser friends.* Berkeley, CA: Wildcat Canyon Press.

VanLear, C. A., Koerner, A., & Allen, D. M. (2006). Relationship typologies. In A. L. Vangelisti & D. Perlman (Eds.), *The Cambridge handbook of personal relationships* (pp. 91–110). New York: Cambridge University Press.

Voorpostel, M., & Blieszner, R. (2008). Intergenerational solidarity and support between adult siblings. *Journal of Marriage and Family, 70,* 157–167.

Voorpostel, M., & Van Der Lippe, T. (2007). Support between siblings and between friends: Two worlds apart? *Journal of Marriage and Family, 69,* 1271–1282.

Waite, L. J., & Harrison, S. C. (1992). Keeping in touch: How women in mid-life allocate social contacts among kith and kin. *Social Forces, 70,* 637–655.

Walker, A. J., Allen, K. R., & Connidis, I. A. (2005). Theorizing and studying siblings ties in adulthood. In V. Bengtson, A. C. Acock, K. R. Allen, P. Dilworth-Anderson, & D. M. Klein (Eds.), *Sourcebook of family theory & research* (pp. 167–181). Thousand Oaks, CA: Sage.

Warhola, J. (2003). *Uncle Andy's*. New York: G. P. Putnam's Sons.

Wegner, D. M., Erber, R., & Raymond, P. (1991). Transactive memory in close relationships. *Journal of Personality and Social Psychology, 61*, 923–929.

Wellman, B., Wong, R. Y., Tindall, D., & Nazer, N. (1997). A decade of network turnover, persistence and stability in personal communities. *Social Networks, 19*, 27–50.

Wellman, B., & Wortley, S. (1989). Brother's keepers: Situating kinship relations in broader networks of social support. *Sociological Perspectives, 32*, 273–306.

Wenger, G. C. (2001). Ageing without children: Rural Wales. *Journal of Cross-Cultural Gerontology, 16*, 79–109.

Wenger, G. C., & Burholt, V. (2001). Differences over time in older people's relationships with children, grandchildren, nieces and nephews in rural North Wales. *Ageing and Society, 21*, 567–590.

White, L. (2001). Sibling relationships over the life course: A panel analysis. *Journal of Marriage and Family, 63*, 555–568.

White, L. K., & Riedman, A. (1992). Ties among siblings. *Social Forces, 71*, 85–102.

Widmer, E. D. (1999). Family contexts as cognitive networks: A structural approach of family relationships. *Personal Relationships, 6*, 487–503.

Widmer, E. D., Castren, A., Jallinoja, R., & Ketokivi, K. (2008). Families as configurations. In E. Widmer & R. Jallinoja (Eds.), *Beyond the nuclear family: Families in a configurational perspective* (pp. 1–10). Geneva: Peter Lang.

Widmer, E. D., Le Goff, J., & Levy, R. (2006). Embedded parenting? The influence of conjugal networks on parent–child relationships. *Journal of Social and Personal Relationships, 23*, 387–406.

Widmer, E. D., & Sapin, M. (2008). Families on the move: Insights on family configurations of individuals undergoing psychotherapy. In E. Widmer & R. Jallinoja (Eds.), *Beyond the nuclear family: Families in a configurational perspective* (pp. 279–302). Geneva: Peter Lang.

Wild, R. (2000). *Uncles: A tribute to the coolest guys in the world*. Chicago: Contemporary Books

Wilkes, L., Beale, B., & Cole, R. (2006). Aunties and Uncles Co-operative Family Project Ltd.: Volunteers making a difference in the lives of children and parents. *Contemporary Nurse, 23*, 291–302.

Wood, J. T. (2000). Gender and personal relationships. In C. Hendrick & S. Hendrick (Eds.), *Close relationships: A sourcebook* (pp. 301–313). Thousand Oaks: Sage.

INDEX